'Jeff Apter tells the Malcolm Your
as momentous as the AC/DC legend played guitar.
From Scotland to Sydney's Villawood Migrant Hostel
via Ashfield Boys' High and his sad end at Lulworth
House, in Apter's hands it is a story as spellbinding as
one of Young's guitar riffs.'

Helen Pitt, author of *The House*

★

Jeff Apter is the author of more than 20 music biographies,
many of them bestsellers. His subjects include Johnny
O'Keefe, Keith Urban, John Farnham, the Bee Gees, the
Finn brothers and Angus Young of AC/DC. As a ghost-
writer, he has worked with Kasey Chambers, Mark Evans (of
AC/DC) and Richard Clapton. Jeff was on staff at *Rolling
Stone* for several years and has written about legends such as
Aretha Franklin, Patti Smith, Robbie Robertson, Bob Dylan,
Chrissie Hynde and Lucinda Williams. In 2015, he worked
on the Helpmann award–nominated live show *A State of
Grace: The Music of Jeff and Tim Buckley*. Away from music,
Jeff has also worked on books with soldiers and diplomats
and sports greats such as Michael Slater and Tim Cahill. He
lives in Wollongong, New South Wales, with his wife, two
children, a cat that's so damned cool it needs no name, and
a very blue dog named Neela.

www.jeffapter.com.au

MALCOLM YOUNG

THE MAN WHO MADE AC/DC

JEFF APTER

ALLEN&UNWIN
SYDNEY · MELBOURNE · AUCKLAND · LONDON

First published in 2019

Copyright © Jeff Apter 2019

Allen & Unwin
83 Alexander Street
Crows Nest NSW 2065
Australia
Phone: (61 2) 8425 0100
Email: info@allenandunwin.com
Web: www.allenandunwin.com

 A catalogue record for this
book is available from the
NATIONAL
LIBRARY   National Library of Australia
OF AUSTRALIA

ISBN 978 1 76052 875 1

Internal design by Post Pre-press
Set in 12.5/17 pt Adobe Garmond by Post Pre-press Group, Australia
Printed and bound in Australia by Pegasus Media & Logistics

20 19 18 17 16 15 14 13

For Peter

Prologue

In 2016, when I was writing *High Voltage*, my biography of Angus Young, I subtitled the book 'AC/DC's Last Man Standing'—and for good reason. The months and years leading up to this flashpoint in Angus's and the band's long and winding career had been chaotic. In the midst of their *Rock or Bust* tour—a prescient title if there ever was one—they'd lost their singer, Brian Johnson, who was fast going deaf, and their drummer, Phil Rudd, under house arrest for various crimes and misdemeanours. (And you simply cannot play the drums while wearing an ankle bracelet.) Then their bassist of almost 40 years, Cliff Williams, announced that he'd retire at the end of the tour. It was pretty much the first thing he'd said publicly since joining the band in 1977. And then Axl Rose, Johnson's surprise replacement, broke his foot on the eve of his first gig; Rose made his AC/DC debut seated on a throne.

If rock and roll wasn't such big business, it would have been hilarious, like something straight out of *This is Spinal Tap*. (Mind you, it's been reported that Rudd, Johnson and

Williams have all returned in 2019 to work on a new AC/DC album, which goes to show that this band is a tough outfit to quit.)

As if all this wasn't calamitous enough, a long, dark shadow had been cast over the *Rock or Bust* tour before it even began. In 2014, Malcolm Young, the heart and soul of AC/DC, the man who'd gotten this rock-and-roll behemoth rolling back in 1973, had become a resident of Lulworth House, an exclusive Sydney nursing home. He was suffering from dementia. The news was devastating.

The preceding few years had been tough enough for Malcolm, who'd endured lung and heart operations—he'd even had a pacemaker fitted. But dementia was the cruellest blow of all; the sight of Malcolm, that tough little bantam of a rocker usually seen in his trademark boots, blue jeans and singlet—his preferred menswear store was cut-price Sydney emporium Gowings—being led by the arm around the grounds of Lulworth was enough to break even the hardest of hearts.

So, as I set out to write my Angus bio, the subtitle seemed very fitting. *Right.*

But within months of the book's release in September 2017, 'The Last Man Standing' took on a totally new and quite uncomfortable meaning, one I'd never envisaged when I started writing. Both Malcolm and his big brother George— mentor, producer and touchtone for AC/DC—were dead.

Despite knowing about Malcolm's failing health, I found it really hard getting my head around the fact that he was dead. Okay, he had never been an athlete—even in his prime, Malcolm had been ghostly pale and rake-thin, and he smoked like a Rasta—but he'd always seemed tougher than old boots, a livewire with magic in his right hand, the best rhythm guitarist this side of Rolling Stone Keith Richards (and perhaps even better).

Malcolm, to me—a fan and observer—was bulletproof, unbreakable. Maybe it had something to do with his rough-as-guts upbringing; his were the kind of hardscrabble roots a working-class guy like me could relate to. Not surprisingly, his early years toughened Malcolm up (although I reckon he was tough from the cradle onwards) and gave him the tools to deal with pretty much anything thrown his way—chairs, bottles, fists and more, in the case of early AC/DC.

Call me delusional, but I'd figured that his toughness could also help Malcolm survive his dementia diagnosis. But, as anyone who's witnessed dementia up close knows, it's a cruel bastard of a disease. It strips you of the very thing we all prize the most: memories. Clearly, judging by the few photos that emerged from the Lulworth years, dementia sank its fangs deep into Malcolm. There was a faraway look in his eyes; he seemed fearful, lost. Already gone.

Yet even now, as I write this biography of Malcolm, I still find it hard to grasp that he's not around anymore. In my mind I can picture him on stage, occupying his few square metres to the right of Phil Rudd's drum kit, his scrawny limbs wrapped around that hefty Gretsch guitar. Heaven help anyone who trespassed on his domain; that part of the stage was Malcolm Young's rightful place, his territory. *His turf.*

And perhaps that's the best way to remember Malcolm Young—he truly belonged on that stage, rocking the signature songs that he'd brought into the world, crunching out one titanium-strength riff after another, lost in music. *Still very much alive.*

3

1

'I always wanted to be a star soccer player.'

Before he fell in love with guitars, Malcolm Mitchell Young was mad for football. It was one of the few escapes to be found on Glasgow's Cranhill housing estate, where he lived until he was ten. 'I always wanted to be a star soccer player,' Malcolm once said. 'Music was something we wanted to do, but we didn't take it all that seriously.' Not at first, anyway.

Malcolm, who was born on 6 January 1953, would kick a ball around the streets of the housing estate, dreaming he was scoring the winner in the Scottish Cup Final. Malcolm was the seventh of eight children born to William and Margaret Young. The youngest Young, Angus, was born on 31 March 1955; by then, the family's eldest sibling, big brother Stephen (Stevie), was almost 22, and sister Margaret was twenty. George was born in 1946, William Jr in 1940, Alex in 1938, John in 1937. Malcolm's parents were 42 and 40 when he was born.

Malcolm's team was the Rangers. 'We've always been Rangers fans,' he once stated, and he always would be.

Perhaps it was no coincidence that the Rangers' team, just like AC/DC, was also formed from a band of brothers; among its four founders way back in 1872 were siblings Moses and Peter McNeil. The fervent supporters of the 'Old Firm', as the teams of Rangers and arch rivals Celtic were known, reflected the key religions of the area, with the staunchly Protestant Unionist community cheering on the Rangers, while Catholics sided with Celtic FC. The Youngs, however, weren't especially big on God. Malcolm's father William developed an aversion to religion after spending a weekend wallpapering the house of the local vicar. His work completed, the vicar offered him a 'God bless you' as payment and showed him the door. The Youngs and the church subsequently gave each other a wide berth.

If the Youngs had a religion, it was football. Many of the teams playing in Scotland reflected the very blue-collar, working-class roots of such clans as the Youngs—the Burntisland Shipyard team and the Inverurie Loco Works would line up against such teams as Forres Mechanics ('The Mighty Cans'). Football was a welcome escape from the workaday grind or, tougher still, life without work, a situation that William Young often found himself in.

One of Malcolm's earliest memories was catching a Rangers game at local stadium Ibrox, along with younger brother Angus, also a staunch Rangers supporter. 'And, of course, we won, 2–1,' Malcolm recalled. Rangers not only made the Scottish Cup Final in 1953, the year Malcolm was born, they beat Aberdeen 1–0, in a replay, before a crowd of more than 110,000 at Hampden Park.

Cranhill produced its share of highly regarded footballers, too, such as winger Kenny Aird, who played for St Johnstone, and brothers Jimmy and Joe Smith. Midfielder Jimmy was good enough to wear the Scottish strip.

Located on the eastern outskirts of Glasgow, Cranhill was a public-funded housing scheme (as it was known locally) established in the early 1950s. About 10,000 people crammed into its four-storey tenement blocks. They were just a few local shops, so mobile traders plied their wares up and down the estate's streets, flogging paraffin oil and coal, sweets and ice cream, and bread from the bakery van. Though an improvement on the old Glasgow slums, Cranhill's conditions were still relatively spartan: the Youngs, who lived at 6 Skerryvore Road, shared just a few bedrooms and a very basic kitchen. Given the size of their family, it was a very full house. Still, a bathroom of their very own was a welcome feature; it was a luxury in working-class Glasgow.

Cranhill helped to forge the character of Malcolm Young. If he had a credo, it was 'cut the crap'. Malcolm had no time for ego or pretension, the type of personality flaws that would be sorted out pretty quickly on the estate.

'It was rough,' Malcolm said about Cranhill. 'You never got ahead of yourself. If you get too big for your boots, if you've got big dreams, you're gonna get them broken or shattered. You never take anything for granted.'

Cranhill would be permanently etched in the memory of Angus Young, too, but not necessarily for sentimental reasons. 'All I remember,' he would recall much later, 'was being hit by a car and playing football in the streets near the housing estate where we lived.'

Music was a constant at the Young family HQ. Older brother Stevie played accordion; John and Alex played guitar—John was a particularly strong musical influence on Malcolm. Soon enough, George was playing too, then Malcolm and Angus, as instruments were handed down from sibling to sibling. Some families handed down clothes; the Youngs shared guitars. 'We never realised that we were learning guitars,' said Malcolm. 'They were always just there. We thought that everyone was like that.'

The Youngs weren't the only Cranhill locals with a musical bent. William 'Junior' Campbell, who had a paper route on the estate, played in sixties band The Marmalade—who, like AC/DC, made their mark with a residency at London club Marquee—before graduating to compose songs for the *Thomas the Tank Engine* TV show. 'Accidents Will Happen', one among many Island of Sodor musical gems, was the handiwork of Campbell.

The Young household had an open-door policy. William and Margaret would regularly host parties, at which neighbours and relatives would gather around an old piano and bang out tunes. And the Young boys always seemed to be working on something musical, as Angus would recall in the documentary *Blood and Thunder:* 'Each brother would show you little bits of music, of what they liked. Even my elder brother Stevie was trying to put me behind a piano—"No, you do it like this, with these fingers".'

Malcolm once gave Angus some advice that summed up his approach to the guitar and life in general. Frustrated by Angus's reluctance to make some real noise, he told him: 'Don't tickle it. Hit the bugger!'

Why fuck about?

Much of the early music going round the heads of Malcolm, Angus and George came from records brought home by sister Margaret. Margaret was tough; when she spoke, her siblings usually listened, especially Malcolm and Angus. According to Malcolm, 'She just kept the peace, if you know what I mean, in amongst all the brothers. If she shouted, everyone shut up. No one would touch my sister, the respect she had.'

Living in Glasgow had its advantages for a music fan like Margaret. Thanks to the proximity of Port Glasgow, she found it relatively easy to obtain a lot of new American records, which reached Glasgow by boat. Elvis, Little Richard, Fats Domino and Chuck Berry were big favourites of hers—and all would have a massive influence on her three younger brothers. Margaret's role in the three Young brothers' musical evolution should not be underestimated. Chuck Berry became such an inspiration for Angus, in fact, that he'd swipe Chuck's on-stage duckwalk when he started performing. Malcolm, too, was a big fan.

Yet for all Malcolm's love of rock and roll, and his desire to master the guitar, a career in music was something he simply couldn't contemplate. It just seemed so unlikely. The Youngs were working-class Scots; they were expected to stay in school only until they were old enough to leave, then get a job, raise a family, get old and die. That was the script.

At least it was until the family moved to the other side of the world.

*

William Young had trouble securing steady work. He'd served in the RAF during World War II, as a flight mechanic, but since the end of the war had bounced between jobs, working as a spray painter, and a machine operator at local manufacturer Turner & Newall. He'd also worked for a printer and did time as a postman. To those who knew them, the Youngs were a solid couple. 'They were honest, decent, fair people,' said one family friend. But they were doing it tough, especially with a brood as sizeable as theirs.

With steady employment scarce, it was no huge surprise that William's eyes lit up when he saw an advertisement spruiking a new life in Australia. The ad for the Assisted Passage Migration Scheme was a milestone in tourism; it made the far-flung colony, only 100 years back a dumping ground for Britain's crims and crooks, sound like heaven on Earth. 'Come over to the sunny side now!' urged the voice-over. 'Australia: a great place for families. Opportunity for you, fine for your wife, great for your children. You could be on your way over to a sunnier future in the new year—on your way to Australia, a great place for families.'

And the cost of the fare? Ten quid. Who, in their right mind, could resist?

It was also 1963, the year of the 'big freeze', one of the coldest UK winters on record. The weather was so bitter that water froze in the taps and life slowed to a crawl. The 'big freeze' dragged on for three months. No one could blame William when he signed up for the Assisted Passage Migration Scheme and transformed the Youngs of Cranhill, Glasgow into 'Ten Pound Poms'.

Unlike most Ten Pound Poms, who underwent a lengthy, stomach-churning sea journey, the Youngs got lucky: they were able to fly from the UK. Alongside a mixture of German and British immigrants, they travelled in relative comfort on Qantas flight QF738064, arriving in Sydney on 22 June 1963. William and Margaret brought with them Angus,

Malcolm, George, Stephen and William Jr. Also travelling was sister Margaret, now Margaret Horsburgh, who travelled with her husband Samuel and their son Samuel Jr. Another Young sibling, John, was already in Australia, while Alex Young stayed behind, much to the dismay of his parents, having moved to Hamburg with his band Grapefruit, where he played at the Star-Club and befriended The Beatles. He was the first Young to defy the working-class script and try his luck with music.

At the time of the Youngs' departure from the UK, the Merseyside musical revolution was in full force, and it left its mark on brother George as well as Malcolm, both becoming avowed Beatles fans. At the end of May 1963, The Beatles' 'From Me to You' was top of the UK singles chart, having dethroned Gerry and the Pacemakers' 'How Do You Do It?' (recorded but rejected by The Beatles), the previous number 1. Songs like these made the old guard of the charts—Cliff Richard, Brenda Lee, Aussie crooner Frank Ifield and the rest of them—appear as dated as the clothes they wore. They were the sound of another generation altogether.

Yet that musical tsunami hadn't yet hit Australia. In mid-1963, the charts were still dominated by lightweight pop and folk songs such as 'Hey Paula' and 'Puff the Magic Dragon' and Cliff Richard's 'Summer Holiday', but late in the year The Beatles began to make inroads: 'She Loves You' and 'I Want to Hold Your Hand' would become two of the biggest singles of 1963. Oz rock trailblazers Johnny O'Keefe and Col Joye, who'd been huge just a few years earlier, had already begun experiencing the same kind of decline as the Americans they worshipped: Elvis, Little Richard, Jerry Lee Lewis, Bill Haley. But unlike good ole boy Jerry Lee, O'Keefe and Joye couldn't get arrested—Joye had just one charting single in 1963 (he'd had five in 1959), while O'Keefe charted only twice. The Liverpudlian long-hairs were gradually taking over.

The broader culture of the Youngs' new home reflected a country unsure of its place in the world: was Australia Little Britain or some brave new southern land? The former seemed to be the case in 1963. *Coronation Street* was the TV soap opera of choice, for those who did have a TV, while Prime Minister Robert Menzies, by his own admission, was 'British to the bootstraps', a diehard Anglophile. When Queen Elizabeth II graced Australia with her presence just two months before the Youngs arrived, Menzies, like much of the nation, fell into a fair old swoon. 'I did but see her passing by,' he gushed, quoting the poet Thomas Ford, 'and yet I love her till I die.'

Malcolm and his family had more immediate concerns, though. They were on their way from Mascot Airport to the Villawood Migrant Hostel. And the rain that set in as they rode the bus would last for the next six weeks. So much for a sunnier future.

The Villawood Migrant Hostel, which opened in December 1949, was on the suburban outskirts of Sydney, 40 kilometres to the west of the city. The camp was populated entirely by 'New Australians' like the Youngs. (Twenty of these camps were scattered across New South Wales.) Fifteen hundred people lived at Villawood in horseshoe-shaped, World War II–era Nissen huts, built from corrugated iron.

Each of these Nissen huts was shared by two families, while cooking, cleaning and bathing facilities were communal. Residents—'inmates,' as some jokingly referred to themselves—slept in Army-style bunk beds. A portrait of Queen Elizabeth II hung in the dining room; it seemed as though she was casting a wary eye over all of the residents of Villawood. The place was rampant with native creepie crawlies and with violence, too; the local constabulary wore a path between their station house and the hostel as they were called in to control regular flare-ups between residents. They were frustrated by many things: their search for a job, the delayed start to their new life in Australia, the lack of anything resembling privacy, the weather—the hostel was wet and muddy in winter and swarmed with flies and heat in the summer.

Violence wasn't strictly in-house. The locals who lived nearby would entertain themselves by wandering into the hostel grounds and beating up anyone they could lay their hands on. They referred to families like the Youngs as the 'hostel hillbillies'. Big brother George, however, was handy with his fists—and his forehead, if required. He may have been from Glasgow but George could administer a pretty fair 'Liverpool kiss', which proved handy both at Villawood and, later on, in the rowdy bloodhouses of suburban and rural Oz. (He actually met future Easybeats Harry Vanda and Dick Diamonde during a brawl at the hostel.) Malcolm, too, could hold his own, while the pint-sized Angus had the benefit of being quick on his feet.

On their first night at the hostel, one of the Young siblings walked in on their parents, who were both in tears. Many years later, George revealed that his parents had seriously considered moving back to Glasgow.

★

On Thursday, 11 June 1964, at 7.45 a.m., The Beatles arrived in Sydney for their first (and as it turned out, only) Australian tour. Despite an almost biblical rain storm, thousands of fans turned up at the airport, screaming their throats raw, striving to get close to their new idols. The event was broadcast live on TV. The Fab Four (well, three, if you excluded stand-in drummer Jimmy Nicol, deputising for an ill Ringo) tried to take cover beneath flimsy umbrellas provided by airline staff, but a howling gale quickly dispatched their brollies in the general direction of New Zealand. It was a bizarre sight: the biggest pop culture phenomenon since Elvis, frozen and drenched, paraded before their fans like some weird exhibit.

Next stop was Adelaide, where things got even crazier: 250,000 people lined the route from the airport to their hotel in the city. It was more in keeping with a royal visit, which it was, in some ways—The Beatles were pop royalty. The next night they packed Adelaide's Centennial Hall, the first of a week of wildly received Australian shows—all for the outrageously low fee of £2500 per week, a fraction of their 1964 asking price of £25,000 *per show*. Canny promoter Kenn Brodziak had secured the band's services in 1963, just before they exploded internationally. 'You got us for the old fee, didn't you?' John Lennon said with a wry chuckle to Brodziak, perhaps the luckiest promoter on earth.

On 18 June, the Fab Four, now with Ringo back in the fold, played on a revolving stage at the Sydney Stadium, the first of six gigs over three days (more than 70,000 fans attended the shows). Local daily *The Sun-Herald* captured the craziness. 'Thousands of girls under 16, who occupied the most expensive seats,' the paper reported, 'seem to be in a state of delirium ... laddering stockings and losing their shoes. Many were hurried off to the first aid room, too excited to stand anymore.'

In the midst of the Sydney Stadium mayhem were Malcolm, George and Margaret Young, taking in the chaos, but perhaps in a slightly different way to the majority of the crowd. George and Malcolm wanted to understand how The Beatles created these amazing songs. Angus insisted that he too was at the gig, though that was unlikely—when he boasted to a future bandmate that tickets for the concert 'cost a couple of bucks', it was pointed out to Angus that decimal currency wasn't introduced to Australia until 1966. (The best tickets actually went for £1 17 s.)

The impact of The Beatles tour of Australia—not only to the Malcolm Young story, but to the entire culture—was massive. It was as though Australia changed overnight from black and white to colour; young men let their hair grow and dressed sharper, emulating their heroes. Women's hemlines started to shorten. The Beatles' 1964 tour can also be held directly responsible for the formation or evolution of dozens of other local acts, among them a trio of toothy siblings residing in suburban Sydney who called themselves the Bee Gees. And without The Beatles, The Easybeats would not have happened, and without The Easybeats, there would have been no AC/DC.

When listening to The Beatles, Malcolm tuned in closely to the guitars of Lennon and George Harrison. That's where the magic lay. 'I tended to pick up on the chords,' he said, 'the whole picture around the guitars.'

By the time of The Beatles' Sydney gig, George Young had already met fellow resident and musician Johannes Jacob van den Berg (aka Harry Vanda) in the communal laundry room at Villawood, but now their jam sessions took a more serious turn. *Australian Musician* magazine would rate the meeting of George and Harry at Villawood as 'the most important moment in local music history'. The Youngs' destiny had been changed forever.

Vanda had some form as a musician, having played in a band called The Starfighters back in his native Netherlands, and he and George roped in some fellow locals: bassist Dick Diamonde, drummer Gordon 'Snowy' Fleet and singer/troublemaker Stevie Wright, to form a group called The Easybeats. Their name was a neat lift from The Beatles, as was their guitar-powered sound. The band that would soon become Australia's first internationally successful rock group comprised two Dutchmen, a Scot and a pair of Poms, yet they'd proudly refer to themselves as Aussies. It was a conundrum that Malcolm would one day tackle as part of AC/DC, another band of post-war immigrants.

The Easybeats rehearsed in the Villawood laundry room and in a shed at the rear of the Diamonde family home. Their every move was studied by Malcolm.

'Me and Angus used to hang out there with them thinking, "This is the way to go!" That planted the seed for us and made us play more, try harder.'

★

In March 1965, having signed to Albert Productions—the record label offshoot of Sydney family business J. Albert & Son, a company whose fortune had been built on selling sheet music and the very popular Boomerang harmonica—The Easybeats released their debut single, 'For My Woman'.

It was produced by 28-year-old Ted Albert, a scion of the Albert dynasty and a friend of the band's manager Mike Vaughan. Albert was determined to modernise his company and steer it in the direction of rock and roll—he saw The Easybeats as the future. The Easybeats found a home at a venue called Beatle Village (having been turfed out of another Sydney club for being 'too loud and too filthy'), where they crafted their live act. Two months later, 'She's So Fine' (co-written by George and Stevie Wright) became their first Australian number 1 and 'Easyfever' erupted all over the country. Australia had its very own answer to The Beatles.

Easyfever really hit home for Angus one day when he returned home from school to his home at 4 Burleigh Street, Burwood. The family's first proper Australian home was a modest, brown-brick, semi-detached house, built in the early 1900s, in a quiet suburban street. But on this day it was surrounded by 300 screaming female fans on the lookout for his brother George. A handful of police struggled to maintain order.

'Let me in,' Angus demanded, pushing his way through the crowd. 'I live here.'

'That's what they're all saying,' replied one of the men in blue.

Angus was forced to jump the back fence to get inside, only to find a dozen or more Easybeats fans inside his home, grabbing anything and anyone they could get their mitts on. It became a regular occurrence. Sleepy suburban Burwood had never seen anything like it.

The neighbours may have hated the madness, but twelve-year-old Malcolm Young was very impressed. 'Those were great days. I was just going into puberty and we were getting all these screaming girls, a couple of hundred of them, hanging outside our house for a glimpse of The Easybeats, who were like Australia's Beatles. You've got reporters on your doorstep, a famous brother, a famous band.'

Malcolm idolised his superstar sibling and began introducing himself as 'the brother of George Young from The Easybeats'. It was a hell of a calling card for such a young kid. The idea of a life playing music was starting to seem not so crazy to Malcolm after all. Football was off the cards; his height, or lack of it, had short-circuited that possible career. He had looked on forlornly as his buddies underwent teenage growth spurts, while he remained stuck at five foot two.

Angus, meanwhile, was intrigued by the sound of The Easybeats, especially the interplay between guitarists Vanda and Young. It would prove to be a very handy lesson in what he could later achieve with his brother. 'Harry was doing the same thing I'd do with Malcolm,' Angus stated in the documentary *Blood and Thunder*. 'George had that very high rhythm and Harry provided the highlights, the colour.'

The Easybeats' debut album *Easy* was released in September 1965. 'Wedding Ring', a Top 10 Australian single, was their next hit, also out in September. Despite their success—hit records and sold-out shows—the band survived on a wage of just £5 per week.

At the 4BC Sound Spectacular at Brisbane's Festival Hall in December, the plug was pulled on The Easybeats' set after just seventeen minutes when a riot erupted among the 5000-strong crowd. Dozens of fans were injured in the crush. The band made their escape in a taxi but were set upon when the driver stopped for a red light; the cab was almost overturned by rabid fans (and the odd angry boyfriend).

'That's where all the bullshit started,' George Young told *Rolling Stone* in 1976. 'We weren't really playing anymore, we were just satisfying demand. From then on, the gigs became a chore.'

For Malcolm, school became less and less a priority as Easyfever erupted. Music was way too exciting. In fact, Malcolm's reputation at school was so lousy that Angus was caned on his first day at Ashfield Boys' High purely for being Malcolm's brother. Malcolm may not have been one for formal education, but he was undertaking a rock-and-roll masterclass, virtually by osmosis, courtesy of brother George and The Easybeats.

2

'I was over the moon . . . the only kid in town
with a Gretsch.'

Malcolm Young and Ashfield Boys' High went their separate ways in 1968, as soon as Malcolm turned fifteen. Their differences were irreconcilable. William Young was firm with his son, who'd grown into a good-looking if pint-sized teen, his dark eyes hidden behind long hair. He told Malcolm that if he was quitting school, he had to 'get a trade'. Malcolm began working as a line fitter at the Berlei lingerie company, having failed to secure a gig as an apprentice piano tuner, his first choice.

But his eyes stayed firmly fixed on the real prize: a life in rock and roll. He worked out pretty quickly that music had to be better than a regular job, although the repetitive clang of the Berlei factory machinery may well have set in motion Malcolm's fixation with heavy, industrial-strength rhythms. The volume was intense.

And 1968 was a key year for Malcolm for another reason: he acquired his first 'real' guitar, a 1963-model Gretsch Jet Firebird. It was a hefty beast, blazing gold in colour. Up until then he'd been playing hand-me-downs, and while this was no different, there was a twist: it was a gift from Harry Vanda. That was a good omen, surely, and something of a statement from Vanda, too—the kid *was* worthy.

'I was over the moon,' Malcolm would recall in 1984. 'The only kid in town with a Gretsch.'

'I had all these guitars and here was this talented kid who had nothing decent to play,' Vanda told writer John Tait. 'We didn't need to give Malcolm any tuition though. He's a shit-hot guitar player.'

Malcolm even had a shot at forming his own band, an outfit with the devilish name of Beelzebub Blues (sometimes known as the Rubberband, other times as Red House, a nod to the Jimi Hendrix cut of the same name), whose members included Larry Van Kriedt, a guitarist who jammed with Malcolm after forming a bond with Angus over Gibson guitars and Van Kriedt's ability to play blues guitar. For the better part of nine months, as Van Kriedt recalled via email, he was a regular at Burwood. 'I used to go to their house every weekend and stay there from Friday till Sunday evening. [Malcolm's] family was very welcoming, especially his mother.'

At rehearsals, Beelzebub would work their way through sixties rock classics: they played the bulk of *Fresh Cream*, Cream's debut LP, and Jimi Hendrix's *Are You Experienced*. These were gutsy, challenging choices for a bunch of kids in their teens. But perhaps the key thing that Malcolm gained from the experience was a towering black speaker box, custom made for him by a buddy of the band named Bevan Boranjee. It was massive, much bigger than Malcolm, a behemoth that put the fear of God into anyone who accidentally ventured into the scout hall in Rhodes where Beelzebub rehearsed.

As for big brother George and The Easybeats, it hadn't all been champagne and groupies. After firing off a succession of memorable hit singles—'Women (Make You Feel Alright)', 'Come and See Her', 'I'll Make You Happy (Just Like Your Mama Wants)'—they undertook a rite of passage for any ambitious Aussie band and prepared to leave the country. But on 9 July 1966, the night before their departure to London—the epicentre of Planet Pop—Harry Vanda's wife, Pam, committed suicide, taking an overdose of sleeping pills. It was a terrible shock; most people didn't even know Harry was married, let alone had a baby son, Johan.

On their way to London the band stopped in Perth, where a performance had been hastily arranged on the tarmac alongside a Lancaster bomber. But even here the inevitable happened and the 4000-strong crowd surged forward, seemingly as one screaming mass, and the local police had to intervene. 'At one stage,' reported *The Canberra Times*, 'several hysterical girls were being carried away or led off the tarmac, displaying bare midriffs and thighs as they struggled with police.'

When the band finally boarded their London-bound 707, there was another problem—a bomb scare—and they rushed off in a police wagon to a remote part of the airport. Bad omens were everywhere: Pam's death, the crowd invasion, a bomb scare. Was someone trying to tell them something?

There were changes happening in-house, too: soon after reaching London, George began writing with Harry Vanda rather than Stevie Wright, and a formidable musical relationship was consummated. The music they'd make now would grow more sophisticated, more ambitious and not always strictly commercial.

A few months into their UK sortie, and yet to make any real impact, Harry and George slacked off one afternoon, catching a movie featuring a performance from The Swingle Singers, an eight-piece French vocal group. Something clicked, and when they returned to the studio, the distinctive opening notes of what became their signature song, the brilliant 'Friday on My Mind', fell neatly into place. The record was produced by brash American Shel Talmy—who'd already struck gold with The Kinks and The Who—and reached number 6 on the UK charts in late 1966. No Australian rock band had achieved this type of success; The Easybeats were trailblazers. (In May 1967 'Friday' entered the US charts, peaking at number 16.)

Back in Australia, Malcolm's mind was duly blown. Since his departure, George had been regularly sending back records that he thought his siblings might connect with, as well as clippings of The Easybeats' progress, but this was different: George now was a star. A framed gold record of 'Friday' took pride of place on the mantelpiece at the Young home in Burwood.

'Geez, how did this happen?' Malcolm said to Angus as they toiled away on their guitars, even more determined to emulate their brother.

Malcolm was so impressed, in fact, that one day he and a friend skived off from school, came home, lifted the framed gold record of 'Friday' off the wall and decided to play it on the family stereo. Malcolm simply couldn't contain his curiosity: what did a gold record sound like? Not like 'Friday on My Mind', weirdly; the song that played was 'Sorry', one of The Easybeats' earlier hits.

With George as his guide, Malcolm's musical vocabulary developed pretty swiftly: he was now heavily into guitarists like Eric Clapton, especially when Clapton was with John Mayall & the Bluesbreakers, and Fleetwood Mac co-founder Peter Green. There were also the bluesmen, Muddy Waters in particular. Malcolm felt a real connection, as he'd recount years later to the *Chicago Tribune*: 'We would relate to what they were singing about. When a family uproots itself and moves to the other side of the world because your dad couldn't get a job, you didn't feel part of the system, if there even was a system. The blues singers were talking about everyday life, and they pushed a button [in me].'

Then there was Chuck Berry—Malcolm was as mad for Chuck as Angus was. 'I mean, just about everything he did back then was great,' Malcolm said of Berry's hot streak in the 1950s, which produced such hits as 'Maybellene' and 'Roll Over Beethoven'.

Another song to have a huge impact on Malcolm was The Who's 'My Generation' (produced by none other than Shel Talmy); it altered his way of thinking about what a three-minute pop single could be. To Malcolm, it was an incredible record, very powerful, heavier than anything by The Beatles or The Rolling Stones. 'That changed my whole thing,' Malcolm said.

As George and Harry struggled with a follow-up to 'Friday' in the UK, Malcolm and Angus caught one of many big shows that rolled into Sydney. On 21 January 1967, the Yardbirds played the Sydney Stadium, the same venue that The Beatles had filled two and a half years earlier. (The Yardbirds' 'I'm a Man' was one of the first records that Angus ever bought.) It was a stellar bill: also playing were

Roy Orbison, the Walker Brothers and an assortment of local talent, including pop star Johnny Young (no relation).

'It was just a great atmosphere,' Angus said of the show. 'They came on, they played, they were really short and sweet. I thought, this is very flash.' Angus was particularly impressed by the sight of then-Yardbird Jimmy Page playing his guitar with a bow. Yardbirds' singer Keith Relf also impressed the Youngs; he was no poser. 'He didn't dazzle you with his hips—he concentrated on what he was there for: to make a bit of rock and roll.'

George and his fellow Easybeats returned to Oz in mid-May 1967—and things had changed. Gone were the matching suits and high collars of their early days. Disembarking from their flight, George looked every inch the rock star in a flowing scarf and Carnaby Street clobber, while Stevie Wright's tired eyes were hidden behind outrageously oversized, oval-shaped shades. Harry Vanda sported a black leather vest-cum-shirt. They looked impossibly cool, though clearly exhausted—the very same fatigued look that the members of AC/DC would wear on their returns from the UK during the 1970s.

A civic reception was held for the band in Sydney, attended by the Lord Mayor of Sydney. 'Three years ago,' noted a reporter at the event, 'the boys were playing in a laundry at Villawood Hostel—only for their own amusement.' As they left the reception, the band was mobbed by female fans, but that was hardly a surprise. It was almost expected.

Yet despite the playful sparring between Stevie and George at a Sydney meet-and-greet with the press—'I've got talent,' Wright laughed. 'Can you sign me up?'—behind the scenes The Easybeats were starting to come undone. Wright felt shut out of the creative process; drugs were leaving their mark on the band and, despite their success, they were broke. They were actually in debt, as the bills started to mount for their long and sometimes unproductive sessions in the studio.

Despite some great musical moments, what ensued for The Easybeats was a classic study in how *not* to make it big. In August 1967 they toured the US with crooner Gene Pitney—hardly the neatest of fits for a band now dabbling in psychedelia. They did make some friends in high places while in the US—expat Aussie writer Lillian Roxon, an influential figure, became a much-needed advocate of the band. She rated George 'a genius'. Max's Kansas City nightclub regular Lou Reed fell so deeply in love with Vanda and Young's 'Falling Off the Edge of the World' that he'd play it repeatedly on the jukebox in Max's back room. 'This is one of the most beautiful songs in the world,' he told Roxon.

But they simply couldn't repeat the global success of 'Friday on My Mind'. 'Hello, How Are You' did reach the UK Top 20 in April 1968, but George hated it, writing it off as 'cornball schmaltzy shit'. Two months later their single 'Good Times' gained a high-profile fan in Beatle Paul McCartney, who allegedly pulled off to the side of the road on hearing the song and called the BBC, demanding they play it again. Still, it wasn't a hit. In July they played the Royal Albert Hall at the Sounds '68 concert, part of a highly impressive lineup: The Move, The Byrds (with Gram Parsons), Joe Cocker, The Bonzo Dog Doo-Dah Band and The Alan Bown Set all played. But by August 1969 The Easybeats were as good as done, leaving behind one more classic single, the soulful, red-blooded 'St. Louis', which, ironically enough, scraped into the US Top 100 well after the band had given up on any further attempts of going global.

The Easybeats returned home for a five-week, 35-date tour in October 1969. More changes had taken place behind the scenes: Harry Vanda was engaged to 21-year-old Melburnian Robyn Thomas. Stevie Wright had been engaged to his fiancée, Gail Baxter, since the time they left for London. Bassist Dick Diamonde was also engaged, to actress Charlene Collins. They weren't just pop stars anymore; they were about to become family men. *The Australian Women's Weekly* reacted with due shock: 'Female fans of The Easybeats . . . will be dismayed to find out that three of their idols will soon cease to be bachelors.'

When asked about The Easybeats' future, the band members refused to admit they were about to split, but insiders knew this was their last hurrah.

On this final tour they were supported by The Valentines, a bubblegum-pop band from Perth who'd covered Vanda and Young's 'Peculiar Hole in the Sky'—when not playing current chart hits such as 'Build Me Up Buttercup'. One of the two singers in The Valentines was a larrikin named Bon Scott, a wild child with a police record and a devilish glint in his eye. The Valentines dressed in matching red velvet outfits, Scott's tattoos hidden beneath several layers of foundation.

After playing to a near-empty room in Wollongong on 26 October, The Easybeats were done. It was hardly the most dignified of farewells for the trailblazing band. After five Australian number 1 hits and the global success of 'Friday on My Mind', they somehow wound up $85,000 in the red.

Vanda and Young returned to the UK to work as a song-writing and production team, hoping to erase some of their debt and fine-tune their studio skills. They also made a pact that whoever they worked with in the future would not make the same business mistakes as The Easybeats, who had committed such rookie errors as signing conflicting record deals—in the same country. Creatively, The Easybeats had lost themselves in baroque pop, trying to craft their own *Sgt. Pepper's,* when their real strength lay in rocky belters such as 'St. Louis'.

Over time, Malcolm Young would come to be the beneficiary of George's new musical manifesto: keep it simple; find out what you do best and stick with it. No more 'cornball schmaltzy shit'. Don't fuck about. And when it comes to business, never, ever get screwed over.

★

It was also a time of change for Malcolm. One day in late 1970, Angus yelled to him from the front door of their house at 4 Burleigh Street: 'Some guys are looking for you.'

He had visitors.

Standing in the doorway of their home were some musicians from a Sydney band named Velvet Underground—drummer Herm Kovac, guitarist Les Hall, bassist Steve Crothers and singer Andy Imlah. The band had been around since 1967, finding steady work on the dance circuit playing the hits of the day. Now they were on the hunt for a new guitarist. At a recent gig at the Toowoomba Show in Queensland, headliner Stevie Wright had approached the band with a suggestion—and a hot tip.

'You'd be heaps better with another guitarist,' Wright told them. 'And I know just the guy. His brother is George Young from The Easybeats.'

With that he tore a poster off the wall and wrote down Malcolm's name and address. The Easybeats may have been done and dusted, but George's name still carried plenty of weight.

The Youngs didn't seem to have a phone, so Kovac and the others decided on the direct approach, simply rocking up in the hope that Malcolm would be home. Yet they almost turned around and ran when they reached 4 Burleigh Street: the door was opened by a pint-sized skinhead, his hair shaved back to the skull, wearing bovver boots and a menacing grin. His teeth were a curious shade of green.

'Erm, we came to see about a guitarist,' someone stammered, as the others took a few steps backwards. The visitors were startled: who, or what, the hell was that?

The scary dwarf—aka Angus Young—nodded and disappeared back inside the house, shouting out to his brother.

Calm was restored, however, when Malcolm's parents, William and Margaret, welcomed the visitors in and immediately made them feel at home. This was a family home, small but neat and orderly. The gold record for 'Friday on My Mind' was up on the mantelpiece, but that was pretty much it for rock-star trappings. A photo of George and his wife Sandra on their wedding day sat alongside the gold record. Malcolm and Angus shared a bedroom, set off from the living room.

Malcolm's mother headed into the kitchen to make tea. Sister Margaret, who lived at the rear of the house with her husband Sam (who had worked as a roadie for The Easybeats) and their ten-year-old Sammy Jr, entered and introduced herself. Margaret quickly warmed to Kovac, especially when she found out he was a teetotaller who went to Mass every Sunday. She felt he was mature, a good influence. Margaret christened him 'Uncle Herm'.

Malcolm then swaggered into the room, wearing his standard uniform of jeans and favourite green T-shirt. Kovac was impressed by the way that Malcolm carried himself. He looked like he meant business.

'I didn't know if it was a self-aware thing,' Kovac would later explain, 'but . . . I got to see it hundreds of times over the next 40 years: the look on his face and spring in his step was always the same.'

As they talked, Kovac had a question for Malcolm.

'What's that language you all talk in?' he asked. He couldn't understand a word any of the Youngs were saying. The family may have left Scotland, but they'd hung onto their pea-soup-thick accent.

'You'll have to become a Scot,' Malcolm replied, grinning wryly.

Kovac and the others invited Malcolm up to Mona Vale, where the band lived, for a jam. The visitors were surprised at how casually Malcolm delivered the news to his mother. Mona Vale was a good hour's drive away, maybe more, way over on the northern side of the city.

'Hey, Ma, I'm going ooot,' Malcolm said. 'Be back tomorrow.' And that was that.

But Angus refused to let them leave without displaying his own virtuoso skills. He enticed the visitors into the room he shared with Malcolm, where he proceeded to run amok on his Gibson SG guitar, leaping from bed to bed, rolling around on the floor, pulling demented faces—essentially, all the antics that would later become his onstage trademarks. The guys from Velvet Underground were savvy enough to know that he could play, but that didn't mean Angus was beyond criticism. He was only fifteen, after all—just a kid.

His one-man show over, Angus turned to the gathering and asked, 'Well, waddya reckon?'

Kovac thought this through for a moment.

'Do you know any chords?' he teased.

The jam in Mona Vale went well, even better than Malcolm or the band could have hoped. They worked their way through a hefty and reasonably tasty song list: The Stones' 'Jumpin' Jack Flash', Free's 'The Stealer' and 'All Right Now', Dave Edmunds's 'I Hear You Knocking', Deep Purple's 'Black Night', Gary Wright's 'Get on the Right Road' and Shocking Blue's 'Venus'. Malcolm made it clear that not only was he a rock-steady rhythm guitarist but he could also fire off a solo when necessary, taking the lead on 'I Hear You Knocking', 'Venus', 'Get on the Right Road' and Badfinger's 'No Matter What'. Les Hall asked if he'd be willing to share lead guitarist duties; Malcolm agreed in a heartbeat.

'Malcolm was a natural musician,' said Kovac. 'He picked up new songs incredibly quickly.'

'Malcolm fitted in without a ripple,' said bass player Steve Crothers. 'The thing about him was he had no ego. He was never in a bad mood, either. He was always up for a laugh and if something displeased him, he just went quiet, and shook his head.'

Crothers figured that there were a lot of things that Malcolm liked about Velvet Underground. 'We had long hair. We owned a van. We had a record out. And we had so much work we were full-time.' Malcolm was still pretty green; how could he not have been impressed?

The record Crothers referred to was a version of Jefferson Airplane's 'Somebody to Love'. It had been released by Festival in early 1970 and although it flopped, it was a professional recording.

Back at Burwood, Malcolm broke the news of his recruitment to his family. His parents were ambivalent; while they encouraged their kids to play music, they weren't convinced that rock and roll was a reliable career, especially after the dramas George had experienced with The Easybeats. They were also concerned—with due cause—that this might spell the end of Malcolm Young, apprentice fitter and turner. *What if he had nothing to fall back on?*

But Angus was thrilled. 'Can I come to your gigs?' he asked Malcolm.

Malcolm wasn't sure this was such a great idea, but then sister Margaret spoke up.

'Only if Uncle Herm keeps an eye on you.'

A deal was struck. Despite being under-age, Angus was allowed to tag along and see his brother play if Kovac watched out for him. In return, Angus agreed to make Vegemite toast and Ovaltine for the band after every gig. He'd become their caterer, purely by accident.

★

Malcolm had also come to the attention of Ted Albert, the businessman/producer who'd championed The Easybeats and continued to run the Alberts family empire. In the wake of The Easybeats' demise, Alberts struck paydirt with expat Englishman Ted Mulry, a sometime visitor to the Young household, and his lush 'Falling in Love Again', a Top 10 hit in March 1971. The song was written and produced by—who else?—Vanda and Young. Mulry's days as a bulldozer driver for the Department of Main Roads were coming to an end, while Harry and George's hot streak had officially begun.

Ted Albert had a smart approach to business: he would sign acts to his in-house label, Albert Productions, then he'd hire a studio to record and produce the music (until Alberts built their own, in 1973, on the fifth floor of a family-owned building in Sydney's King Street). The finished product was then leased to major label EMI, who'd press the vinyl, as well as handle marketing and distribution. Artists were also encouraged to sign with J. Albert & Son, their in-house publishing arm. Alberts was a one-stop music shop.

One day at Burwood, William told his boys that 'the man from the record company is coming over'—Ted Albert, who felt a strong connection to the Youngs, sometimes checked in with the family. Albert arrived and started speaking with William, but stopped when he heard music coming from somewhere in the house.

'Who's that?' he asked.

'That's Malcolm and Angus,' William replied.

Albert had first met Malcolm and Angus in the mid-1960s, during an Easybeats recording session, and had given them a tape recorder to experiment with at home. Now he could hear that the brothers were developing as musicians.

'Well,' Albert said, listening closely, 'if they ever want to do anything, send them to me.'

A relationship that would stretch over 40 years was set in stone that day. Clearly, Ted Albert's radar for quality rock and roll remained fully functional.

Albert was a man who deserved respect, as confirmed by Herm Kovac, who went on to record for Alberts with the Ted Mulry Gang. 'When Ted [Albert] spoke we listened; he reminded me of the headmaster that everyone liked . . . You immediately warmed to him.'

★

Malcolm made his debut with Velvet Underground at Parramatta in April 1971, at a venue named The Rivoli. Their set list was deep with covers: The Rolling Stones' 'Brown Sugar' and Blues Image's 'Ride Captain Ride', as well as Deep Purple's 'Black Night' and songs from Badfinger and Slade—even George Harrison's 'My Sweet Lord', an uncharacteristically mellow number, somehow made its way into their set, with Malcolm playing lead guitar, no less.

Malcolm also liked to play Simon & Garfunkel's folk-rocker 'Mrs Robinson'; he especially loved the catchy guitar intro and would borrow Kovac's acoustic in order to master it. Malcolm had a softer musical side that few people knew about. He owned copies of Elton John's earliest albums and some of Paul McCartney soft-pop solo work; he had a real thing for melodic singer-songwriters.

Malcolm was also happy to share Easybeats stories with his bandmates. Sometimes a song would come on the radio and he'd note, with some pride, 'My brooder wrote that.'

The Velvets played a gig at Santa Sabina College, a high school in Strathfield not far from the Youngs' home. It was quite the gig, too; Malcolm and Les Hall locked into a guitar duel during The Stones' 'Can't You Hear Me Knocking' and the song ran for some twenty epic minutes. Angus, who was looking on, was a convert; it's likely that this was the moment when he decided that rock and roll was his future. The Ovaltine was especially sweet that night.

Soon enough, Malcolm and Kovac wrote their first song; it was called 'Coming Home'. The pair argued over the second chord in the chorus.

'You can't play that,' Kovac told him.

'Why not?' Malcolm replied.

'You're playing open strings in standard tuning. That's not right. What's the name of the chord, then?' Kovac said, challenging his bandmate, who was breaking all the rules.

'I dunno,' said Malcolm, looking down at his guitar, shrugging his shoulders. 'But it sounds good.'

Kovac couldn't argue with him—and the song remained unchanged.

One of the Velvets' earliest road trips was to Muswellbrook, a few hours north of Sydney, for a show at the town's School of Arts Hall. In the hotel across the road from the gig, Malcolm and Kovac sat opposite each other in their room, Kovac strumming chords on his Maton while Malcolm perfected his guitar licks—this became a regular event whenever they travelled. When they were closer to home, Malcolm would spend Sunday afternoons at Kovac's place, the pair jamming jazz for hours on end. They were growing close. 'He was a great jazz guitarist. Knew all the chords and licks,' Kovac remembered.

There was a steady flow of work for the band. Sydney had at least half a dozen venues that offered them gigs. 'It was more than The Beatles did in Hamburg,' noted bassist Crothers. 'It was often boring and tedious, but it certainly made us good musicians.'

Word spread quickly—the Velvets had a solid reputation, and they now had George Young's brother on board—and the band was profiled in *Go-Set* by a writer using the by-line Aunty Agnes. 'Act Two [of Velvet Underground] begins in April 1971,' she wrote. 'There are now five happy looking faces on stage, and rock music is driving from the wall of amps situated at the back of the stage. Velvet Underground is rocking again; the line-up has changed slightly with . . . the addition of a second guitarist, Malcolm Young.

'Velvet Underground have changed,' concluded Aunty Agnes, 'for the better.'

Malcolm was very impressed by the world of the Velvets. He certainly hadn't played in such a professional outfit before; his previous groups had rarely gotten out of the scout hall. 'I think when he first started with us,' said Crothers, 'he was a bit blown away that everybody could play just like the record, and that we played big venues.'

The hard part, Crothers laughed, 'was getting him to swap the green T-shirt and jeans for something a bit flashier.'

Malcolm made it clear how much he respected the guys in the band when they stopped in at Burwood on the way to a gig. Malcolm not only offered them a cup of tea, he actually ducked into the kitchen to prepare it. No one in his family had witnessed that before from Malcolm, whose only relationship with the kitchen was to forage for food. Angus feigned a heart attack. Malcolm's mother was speechless.

Malcolm and Angus continued their fieldwork in May 1971 when they were among the 30,000 punters who travelled to Randwick Racecourse for another huge outdoor show. The headline act was Deep Purple, and Manfred Mann's Earth Band was also on the bill, but the Youngs were far more interested in British outfit Free. This was the kind of band Malcolm could imagine himself leading one day; they were raw and rockin', with a heavy case of the blues, and they had a soulful singer out front (Paul Rodgers), while out the back they had a rhythm machine named Simon Kirke on drums. They also had an impressive, inspired guitarist in Paul Kossoff, who shared many of Malcolm's influences: Eric Clapton and Jimi Hendrix were two of his touchstones. Malcolm had no idea, of course, as he watched the show that day at Randwick, that his and Kossoff's paths would inter- sect in just a few years' time, in the strangest possible way.

3

'Don't worry. Socks kill spunk.'

Even though Velvet Underground regularly filled venues such as the Wollongong Youth Centre and the Forum in the northern Sydney suburb of Brookvale, Malcolm continued to hold down a day job at Berlei. Every Tuesday and Thursday, the band's roadie Ronnie would collect Malcolm after work, drive him to the Northern Beaches for rehearsal, then drop him home afterwards. After playing their weekend gigs, every Sunday night Ronnie the Roadie would drive Malcolm back to Burwood, so he could get to work the next morning. Malcolm was holding down a lively schedule, which he'd maintain for the first six months of what would be close to three years with the band.

Malcolm's world view was still pretty limited. That was made clear during a road trip to Newcastle for a gig. When the band pulled over for a toilet break, Malcolm gazed at the wilderness that surrounded them. 'Look at all the fucking trees!' he exclaimed, his eyes wide open, taking in the huge eucalypts. His bandmates couldn't quite work out why he was so overawed, but then it hit them: Malcolm had seen little of the world beyond Cranhill, Villawood and Burwood. He couldn't have been any greener. (Malcolm would become equally excited at the sight of the Ettamogah Bunyip, a coin-operated installation at a wildlife sanctuary near Albury. There weren't many bunyips in Burwood, mechanical or otherwise.)

While with Velvet Underground, Malcolm also travelled by plane for the first time since his voyage from the UK to Australia almost a decade earlier.

'Make way for the jetsetter!' he proudly told the others as he stepped onto the plane, destined for the New England region, where some shows had been arranged by local radio station 2MO. He carried his belongings in a brown Samsonite school case. Malcolm couldn't believe that they served tea and biscuits on the flight, he was so inexperienced.

Malcolm may have been a tad unworldly, but he didn't lack ambition. His plan, even at this early stage, was to bring together a band of his own that could take on the world, much as George had done with The Easybeats. Malcolm certainly looked like a man on a mission when the band was again profiled in *Go-Set* during mid-August 1971. In the group photo, Malcolm was the only one seated, and he stared directly at the camera, as if to say *Don't fuck with me. I mean business.*

'We're not anarchists or anything like that,' the band told *Go-Set*'s reporter, probably in response to a question about their name, which was taken from the same Michael Leigh cult novel that had grabbed the attention of Lou Reed and John Cale in New York. 'But we know what we like and the kids like it, too.'

'Their average age is 20 years,' the article stated, 'and not surprisingly they play mainly at suburban dances and halls, where the kids want to hear the kind of music the Velvet Underground specialises in: "thumpy rock".

'They make no claims that their music is art, just good old rock 'n' roll . . . of the type that Stones used to play in 1965.' Malcolm would have appreciated the comparison to The Stones, a band he particularly loved.

★

Bon Scott and his new band Fraternity were also receiving their share of press ink, much of it courtesy of Vince Lovegrove, Bon's old buddy from The Valentines. Writing in *Go-Set*, Lovegrove described the alternative community that Fraternity was trying to build in the Adelaide Hills and made it seem as though Scott and his bandmates had found the same kind of bucolic retreat that The Band, Bob Dylan and many others had discovered at Woodstock in upstate New York.

'[Fraternity] live like no other band in Australia, in a house in the hills 17 miles from Adelaide,' wrote Lovegrove. 'It's surrounded by seven acres of bushland. They're far from everything but nature. What a buzz! Once a week they come into the city to have a meeting with their management and collect their pay. They only leave their pad to play gigs.'

Bon, who sang and played the recorder and timbala in the band, spoke in a language befitting the counterculture scene he'd bought into; it was hard to believe that he'd one day be writing raunchy songs like 'Whole Lotta Rosie'. 'The point is, the dollar sign is not the ultimate,' he told Lovegrove. 'We want to try and help each other develop and live. So that the thing inside of us, whether it be creative or not, is satisfied. Something makes us tick and it's up to people to satisfy that something. We are satisfying ourselves and others by creating an environment.'

Scott was sporting a new look—a harsh homemade haircut and a beard that wouldn't have been wasted on the Amish—when he and Fraternity performed a note-perfect cover of The Band's 'The Weight' on ABC TV show *GTK*. He'd moved on from the sticky-sweet pop of The Valentines, but it was still hard to imagine Scott becoming a hairy-chested rock-and-roll icon. He was a hippie.

In July 1971, Scott and Fraternity won the hugely influential band comp Hoadley's Battle of the Sounds, and it was one concession to the mainstream they were happy to make. With the help of the $2000 prize money they decided to trade the Adelaide Hills for London. It was a bad move. London would do to Fraternity what it had done to everyone from The Easybeats onwards: it'd break their spirit, then it'd kill the band. But while in the UK, Fang (as Fraternity became known) supported a band from Newcastle upon Tyne named Geordie, whose lead singer was Brian Johnson. Scott paid close attention when Johnson waded into crowds with the band's guitarist riding on his shoulders. Johnson was quite the showman—and the crowd lapped it up.

While Bon Scott froze in London's winter, Malcolm made yet another pilgrimage to Randwick Racecourse, in late February 1972, again with Angus in tow. There they witnessed Jimmy Page doing his thing for the second time, this time with supergroup Led Zeppelin, whose early records had impressed the Youngs.

But Malcolm didn't like Robert Plant's wail, or his stage manner. Way too much flash.

'Singer was a blond fella,' he'd say, dismissively. 'Bit of a poser.'

Angus's reaction to Plant was pretty similar: 'He'd sing like he was picking his nose.'

A few weeks later, Velvet Underground played at half-time during a rugby league match between Sydney clubs Manly and Penrith at suburban Brookvale Oval, the first of a series of weekly half-time gigs. Also on the bill was Ted Mulry. Not long after the Velvets began their set, a stray football flew through the air and crashed into Malcolm's guitar, rendering it useless. While a mercy dash was undertaken for a replacement axe, an Aboriginal man throwing a boomerang stepped in to entertain the 13,000-strong crowd. The rock-and-roll show, eventually, went on.

The half-time segment was sponsored by hair product company Pantene, and 'they couldn't have found a better advertisement than all these straggly mops', sniffed a reporter from *The Manly Daily*, who smugly referred to the band's appearance as 'little Woodstock'.

Go-Set magazine also reported on this unlikely meeting of footy and rock and roll, but with far less condescension towards the band, if not the crowd: 'Velvet [Underground] caused a recent sensation among the meat-pie sect.'

★

The idea of following in brother George's big footsteps meant everything to Malcolm—and Angus clearly felt the same, because he dropped out of Ashfield Boys' at fifteen, the legal

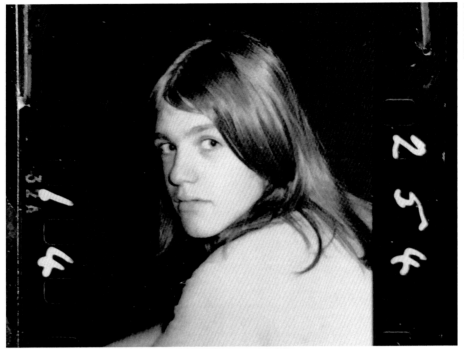

'We never realised that we were learning guitars,' Malcolm said of his teenage years. 'They were always just there.'

With the Velvet Underground, early 1970s. *Clockwise from top left:* Herm Kovac, Andy Imlah, Les Hall, Mick Sheffzick and Malcolm Young.

Malcolm (middle) in action with the Velvet Underground.

Malcolm poses in front of his impressive Marshall amplifier, purchased on the 'trust-you-once' scheme.

Malcolm (bottom row, left), again with the Velvet Underground, which would morph into the successful Ted Mulry Gang. Malcolm, however, had other plans.

AC/DC at their first studio shoot, in early 1974. *From left:* Dave Evans, Rob Bailey, Peter Clack, Malcolm and Angus Young.

AC/DC with producers/mentors George Young (far left) and Harry Vanda (to Bon Scott's right), 1975

Bon Scott (right) and Malcolm (left) lead the charge at Sydney's Victoria Park on 7 September 1975.

An early promo shot for the *High Voltage* album. *Clockwise from top:* Angus Young, Malcolm, Bon Scott and Phil Rudd.

At the piano in Alberts, with Angus (left) and George (right) who gave his brothers this advice: 'You can't polish a turd.'

Malcolm (left), inside Alberts studio with Angus. Malcolm is playing the guitar given to him by AC/DC co-producer and former Easybeat Harry Vanda.

PHILLIP MORRIS

A promo shot from 1975, with bassist Mark Evans (right) now in the fold. Alberts staffer and band confidante Fifa Riccobono looks on.

From left: Angus, Mark Evans and Malcolm bring the thunder in Alberts studio during sessions for *Dirty Deeds Done Dirt Cheap*, 1976.

leaving age. By this time Malcolm had quit his job at Berlei and gone full-time with Velvet Underground. Angus's cards had been marked from that fateful first day at school, when he was singled out and caned simply for being Malcolm's brother. But, just like Malcolm, he was hardly a model student. As one former classmate, Neil Litchfield, recalled, Angus 'was the head of the smoking brigade at school', a gang of junior reprobates who'd cut class to smoke ciggies. A rare photo of Angus at school, with the class of 1963, captures him sporting a mile-wide grin. He was cheeky, a troublemaker.

Angus almost coughed up a lung when he was once asked if he, or Malcolm, were seen as famous former alumni of their school. 'I think they hung up garlic cloves to keep us away,' he snorted, although he would, in time, find good use for his Ashfield Boys' uniform.

Again, just as he had with Malcolm, Angus's father insisted that he get a job, and Angus found work in a printing company, allegedly producing copies of porno rag *Ribald*. At the same time he put together his own band, with a little help from ubiquitous 'Uncle Herm' Kovac.

'I was teaching drums to a kid named Trevor James,' said Kovac, 'and suggested Angus jam with him as it would help him to play with another instrument. At that stage Angus was into [American rock guitarist] Leslie West and Mountain so they played all of that. Velvet Underground took them as a support for gigs down at Ulladulla and Batemans Bay.'

The band was called Kantuckee—sometimes Kantucky— both misspellings of Angus's favourite fast-food chain. The other members of the band were singer Bob McGlynn and bassist John Stevens.

Apart from Mountain covers, Kantuckee's set list included an original, 'The Kantuckee Stomp', and they also covered Cactus's 1972 album *'Ot 'n' Sweaty* from beginning to end. Angus, again like Malcolm, had grown his hair long. Printed on top of his amp, which towered over him, was this ominous warning: HIGH VOLTAGE.

Angus's band soon underwent another name change— to Tantrum—and played some shows at Sydney nightclub Chequers, where AC/DC would stage their own 'coming out' in the not-too-distant future. The 550-capacity club had been the Sydney venue of choice for the glamorous and elite; Prime Minister John Gorton was once seen slipping backstage at Chequers to chat with Liza Minelli, while gossip columnist Rita Cobb documented every crucial coming and going. Big acts such as Shirley Bassey and Sarah Vaughan would command upwards of £5000 for a week's work. But times had changed. Chequers was now more grimy than glamorous, the domain of sweaty young rock bands like Tantrum, all hustling for a buck (rather than 5000 quid). And Angus, taking his cue from Malcolm, was now introducing himself as 'Angus Young, brother of George Young from The Easybeats, also the brother of Malcolm Young'.

Malcolm and Angus were contrasting characters in some ways. Malcolm didn't mind a drink, or anything else going around, whereas Angus had no interest in getting wasted. He'd rarely drink alcohol, let alone smoke grass; it's likely he saw Easybeats' singer Stevie Wright come undone in a blur of booze and dope, which was enough to scare anyone straight. (Drug-takers were 'hippie cunts', according to Angus.) Angus did, however, have a weakness for chocolate milk, Benson & Hedges cigarettes and spaghetti bolognaise, which, when combined, would cause him to spray snot and saliva in all directions as he played. One bandmate would describe it as Angus's 'snot cyclone'. Anyone down front at a Tantrum gig would wear the lot. It was no wonder that when the brothers did play together, Malcolm opted for stage right, well out of his brother's line of fire.

Angus would admit that 'the only one that had a problem with it'—his diet, that is—'was my dentist'. A future member of the AC/DC crew, Pat Pickett, said of Angus's teeth: 'If there's a white one in there he'd have a snooker set.' The good-looking Malcolm, not surprisingly, was the Young brother who tended to get the girls.

Malcolm's fondness for a tipple didn't extend to all his Velvet bandmates. He actually had to talk straitlaced drummer Kovac into his first drink, one afternoon after a gig at the Spinning Wheel Disco in Narrabeen on Sydney's Northern Beaches.

'Come on, Herm,' Malcolm said, after the drummer had finished his first. 'Just one more.'

Kovac reluctantly obliged. Bad move.

A few hours later, when Kovac started to regain some of his senses, Malcolm showed him a polaroid. Someone had drawn glasses, a moustache and a beard on Kovac's face with a texta; he was snapped while standing in the shower, wearing a duffel coat and a sign around his neck that read 'Spy in the rain'. Malcolm thought it was hilarious and would dine out on the story for years afterwards.

Malcolm also had a favourite joke that he'd repeatedly tell the guys in the band: 'A little horny flea is flying around, looking for sex. He spots an elephant and goes for it. At the same time a bee decides to rest on the elephant. The elephant tries brushing the flea off with his trunk, only to be stung by the bee. The elephant screams in pain. "Suffer, baby, suffer!" cries the flea, madly humping away.'

Malcolm thought it was the best joke he'd ever heard. Sometimes he'd say good night to the others, but would suddenly stop and ask, 'Hey, did you hear the one about the flea . . . ?'

Things were on the improve for Malcolm Young, ladies' man. After a Velvets gig at the Tamworth Town Hall, Malcolm and Kovac adjourned to the nearby Flag Motor Inn with a couple of friendly females. They both seemed in for a good night when they realised they only had one condom between them.

'Don't worry,' Malcolm told Kovac, keeping the straightest of faces. 'Socks kill spunk.'

He somehow convinced Kovac that a nylon sock was a perfectly viable form of contraception. But because they were sharing a room, it didn't take long before Kovac realised that Malcolm was pulling his, erm, leg.

'Suddenly,' Kovac recalled, 'the lights came on and Mal was in hysterics; he saw me hunched over, trying to make the sock, which was way too big, stay on.'

Malcolm started referring to Kovac as 'Soggy Socks Herm'. This was another story he'd repeat endlessly.

The drummer did get his revenge. Whenever Malcolm would bring an eager fan back their room and Kovac had struck out, he would grab his trusty harmonica and blow a few notes of 'Oh! Susanna', a mood-killer if ever there was one.

On stage, Malcolm was now the proud owner of an imposing Marshall amp, which he'd bought from a music shop in Brookvale. The shop owner, Barry Farrell, had sold gear to Herm Kovac and others on the proviso that they'd pay him whenever they could, as long as they handed over at least $100 per month. This was referred to as his 'trust you once' scheme. Kovac brought Malcolm into the shop, introduced him as a friend—which qualified him for 'trust you once'—and he walked out with a brand-spanking-new Marshall amp and Quad box.

The rig was huge. 'Mal looked like a pixie next to his [speaker] tower,' said Kovac.

Angus, meanwhile, continued to cater for his brother's band. He was crafty; he knew that Kovac owned a pristine copy of Jeff Beck's 1968 single 'Hi Ho Silver Lining' (with 'Beck's Bolero' on the B-side), a record that Angus craved. Angus offered him $2 for the record, and in order to sweeten the deal, quite literally, ensured that an extra scoop of sugar made its way into every cup of post-gig Ovaltine that he served Kovac. Kovac finally relented and sold the record (which Angus still has, some 40-odd years later).

*

Harry Vanda and George Young's exile in London came to an end in early 1973. George Young and Ted Albert regularly exchanged letters and Albert floated the idea of George and Harry becoming in-house producers for Alberts, with plans to build a studio for their use.

Vanda and Young agreed to resettle their families in Sydney; Albert loaned them both money to buy a home. Harry had married his fiancée Robyn Thomas, while George Young and his wife, Sandra, now had a daughter named

Yvette (known as Evie). Among the items George brought back with him from London was a candy-striped shirt he'd once snapped up at The Beatles' famous (and short-lived) Apple Boutique, which he gave to Malcolm. John Lennon had worn a similar shirt in the *Let It Be* movie. It wasn't a bad talisman, all things considered.

Ted Albert had once given George Young some advice, and now George and Harry adopted it as their own mantra. 'Get it right, get the song right, get the music right, get the mix right,' Albert had told him. 'And only then—when you are happy that you have the absolute best out of the song, out of the record, out of the mix—then you release it. You do not release records to schedules or deadlines, or because the manager or a radio station has to have it on their playlists. You release the record when the record is finished.'

Vanda and Young now had their mission statement: the song came first.

Malcolm, and Angus, quickly became part of the first Vanda/Young project in Australia. The roots of the project, which became known as Marcus Hook Roll Band, took seed while Vanda and Young were still in London, when engineer Allen 'Wally' Waller invited them into the legendary Abbey Road studios to record a few tracks. A song called 'Natural Man' came from that session; Capitol Records in the US were keen on 'Natural Man' and wanted to hear more.

Waller scored a free trip to Australia out of the deal, while the duty-free booze he brought with him would provide the album with a name, in honour of Old Grand-Dad bourbon, a favourite tipple during the ensuing recording.

The Marcus Hook Roll Band sessions, which took place during July and August 1973, marked the first occasion when either Malcolm or Angus had been inside a real recording studio, having been invited by George and Harry. Malcolm learned a lot from the sessions, not all of it good, while for George it was all a bit of a drunken lark.

'We thought it was hilarious, it had just been a joke to us,' George told *Bomp* magazine when asked about the Marcus Hook Roll Band. 'We all got rotten, except for Angus, who was too young, and we spent a month in there boozing it up every night. That was the first thing Malcolm and Angus did before AC/DC. We didn't take it very seriously, so we thought we'd include them to give them an idea of what recording was all about.'

Much of the finished album, *Tales of Old Grand-Daddy*, contained hints of future AC/DC tracks; that driving, insistent rhythm guitar sound would become their trademark. Malcolm's rhythm guitar playing throughout was rock solid; clearly, he was a quick learner. But he also had an epiphany in the studio—Malcolm now understood how modern records were made, and how reliant they were on overdubs and repeated takes. While he was all the better for the in-studio hours, to him it was too laborious, it sucked the energy out of a hot take. He sensed that the type of music he wanted to make was best captured live and raw; he wanted the same kind of spontaneity heard on some of his favourite blues records, or The Stones' live LP, *Get Yer Ya-Ya's Out!*

In a symbolic gesture, he came home one night and binned all his Elton John and Paul McCartney LPs. Enough with that over-produced guff.

In the album credits, Angus and Malcolm were listed among the band's 'main personnel', as was their brother Alex, who'd been playing with UK band Grapefruit (also produced by Vanda and Young) and were signed to The Beatles' Apple label. With George co-producing, it was a rare instance of four Youngs working on the one project.

The album only got a limited release (at least until 2014, when it got a full digital re-package/do-over), and nothing came of the interest shown by Capitol, but it was an invaluable education for Malcolm. In some ways, it was a case of discovering what he didn't like.

A few months before those sozzled Marcus Hook sessions, Malcolm had caught yet another show that left a mark on him as indelible as a tattoo. The Rolling Stones hadn't toured Australia since 1965, when their concerts comprised hastily played songs, lots of screaming, stage invasions and swift, stealthy exits. This time around, though, they gave a show that no one could possibly forget. They entered the Randwick Racecourse on 27 February 1973 in a horse-drawn carriage and departed in a blaze of fireworks that lit up the Sydney sky. Malcolm wasn't mad for razzle-dazzle, but this was The Stones, after all. It was impossible not to be impressed by the spectacle.

The show began with 'Brown Sugar' and finished, fifteen songs later, with 'Jumpin' Jack Flash' and 'Street Fighting Man'. These songs packed the same kind of powerhouse riffs and bluesy swagger that Malcolm himself would soon be creating.

In 1973, The Stones radiated some serious rock-and-roll attitude, too. At their Sydney press conference, Keith Richards was at his broody best; he slouched into the room, sprawled cross-legged on a couch and sparked up the first of an endless series of ciggies.

'You look kind of different to what we expect people are

expected to look,' asked a hapless journo. 'Is this the way you like to dress, Keith?'

'Maybe it's because you live down here and I live somewhere else,' Richards sniped, as an elegantly wasted Mick Jagger fell about laughing.

'Australia doesn't have a good reputation as far as bands are concerned,' added Richards, 'as far as hospitality. You're known as the most inhospitable country.'

Malcolm would one day have good reason to agree with The Stones.

4

'We didn't know what the name [AC/DC] meant.
We just liked the sound of it.'

By the time of The Stones' Sydney extravaganza, Malcolm's
time in Velvet Underground was coming to an end. In late
1972 they'd changed their name to Pony, a nod to the Free
song 'Ride on Pony', but that only lasted six months. Despite
a reassurance from the band to the press that they were still
trading in 'good, straight, rock'n'roll', they were heading in an
entirely new direction. Ted Mulry, recently returned from an
unsuccessful tilt at the UK market, began using Pony more
frequently as his backing band. They shared a booking agent
named Dal Myles (later a Channel 10 newsreader) and often
played the same venues. This was something that rankled for
Malcolm in particular. It got to the point where he sometimes
refused to go on stage when Mulry began a set with Pony
behind him.

'He only needs Les, anyway,' Malcolm said dismissively.
As far as he was concerned, Mulry had no use for two
guitarists.

Then, after another gig, he spoke on the quiet with bassist
Steve Crothers. Malcolm was clearly pissed off.

'We shouldn't be backing Ted,' Malcolm said. 'It makes us look like a backing band—and we should be the stars.'

This was most likely the moment that Malcolm seriously started considering blazing his own trail and forming his own band. He didn't lack ambition.

There was a complication, though: his friendship with drummer Kovac. They'd grown so close that they sometime shared a bed in a caravan on the road when money was tight. They had some lively shared history, too—the 'soggy socks' incident, the 'Spy in the rain' photo and their attempts to co-write songs. There was also a freezing cold night in Armidale when they returned to their hotel room and Malcolm said, upon climbing into his bed, 'You know, the bottom half of my bed feels like a bare mattress.' 'Me, too,' said Kovac. They both stood up, pulled down the blankets and saw that they were right—the stingy proprietor had cut a single sheet in two and dressed each bed with the top half, to give the appearance that each was fully made.

Together they'd had almost three years of gigs and travel and adventures. They'd become best friends, so it wasn't surprising that Malcolm struggled to be as candid with Kovac as he had been with Crothers.

'I want to leave the band,' he finally managed to stammer.

Kovac was stunned. He knew that Malcolm didn't like backing Mulry, but had no idea he felt so strongly about it.

As Kovac said in 2018, 'I was not expecting it and I could see he was getting upset, as he was fumbling for reasons. I knew that he wasn't keen when we backed Ted, but I didn't think that would be a reason to leave.'

'Mate, it's not personal,' Malcolm told him. 'It's strictly musical.'

He went on to explain that he wanted to play heavier music, 'like Deep Purple. And I know you guys will never go that way'.

Then he sprung another surprise on Kovac.

'I know you're close to Les,' Malcolm said, 'but it'd make me happy if you want to come along with me.'

Kovac was torn, and spent a week kicking around the possibility of joining forces with Malcolm. He was split between his loyalty to the other guys in the group and their possible success with Ted Mulry, and his friendship with Malcolm.

'After about a week, however,' Kovac now admits, 'the penny dropped. It was a no-brainer. I hadn't considered the music part of it and when I did, the decision was easy. I hated heavy rock. I hated Deep Purple. But I loved Ted's songs. That's what I wanted to play.

'And I was headstrong,' Kovac adds, 'and Mal was starting to get that way. I wouldn't have lasted two months in his new band. I would have left or been kicked out and may have lost the friendship that endured.'

He was right; this was by no means the end of his relationship with Malcolm. Their friendship continued, and as the star of Ted Mulry Gang (which included Kovac and Les Hall) began to rise—and it shone very brightly in late 1975, when they were sharing the local charts with Swedish superstars ABBA—the band's path would intersect often with that of AC/DC. Both bands would be signed to Alberts, too—Australia's House of Hits.

*

Having now served his apprenticeship with Velvet Underground, Malcolm turned his attention to what he was hearing on the radio. To his ears, acts like Cat Stevens and James Taylor and the Eagles were all too smooth, too downbeat, too *dull*. When he first heard Little River Band, Australia's answer to the Eagles, play their hit 'Curiosity Killed the Cat', he turned to his mate Kovac and said, 'What a fucking stupid song.'

In 1973, one of the most successful homegrown acts was Brian Cadd, a bearded West Australian piano man cut from the same singer-songwriter cloth as American troubadour Billy Joel. The biggest-selling albums of the year came straight from the middle of the road: Neil Diamond's *Hot August Night*, Wings's *Red Rose Speedway*, Elton John's *Don't Shoot Me I'm Only the Piano Player*. The likes of Lobo, Carly Simon, Roberta Flack, Tony Orlando & Dawn, and the Carpenters dominated the Australian singles charts. This was hardly the type of music that rocked Malcolm Young's world. He may still have had a soft spot for 'Mrs. Robinson' and 'My Sweet Lord', but all this was lightweight stuff.

So Malcolm had plenty to rail against. He wanted to form a band that dealt in gut-level rock, played with heart and soul and balls—a band where wearing the same T-shirt and jeans night after night was not just okay but mandatory.

Always the realist, Malcolm also had a practical reason for forming his own band, as he'd tell a reporter from *Billboard* in 2003. 'Yeah, there was a vision—that was basically that we didn't have to have day jobs and could get out and play guitar for a living, something you loved doing. It was great if you could give up your day job and spend more time on the guitar.

'That was our ambition and our vision, and it just got bigger and bigger as [AC/DC] evolved. But there was no grand sort of plan, not like they have these days. We were just working-class people, and we were just glad you could enjoy yourself making money, even if it was 50 bucks a week.'

★

In the spring of 1973, Malcolm began pulling together his band. His singer was Dave Evans, a flashy, lanky frontman who towered over Malcolm and had spent some time as a singer with Pony. Colin Burgess, formerly of successful local act The Masters Apprentices, was recruited to play drums, while Angus's Beelzebub buddy Larry Van Kriedt was on bass. Angus once remembered this as an interim line-up, saying it was 'me, Malcolm [and] a bass player and drummer that we hired because they had a PA system, and I don't know who we had singing. We're still trying to find out.'

Malcolm's biggest and perhaps boldest step was to ask Angus to join his band. There was a simple reason they hadn't worked together beyond the Marcus Hook sessions: they were siblings, they clashed, there was friction. 'We fought all the time,' Malcolm admitted. Angus, however, did share Malcolm's feelings about the current state of music: it was way too soft, too limp. A swift kick in the balls was required.

'I think the '60s was a great time for music, especially for rock and roll,' Angus would tell a reporter from VH1:

It was the era of The Beatles, of The Stones, and then later on The Who and Zeppelin. But at one point in the '70s it just kind of became . . . *mellow*. When Malcolm put the band together, it was obvious what was missing at the time, another great rock band . . . For us it was a pretty easy choice, especially because Malcolm and myself—we're two guitarists—so from the get-go it was going to be a guitar band.

Malcolm made his intentions clear from the start. 'We just wanted to be a good rock and roll band. That's it, that's all we can do. That's what we do best. Trends come and go . . . but we won't ever change.'

There was another practical factor at work in recruiting Angus: Malcolm knew his younger brother. He didn't have to go through the sometimes tricky process of getting to know a stranger, as he would explain in a 1984 interview. 'It's not like finding a guy you want to play with, and then you find out after a year that the guy's a pig or whatever. At least we knew each other from day one. We knew each other's tempers.'

Their father William wasn't so sure it was a solid idea. In fact, he'd been quietly trying to encourage his boys not to pursue rock and roll as a career, as Angus recalled in an interview with *Guitar Player* magazine: 'My parents thought we'd be better off doing something else.'

When Malcolm broke the news about recruiting Angus, William had to stop himself from laughing. 'It'll last a week!' he told them.

Given the volatile nature of the siblings' relationship, William was convinced one brother was likely to kill the other if (or more likely when) things got heated. While they may have shared a bedroom, the Young boys kept their distance. When Angus was practicing, he would hang a

Playboy poster on the bedroom door as a message to Malcolm to stay out.

Brother George, too, was unsure if their personalities would get in the way, but he did recognise their talent. 'They were extraordinarily good musicians in the style they'd latched onto.'

Others close to the scene had a far more upbeat read on Malcolm's decision. Bandmate Larry Van Kriedt knew Malcolm made the right call by recruiting Angus. Van Kriedt said Malcolm was 'a bit of a visionary'.

There was also another sort of pragmatism at work: the brothers had quickly discovered they weren't cut out for 'regular' work, and a rock-and-roll group, as Malcolm had learned while with Velvet Underground, was a far more exciting way to try to make a living. Malcolm also knew that, Angus being a hugely talented lead guitarist, he would be free to focus on rhythm guitar. He wanted to be the band's own Keith Richards, The Human Riff.

*

Around this time, sister Margaret provided some sage advice. She'd sometimes look on as Angus returned home from school each day, strap on his guitar and start playing. She thought it was endearing, this little fella—Angus was on a par with Malcolm in the height department—bashing away at his Gibson in his school uniform. Malcolm and Angus, when talking with VH1's *Behind the Music,* related a conversation they had. 'Margaret said to Angus, "You still look like a schoolboy. Why don't you wear the uniform when you play?"'

'She used to think it was very cute that I'd come home

from school and be in my little room playing guitar,' said Angus. 'I guess she thought it was cute to see a little man with a big guitar.'

Angus went along with the idea, although everyone figured that it was a look he'd eventually outgrow. At least he'd finally found a use for his Ashfield Boys' High uniform; it wasn't as though he'd got to wear it that much during his student days. He'd spent more time wagging school than attending, sneaking ciggies and causing mayhem. The blazer Angus wore on stage wasn't his; it belonged to his brother-in-law Sam Horsburgh. Only those students who made it to Year 11 received blazers, and that certainly wasn't the case with Angus.

Margaret stepped up again when Malcolm and Angus were tossing around possible band names. For a time, they were seriously considering calling themselves The Young Brothers. One night, Margaret was working away at one of Angus's uniforms on her Singer sewing machine when she noticed the 'AC/DC' sign on the sewing machine. 'That could be a good name,' she offered.

Malcolm and Angus both agreed—frankly, they had very few other options. Malcolm didn't know that there was a certain sexual connotation in 'AC/DC', at least until a cabbie put him straight (so to speak).

'What's the name of your band?'

'AC/DC,' Malcolm replied.

'It means *gay*, mate.'

Malcolm was shocked.

'We didn't know what the name meant,' Malcolm would later tell *Juke* magazine. 'We just liked the sound of it . . . and then people started calling us pooftahs.'

The newly christened band rehearsed in a space in inner-city Newtown.

Apart from Angus's school uniform, they looked nothing like the streetwise AC/DC the world would come to know. Malcolm had briefly ditched his favourite T-shirt and jeans and gone glam, (mis)matching over-sized boots with a satin top. As for the rest, it was a strange mix of hippie gear and glam rock styles.

AC/DC made their public debut in December 1973, at a Cronulla venue called The Last Picture Show. The room was run by Denis Laughlin, a fellow Scot, who would help the band book their first gigs. Even at early shows such as this, Angus discovered the benefits of his uniform. 'Wearing something like that helps me become something else,' he said. 'Normally I'm pretty quiet, I keep to myself, but when I get the school suit on it gives me the advantage of being someone else. It's a bit like going to a fancy dress ball.'

The two-pronged guitar attack of Malcolm and Angus had been unleashed. Australian pub audiences had no idea what was about to hit them.

*

AC/DC rang in the new year, 1974, with a gig at Sydney's Chequers. The band played several hour-long sets, recycling songs as the evening dragged on and the clientele got increasingly wasted. Their set list included covers such as The Stones' 'Jumpin' Jack Flash' and 'Honky Tonk Women', The Beatles' 'Get Back' and 'I Want You (She's So Heavy)', Little Richard's 'Tutti Frutti' and some Chuck Berry standards—'School Days' and 'Nadine'—along with a lengthy jam on the old blues number 'Baby Please Don't Go'. Their rocking version owed quite a bit to the 1964 cover of the song by Van Morrison and Them.

AC/DC were quite the sight on stage at Chequers. Singer Evans sported nut-crunching tights and knee-high platform boots, wearing what could have been a prototype 'mansiere' (man-bra) under his candy-coloured jacket. Angus went with his green school uniform and white sneakers, the word 'left' scrawled in texta on both shoes. He had a satchel slung over his shoulder and wore his Ashfield Boys' High tie, which created a stir among his former classmates.

Malcolm wore knee-high green boots and a white jump-suit with puffy sleeves, open to the waist. He could've been mistaken for a jockey, or possibly a pirate or a pimp. The look wasn't a keeper.

Go-Set photographer Philip Morris was invited to the Chequers gig by roadie Ray Arnold, who was helping the fledgling band. A roadie also supplied some A-grade grass, another big drawcard for Morris. Straightaway Morris, who'd shot The Easybeats and other Aussie greats, sensed that AC/DC packed some real rock-and-roll muscle—and that they were great subjects for any photographer. 'When it came to getting great live shots,' he said, 'nobody beat AC/DC. It was all about the energy.'

Morris conducted the band's first formal photo shoot, outside Her Majesty's Theatre in Sydney and he'd continue shooting the band for the next five years: in the studio, playing live, scrawling graffiti on a city wall. Anywhere, anytime—usually prompted by a call from Alberts.

Much to the delight of Malcolm and Angus, there was a strong teen female contingent on their first night at Chequers, and much of their attention was focused on the Youngs—the rest of the band were too old. The girls gathered at stage left, where Angus held court.

Despite the temporary line-up, Angus was still impressed by what was ostensibly AC/DC's debut gig. 'We had to get up and blast away,' he would tell a reporter, 'From the word go, it went great. Everyone thought we were a pack of loonies—you know, who's been feeding them kids bananas?'

Dave Evans, though not long for the band, had equally strong memories of their Chequers debut. 'It was New Year's Eve, we got that gig and we killed it, we absolutely killed it because everyone was drunk, but anyway. It was a great start to the band to be in the top nightspot absolutely chock full of people going crazy on New Year's Eve. We couldn't have had a better start.'

Even at this early stage, the musical roles of Malcolm and Angus were becoming clear. Malcolm encouraged Angus to play solos, where he excelled. Malcolm preferred to play rhythm guitar, and hit those damned strings hard. '[Malcolm's] right hand is always going,' explained Angus. 'He's very clean, he's very hard. It's an attack. I'm just like the colour over the top.'

'I'm playing rhythm because Angus could really soar with the leads,' Malcolm said when asked about their division of duties. 'Angus, he was just so much better [than me], he just went for it and it was brilliant. My place was sitting with rhythm—and I love rhythm.'

The venue's booker invited the band back for more gigs in the new year. Other promoters started seeking out AC/DC's services too, but perhaps under a misapprehension, as Malcolm would explain.

'It's a funny situation,' Malcolm told a reporter, 'because our sister gave us this name, from the sewing machine [and] we thought it was great. All of a sudden, we found this agent in Sydney'—they'd started working with promoter Michael Chugg—'and a week later we got calls from all the different cities in Australia, wanting us to come down and play. We thought, "This is great . . ." We got down and played to all these transvestites, because of the name of the band.'

Still, a gig was a gig; it put food in their mouths. Now the logical next step for Malcolm and his new band—and it was very clearly Malcolm's band—was to get into the studio with Vanda and Young.

5

'We used to play "Jumpin' Jack Flash" and add fifteen
minutes of bullshit so we could fill up a 40-minute set.'

AC/DC's first recording session took place in January 1974,
when they cut an original called 'Can I Sit Next to You,
Girl', with Vanda and Young producing. Malcolm and
Angus shared the songwriting credits. George Young played
bass on the track; Colin Burgess drummed.

Much to Malcolm's relief, this was a vastly different experience to the Marcus Hook Roll Band sessions. Spontaneity
was now the key; there was no tiresome overdubbing.
Perhaps studio time was an issue—Vanda and Young had
also been working with Stevie Wright on his solo debut LP,
Hard Road, which would see the light of day in early April,
so their availability was restricted. Malcolm played rhythm
guitar on Wright's album, the feature being the epic three-
part 'suite' 'Evie', which would become an enormous success
for Wright and for Vanda and Young, who also wrote the
track. (Malcolm actually played lead guitar on 'Evie [Part
One]'.) Not many 10-minute-plus songs got played on radio,
let alone became number 1 hits.

During AC/DC's debut recording sessions, Malcolm and

Angus were hugely impressed by George's innate ability to get to the heart of a song.

'Working with George . . . everything seemed to be in his head,' said Angus. 'He'll say, "Play us what you've got" and then he'll say, "Let's try this". Just try this, try that. He seemed to be creating things in his head.'

George had a policy in the studio: if the song they were considering could be played on the piano, it could be recorded. It proved to be a rock-steady litmus test.

And if it didn't work?

'You can't polish a turd,' George told his brothers. Fair enough. Lesson learned.

The band cut a few other songs at these first sessions, including 'Rockin' in the Parlour', another Young/Young composition, which would become the B-side of 'Can I Sit Next to You, Girl', as well as 'Sunset Strip' (aka 'Soul Stripper') and 'Rock 'n' Roll Singer', early cuts that were later re-recorded for the *High Voltage* and *T.N.T.* albums.

As first recordings go, 'Can I Sit Next to You, Girl'—while not exactly a ball-tearing rocker long for the AC/DC canon—had enough grunt to give a hint of the direction in which Malcolm was steering the band. And it was a hell of a long way from many of the songs topping the charts at the time, such as Helen Reddy's 'Leave Me Alone (Ruby Red Dress)' or Ringo Starr's 'Photograph'.

A journo once asked Malcolm about 'Can I Sit Next to You, Girl'. Did he think it was a solid first recording?

'The guitars were good,' Malcolm replied. 'The band was good. It was just the singer . . .'

Malcolm had the sense that Evans wasn't the right man for his band. 'He sort of played up this Gary Glitter bisexual thing,' Malcolm said. 'He'd go on with his make-up, blowing kisses, which we just grew not to like.'

'He was more into pop,' Angus would tell a reporter. 'He wanted to be like Rod Stewart.'

Harry Vanda, too, felt that Evans might not be the best fit. 'Dave always leant towards the glittery part of rock,' he said, '[which] I think was pretty alien to the guys, it's not their thing.'

In short, Evans was a bit of a poser, just like that 'blond fella' in Led Zeppelin. It wasn't what Malcolm wanted his band to be about.

*

The band became regulars at Sydney's Chequers, playing there seven times during January and February 1974. A night at Chequers usually required five hours of stage time, no small ask for a band fresh out of the garage. Fresh out of the lounge room, in fact, because band rehearsals typically took place at the Youngs' place in Burwood, using acoustic guitars and a practice drum kit so as not to faze the neighbours, who were probably still recovering from the days of Easyfever and schoolgirls trampling their petunias.

During one of those Chequers shows, the band clashed with another act on the bill. After their gig, as Malcolm and the others were loading their gear in the back alley behind the venue, a car roared towards them at speed, headlights on high beam. The car screeched to a stop and four or five guys jumped out and started making their way to where Malcolm and the others stood, clearly with trouble in mind. In a flash, Malcolm grabbed a piece of pipe from a nearby construction site and ran full tilt at his would-be attackers, waving the pipe as he ran.

'I've never seen anyone move so fast,' singer Dave Evans would tell *Wales Online* many years later. 'They were back in their car and out of there like their asses were on fire. Malcolm was fearless. Nothing fazed him—not ever.'

They also played the front bar of Sydney's Hampton Court Hotel several times during February and late March, pumping out two, sometimes three sets a night. The publican had heard the band rehearsing in the pub and invited them to play some proper gigs.

A rare recording caught the band in action at Hampton Court on 27 February.

'A little bit of Chuck Berry for you,' said singer Evans as he introduced 'No Particular Place to Go', their usual closer. This was an understatement—there were now as many as three Berry covers in their set. The others, 'Johnny B. Goode' and 'Carol', were also keepers, at least until they had more of their own songs.

Malcolm understood that playing these covers was an act born of necessity. 'We were so short of original material. We used to play "Jumpin' Jack Flash" and add fifteen minutes of bullshit so we could fill up a 40-minute set.'

Beyond the Hampton Court and Chequers, AC/DC rocked the Curl Curl Youth Club on the city's Northern Beaches and took a trip beyond Sydney to Gosford on the New South Wales Central Coast, for a school dance on 10 March. They also played Newcastle, a little further north, during March. They even played a Greek wedding reception, on the urging of singer Evans, where Malcolm was pressed into improvising a version of 'Zorba the Greek'. 'Just follow me,' Malcolm instructed the others, who had no idea how the song went. Miraculously, it worked.

★

Malcolm's onstage manner was simple and precise; he had his dedicated space to the right of the drum riser, which he'd only vacate to bark the occasional backing vocal. Then he'd retreat to his few square feet of turf and continue bashing away on his Gretsch, which was plugged into a new and even more imposing Marshall amplifier than the one he'd bought on the 'trust you once' scheme.

But while Malcolm was all about the work and getting the job done, brother Angus was different: something overtook him when he slipped into his school uniform and plugged in his guitar. It was a transformation that Malcolm witnessed from close range.

'As soon as he put on that school uniform he became a monster. Of course, [audiences] jeered and whistled when he walked on . . . but as soon as he struck up, the looks on their faces changed . . . Angus would run around the club, get on their tables; drinks would be going over and more drinks being bought so the club owner loved us.'

Angus felt that his school uniform functioned a little bit like Superman's cape: it allowed him to transform into a completely different person altogether. Larger than life. Super-Ang.

During one of these early shows, Angus had a stroke of dumb luck while playing a solo. He tripped on his guitar lead and landed on the venue's sticky carpet. He had two choices: dust himself off and look like a fool, or just keep playing and pretend it was all part of the act.

68

'I thought people thought I was a fuckin' idiot,' Angus told a reporter, 'so I started bobbin' around on the ground.'

A signature move—known as The Dying Bug—was duly created.

While the work was steady—they played Chequers three times during May 1974 and six more times in June—AC/DC's line-up was anything but. During a Chequers show, Colin Burgess collapsed into his drum kit—he suspected someone had spiked his drink—and was sacked. George Young filled in for the rest of the night. Angus's guitar-loving buddy Larry Van Kriedt was in and then out of the band (among other things, he had a baby son to care for). After sitting in with a local act called Jasper—whose lead singer was a nondescript bloke by the name of Johnny Cave, soon to morph into William Shakespeare, future Alberts pop star—Malcolm poached the band's bassist (Neil Smith) and drummer (Noel Taylor). Ever the pragmatist, Malcolm thought it a big plus that they owned their own PA and a van, but the pair didn't last long, and were replaced by drummer Peter Clack and bassist Rob Bailey. Malcolm, meanwhile, bought a VW Kombi, which became the band's new transport.

Even at this nascent stage, Malcolm was mapping out his and AC/DC's future, telling anyone who cared to listen: 'We're going to England, as soon as I pay off my new amp.' He certainly didn't lack ambition, or drive. Malcolm also knew that he had no fallback plan. The band simply had to succeed.

Malcolm was the band's spokesman when they were granted their first coverage in the music press just after officially signing with Alberts in June, an interview with *Go-Set* magazine. The writer zeroed in on the youthfulness of the band—Angus was nineteen but could have passed for twelve, Malcolm was 21, seemingly going on fifteen—and it was this point of difference that Malcolm talked up. 'Most of the groups in Australia are getting on, rather than getting it on,' he said. '[They're] out of touch with the kids that go to suburban dances.'

A few weeks later, 'Can I Sit Next to You, Girl' was finally released as a single. It did not set fire to the charts. While Alberts labelmate Stevie Wright hogged the number 1 spot for six weeks with 'Evie', AC/DC's debut didn't progress further than number 50 and charted for just ten weeks. 'Evie', meanwhile, charted for a lengthy five months and was the third-highest-selling single of the year. It was Vanda and Young's first chart-topper.

George Young, meanwhile, had been quietly placing some calls about AC/DC, whose members he considered his protégés. He'd spoken with Vince Lovegrove, Bon Scott's former bandmate from The Valentines, who now ran a booking agency in Adelaide. Bon, who was recovering from a horrible motorcycle accident that very nearly killed him, was helping out in the agency's office. Scott was in the midst of a break-up with his wife Irene—and was also attempting to write lyrics.

'My brothers' band are looking for a singer,' said George.

'Bon would be perfect,' Lovegrove told him.

Scott, however, wasn't so sure when he and Lovegrove spoke about it. 'They're too young to know what rock and roll is about,' Scott said dismissively. 'I'm a serious musician.'

What Scott didn't know was that Malcolm was very serious about rock and roll. Deadly serious.

★

Malcolm's belief that AC/DC scored some unlikely book-ings because of the band's sexually ambiguous name was writ large when they were tapped to open for New Yorker Lou Reed, whose first Australian tour was set to start in August 1974. Paul Dainty was the promoter; red-hot rocker Stevie Wright was second on the bill. In theory, a band calling themselves AC/DC opening for the boundary-pushing, leather-clad 'Walk on the Wild Side' Reed made perfect sense. It was something that Angus later laughed about. 'People said, "Oh, AC/DC and Lou Reed—this is gonna be a big bisexual show." Every gay place in the country booked us on the name alone.'

'The Reed tour promises to be one of the smash-hit tours of the year,' proclaimed a press release, which also mentioned AC/DC. Sydney and Melbourne shows sold out in advance.

Of course, Lou Reed had no idea he was touring with the brothers of George Young from The Easybeats, whose song 'Falling Off the Edge of the World' had once moved him to tears. Or that he and Malcolm had shared band names for a time. Reed was too busy having a field day with a bewildered local media.

'You said a little while ago that you sing mainly about drugs . . . Why do you do this?' Reed was asked by a very serious and hirsute Ian Leslie at his Sydney press conference.

'Because,' Reed replied, adjusting his oversized shades, 'I think the government is plotting against me.'

Leslie tried again. 'You like singing about drugs—is this because you like taking drugs yourself?'

'I don't take any,' Reed countered. 'I'm high on life.'

How could AC/DC compete with that? They couldn't—at least not until the roadshow reached Adelaide on 17 August.

While they played, a fracas erupted at the front of the stage. Some punters started heckling and goading Angus.

'Go and get fucked,' Angus snarled, and got back to work.

According to Bon Scott, who was looking on from the crowd, 'There were a dozen guys in front of the stage shouting, "Hey, hey, come on down here ya * * *," and Angus, he walks up to the edge of the stage and screams at them, "Go and get * * *."'

Scott was stunned when the crowd, rather than invading the stage, actually simmered down. It was apparent that Angus could flex some muscle (perhaps it was that school uniform-cum-cape of his). And Malcolm, despite his lack of size, exuded toughness on stage; he didn't look like the kind of guy you'd want to mess with. Fighting skills were a necessity for anyone with the Youngs' background.

Maybe, Scott figured, these guys understood rock and roll after all.

★

During a free night on the Reed tour, AC/DC played the Hard Rock Café in Melbourne. The venue was owned by Michael Browning, a tall, savvy scenester who'd run various successful venues in the city and also succeeded, at least partially, in managing the career of maverick rocker Billy Thorpe. Browning very nearly broke Thorpe in the UK, only for Thorpe to treat a London showcase as he would a festival gig—the one lasting impact he made on the local media was giving them tinnitus. Browning, like Malcolm, was a man with a dream: he wanted to be the first manager to break an Australian band internationally. The two shared more than they probably realised—as a kid, Browning had had a strong work ethic drilled into him by his father. While still in school he cornered the market in selling used golf balls rescued from the creek on the Mount Macedon course (which he'd sell back to the same golfers who'd lost them) and collecting beer bottles for the refund money. In his spare time he mowed the golf course's fairways. Browning was a self-made man, an entrepreneur, who went on to run hip Melbourne clubs such as Bertie's and Sebastian's and immerse himself in a live scene in which acts such as The Loved Ones, Max Merritt & The Meteors, and Doug Parkinson in Focus thrived.

Browning had been tipped off about AC/DC by Sydney promoter Michael Chugg; as soon as Chugg had mentioned the band's Easybeats bloodline, Browning was interested. Yet while Angus's madcap antics grabbed Browning's full attention when AC/DC played—'The little fucker was going off . . . I couldn't take my eyes—or my ears—off Angus . . .'—it was clear to Browning that Malcolm was in charge. He was the one who collected their $200 fee after the Hard Rock gig and said they'd be back in a few weeks, after the Reed tour and some solo shows in Perth. Browning booked AC/DC for subsequent Hard Rock gigs on the spot.

'I couldn't help but notice how polite they were,' Browning said of the Youngs in his memoir *Dog Eat Dog*. 'They were not at all like your typical rockers.'

A few weeks later, Malcolm put in a call to Browning from Adelaide. He sounded like he was in trouble.

'We're stuck,' he said. 'Can you lend us some money— enough to get us to Melbourne and play some gigs, yours included?'

Malcolm spelled out their recent disaster. After the Reed tour, they were booked for a run of dates at Beethoven's Cabaret in Western Australia. After a mammoth trip across the Nullarbor Plain in their ratty tour van, five scruffy, broke and hungry rockers wandered into the venue, introducing themselves as AC/DC. They were not what the promoter, or the punters, had expected; they'd been booked to open for the country's best-known drag queen, Carlotta. The venue's owner had been hoping for sequins and boas, but instead he got denim and T-shirts and some bloke in a school uniform. Their six-week booking was cancelled after a fortnight, and in mid-September the very broke band limped back to Adelaide. It had been a wasted round trip of more than 5000 kilometres, a rough introduction to life on the road.

However, there was one upside to their cross-country ordeal. On 20 September, during a post-party, they'd jammed at the Adelaide home of Bruce Howe, lately of Fraternity. Bon Scott was again looking on, and agreed to get up and sing with the band. Bon slugged from a bottle of bourbon as he staggered about and Angus whispered to Malcolm: 'I'd be surprised if the guy can walk, let alone sing.' But the proof was in his singing—Scott won over the Youngs.

Afterwards, Scott and the Youngs talked and learned that they shared Scottish roots. Malcolm was taken aback by the stories Scott told him about his wild days in the west, cray fishing with 'these really rough, redneck Aussies. And they made him get all these tattoos. Basically, if he didn't get them he'd get the shit kicked out of him'. In spite of their age difference—Scott was seven years older than Malcolm and had a full nine years on Angus—a bond of sorts formed. And Scott made his intentions very clear. 'I can sing much better than that drongo you have at the moment,' he said, nodding towards Evans.

According to Malcolm, connecting with Bon was easy. 'When we met him for the first time it was like we'd known him forever. There was no shit with Bon . . . He almost became a brother. We just said, "You wanna join?" That's how confident we were it was going to work.'

Dave Evans was on his way out—and he wasn't impressed. He told the band they'd be 'finished' with his sacking. But Malcolm and Angus sensed that Scott was a better fit for AC/DC. Not only could he sing, but he had broad audience appeal: he was the type of bad boy that young women fancied, while blokes in the crowd saw Bon as a tough, cool older brother. Maybe he could help write some songs, too.

AC/DC had a more immediate problem—they were broke. Hence Malcolm's call to the Hard Rock. Browning sent him a couple of hundred dollars and the band crawled back to Melbourne.

'I'd be interested in managing you,' Browning told the Youngs, after their return gig at the Hard Rock. A meeting was arranged in Sydney with Ted Albert and George Young and when that went well, Browning got the gig. But he hadn't quite grasped what he was taking on—he'd never be fully welcomed into the Youngs' inner circle. 'I soon learned that I hadn't signed a band; I'd signed a clan,' he later wrote. Malcolm and the others referred to him simply as 'Browning', hardly the warmest of terms. It was all about business.

6

'There'd be a knock on the door at three in the morning
and a bunch of waitresses just off work would be there
with bottles of booze, a bag of dope and everything else.'

Malcolm's dream of world domination might have been a
way off, but his more immediate goal of forming 'a good rock
band' was really starting to take shape. By October 1974,
AC/DC had a new lead singer, Bon Scott, and a new manager
in Browning, who shared Malcolm's goal of going global, as
well as providing a surrogate HQ in the Hard Rock Café.
They also decided to relocate from Sydney to Melbourne,
where they settled into a large, rundown but surprisingly
affordable spread in Lansdowne Road, St Kilda East, deep in
the red-light heart of Melbourne. It was the first time either
Malcolm or Angus had lived away from home.

Manager Browning put each band member on a weekly
wage of $60 ($300 in today's terms), at least for the first six
months, with costs such as PA and gear covered by Alberts.
Browning also offered his new charges some sage advice:
they shouldn't wear watches on stage—he believed rock
musicians shouldn't be restrained by such mundane things
as time—and they should avoid public transport at all costs.
Browning had once spotted local sixties pop duo Bobby &

Laurie riding on a tram, and he'd been appalled. That wasn't how stars were supposed to travel; they were meant to operate on a different level to regular people. AC/DC may have been broke, he figured, but that didn't mean they couldn't look the part. Browning knew that image was important.

Angus explained the reason for their change of cities to a reporter: 'Melbourne's the hub, the heart, where the biggest demand is. If you're big there, you're big all over.'

It wasn't quite as bold as Malcolm's plans to take over the world, but Angus was right—it was a step in a more professional direction for the band. Many of the bigger booking agents were based in Melbourne, and Browning knew most of them very well. These agencies included Premier Artists; its principals included Michael Gudinski and Ray Evans, who'd also set up their own record label, Mushroom, home to the high-flying Skyhooks. (Skyhooks' debut LP, *Living in the 70's*, released in October 1974, would sell more than 200,000 copies, making them obvious rivals for AC/DC.) ABC TV's *Countdown*, which first aired in November 1974 and became a great promotional vehicle for bands on the rise, was produced in the Melbourne suburb of Ripponlea.

And Melbourne had even more live venues than Sydney: there was the Hard Rock, of course, as well as dozens of hefty suburban bloodhouses such as the Matthew Flinders in Chadstone, the Waltzing Matilda in Springvale—which had a capacity of 1200 and a bar that stayed open until 11.30 p.m.— plus the Ringwood Iceland skating rink, the Southside Six in Moorabbin and, further afield, the Sundowner in Geelong. Then there were smaller rooms like the Station Hotel in Prahran. All regularly hosted gigs and would, soon enough, become happy rocking grounds for AC/DC.

The entire band and crew—whose numbers now included Tana Douglas, a teenage escapee from a convent school in Brisbane and one of Australia's first female roadies, and Pat Pickett, a roadie mate of Bon's—shared the place in St Kilda, as did much of the local transient population. Addicts and runaways and street people drifted in and out of Casa de AC/DC, 24/7; it swiftly became the local do-drop-in.

'There was more action happening there than ever since,' Malcolm said of life at Lansdowne Road. 'We drank like there was no tomorrow. We woke up and drank again and continued like that for a long time.'

There was a steady flow of women, including working girls, in and out of Lansdowne Road, too, as Malcolm told a writer from *Mojo* in 2000:

> The prostitutes got to know us. A lot of them would come around—all sorts of women would show up because we were young and in a band. All of a sudden we had what The Easybeats had when we were kids—all the women outside the house. And *inside!* Everything was taken care of: there'd be a knock on the door at three in the morning and a bunch of waitresses just off work would be there with bottles of booze, a bag of dope and everything else. Never a dull moment. You name it, it happened in that house. We were poor but living like kings.

Local coppers were also frequent visitors to Lansdowne Road, drawn by the ungodly racket and the pungent aroma of pot, but their visits were primarily social. 'They let us alone, you know,' said Malcolm. 'They'd just go, "Oh, can I have a go on the drums?"'

Manager Browning did Malcolm and the others in the band a huge favour when he found an accommodating local doctor who ensured the guys received regular shots of penicillin. They duly earned themselves a new nickname: The Seedies. 'We got group rates from the doctor,' chuckled Angus. Malcolm, perhaps not surprisingly, wouldn't have a steady girlfriend for several years.

It wasn't only about partying, though, Malcolm insisted. Some work also got done, almost in spite of their wild life-style: 'We wrote a lot of songs there.'

Bon, being the band's resident elder, commandeered the large rear room of the house as his own. One afternoon, an angry parent—allegedly an ex-con—stormed into the house and found Scott bedded down with his daughter. He dragged the singer across the front yard and through a bed of rose bushes, before laying into him with his fists. During the prickly encounter, Scott lost the dental plate he had had installed after his bike accident in Adelaide.

Bon gave his version of events to a British journalist in 1978. 'This guy comes banging on my bedroom door . . . loud as all hell itself, and I say to him, "Fuck off, I'm having a fuck." Suddenly the door is crashed in and it turns out to be this girl's father and there he finds me on top of his daughter, who I then find out was only sixteen years old. Needless to say, he beats me to a pulp. I lost two teeth in the process.'

Bon, now minus the hippie beard and Jesus sandals he'd worn in his Fraternity days, made his Sydney debut with the band at the Masonic Hall in the suburb of Brighton-le-Sands on 5 October. Their set list was balanced between the usual covers—such as 'Baby Please Don't Go', fast becoming an

Angus showpiece—and a handful of originals, including 'She's Got Balls' and 'Rock 'n' Roll Singer'.

Two weeks later, Scott played his first Hard Rock Café gig with the band. 'With Bon now on board,' wrote Browning, 'the band had acquired a new sense of purpose as well as a sense of humour and uniqueness. Bon was one of the world's best street poets.' Scott would refer to his bawdy, street-smart lyrics as 'toilet poetry' or simply 'rude poems'. Upon sampling his lyrics, Malcolm figured—with some justification—that Bon 'was obsessed with his balls'. (Scott's lyric for 'She's Got Balls' was inspired by his ex-wife, Irene Thornton.)

The band also crossed the border during October, playing several gigs at the Largs Pier Hotel in Adelaide, another of the bacterial beer barns that formed the backbone of the thriving live music circuit. But all this live work was a precursor to their next big step: spending ten days in the studio cutting their debut album with Vanda and Young in November. The sessions, of course, were sandwiched between a seemingly never-ending run of shows. In 1974 alone they'd play close to 80 dates; this would double—and more—in the ensuing years. AC/DC was a working band.

George Young hadn't actually met Bon Scott before, and he gave the singer a wary once-over when he turned up at the Alberts studio. Scott was quite a sight, with his tatts, shark-tooth earring, a smattering of broken teeth and shop-worn appearance. By comparison, George's brothers seemed like wide-eyed kids. (As early as 1975, *Juke* magazine referred to Scott as a 'veteran' of the local scene and the 'one old face' in AC/DC. He hadn't yet hit 30.)

'He's been around the block more than a few times,' George muttered to Malcolm, nodding towards the singer.

However, once he heard Scott sing, he knew that Scott was a perfect fit for the band. Malcolm had been right. 'He's your man, no doubt,' George said. 'You're a rock-and-roll band now.'

As for Malcolm, he was all over the album, which they called *High Voltage*. He co-wrote seven of the eight tracks (the only non-original was their cover of 'Baby Please Don't Go') and played every note of rhythm guitar; he also played bass on several tracks. Malcolm even provided some lead guitar—including a solo on the cut 'Little Lover', and in tandem with Angus during 'Soul Stripper' and 'Show Business'; this was a first for Malcolm. Angus felt that his older brother was an underrated lead guitarist, even though Malcolm preferred to stick to rhythm. 'If Malcolm sits down to play a solo,' Angus said, 'he can do it better than me.'

While Malcolm's reputation as 'the best right hand in the business' was some way off, he sure knew how to cook up a heavyweight riff, leaving the mark of his Gretsch all over such rockers as 'She's Got Balls', 'Show Business' and 'Stick Around'. As for Bon Scott, he got to work tweaking some Dave Evans–era songs, reworking 'Sunset Strip' (which Evans claimed to have co-written) into what became 'Soul Stripper'. But Scott's best work—and the band's—was still to come. As Malcolm later admitted, back then 'we thought [that] a riff was a song. We really didn't know any better'.

Ron Carpenter, a drummer who'd sat in with AC/DC at a few shows, was in the same studio, recording with his band Aleph. He looked on closely as the Youngs worked together and in 2006 related his version of events to the acdc.collector. com website, providing a revealing snapshot of how George got the best out of the band, especially Angus.

'George would show Angus a riff and they would both play it over and over—for many minutes. The room was concrete with Marshalls stacked against one wall . . . the lift well in King Street used to shake when they were riffing.' The decibel level would increase the higher you rose in the Alberts lift. Once you hit the fifth floor, where the studio was located, the sound was deafening.

'After twenty minutes of riffing,' Carpenter said, 'George would signal Harry [Vanda] or go into the control room himself and record a few minutes of Angus. He'd then return to the studio and show Angus the next riff; the process would go on all day and all night.'

When not guiding Angus through his solos, George would sit at the piano with his brothers, checking that every song they were about to record passed the litmus test: if it worked on the piano, it was good to go.

In 2003, speaking with *Billboard* magazine, Malcolm admitted that *High Voltage* wasn't his favourite AC/DC LP, although he thought it had its moments:

I think we had about five songs. They were still rough, just from trying them on stage. They still had to be sorted out with a little bit here and there, and we put the rest together in the studio. We didn't have time to think, to be honest. We just went for it. We'd go to a gig and we'd go into a studio for two hours after the gig, knock out a tune or a backing track, things like that. It was all patchy how we did things, and it was done that quick, everything. At the end of the day you'd hear it and go, 'Shit that is good, isn't it?' So that album was really thrown together pretty quickly.

In between recording the album, the band played four dates with heavy-metal Brits Black Sabbath at Sydney's 5000-capacity Hordern Pavilion, in November. Security proved to be a problem on the first night; the bouncers thumped anyone who got out of hand. 'These guys in their red coats, as soon as anyone stood up, it was like a "smack round the mouth and sit down again",' Ozzy Osbourne told a reporter from radio station 3XY. 'That's not on. They paid to see us. There's no call for any violence.'

This wouldn't be the last time AC/DC and Black Sabbath joined forces. And when they next toured together, it would be Malcolm who was in the thick of the action.

★

ABC TV's *Countdown* was a boon for both the local music industry and for Australian television, providing a much-needed promotional outlet for local artists and some essential weekend viewing for an audience that quickly built to more than one million. There had been many music shows on the box prior to *Countdown*—*Six O'Clock Rock, Uptight, GTK* and *It's Happening* among them—but none had the same impact. One Sunday night appearance on *Countdown* could increase an act's audience tenfold and break them far more quickly than the usual method of relentless gigging and sucking up to radio DJs. The show, and the relentless plugging of bands by Ian 'Molly' Meldrum, made stars of dozens of local acts and boosted the careers of internationals such as ABBA, Blondie and Meat Loaf, some who became stars in Australia before hitting big in their home country.

By the time AC/DC was booked for the fourth episode

of the show, which aired on 29 November 1974, *Countdown* was starting to take shape. Meldrum, a reporter for *Go-Set* and Melbourne music scenester, had been hired as talent co-ordinator, while the first episode had been hosted by Grant Goldman, a radio broadcaster. (Interestingly, Goldman would become the ground announcer at Brookvale Oval, where Malcolm had played half-time shows with Velvet Underground.) Meldrum would move into the host's seat soon enough.

The early guest choices were fairly obvious—episode one featured pop stars Johnny Farnham and Sherbet's Daryl Braithwaite, while Debra Byrne, Stevie Wright and glam rockers Hush appeared on the second. Sharing the bill with AC/DC on episode four were Braithwaite and Byrne in return appearances.

The band chose to perform 'Baby Please Don't Go'. With the help of some of Browning's crew at the Hard Rock, a sort of home-made model of a plane had been pieced together for Angus. He played while seated in this jerry-rigged flying machine, in a white scarf, goggles and leather jacket, grinning like a demented airline captain. Malcolm, who'd temporarily shelved his denim and favourite green T-shirt for silk strides and knee-high boots, faded into the background alongside his flashy younger brother. The ABC paid the band a $160 appearance fee, which wasn't bad for a few hours' work, all things considered.

In a shortsighted cost-cutting move, the ABC erased the master tapes of this and other early *Countdown* episodes. Fortunately, that was just the first in a series of trailblazing appearances for Malcolm and the band, as their reputation quickly spread beyond the east coast. (They'd feature on the show more than 30 times during its thirteen-year run and several of those appearances were documented for posterity.)

The Top 10 on the week of AC/DC's debut on *Countdown*—each episode ended with a chart countdown—was soft pop from top to toe. It featured Olivia Newton-John's 'I Honestly Love You', the Bee Gees' 'Mr. Natural', Carl Douglas's 'Kung Fu Fighting' and Glen Campbell's 'Bonaparte's Retreat'. If Malcolm had needed reminding that what the music world desperately needed was a great new rock-and-roll band, this would have been one hell of a memory-jogger.

★

The band was back at *Countdown* on 20 December, again performing 'Baby'. (The Top 10 now included Sweet's 'Peppermint Twist' and Leo Sayer's 'Long Tall Glasses'.) This time Angus transformed himself into Zorro, all in black—hat, cape, socks. Someone even provided him with a foil, the perfect capper for the outfit.

Bon Scott was also quite the sight: he wore nut-squeezing bib and braces, a grin spread across his face. The mainly young, primarily female audience wasn't quite sure where to look. Malcolm seemed content to let these two take centrestage; he stood his ground, just to the right of the drum kit, and set his Gretsch to stun. Who cared if they were miming?

Countdown host Meldrum, a good man to have on your team, was quickly won over by the band's combination of rock-and-roll muscle, humour and theatricality. Uncharacteristically, Meldrum was able to capture his feelings about the band in one word: 'Fantastic.'

By the time the band plugged in to play Melbourne's Festival Hall on New Year's Eve 1974, to a crowd of around 5000, Malcolm's baby brother was morphing into a cult hero. A chant of 'We want Angus! We want Angus!' went up even before the band started playing. The show was broadcast live on radio; others on the bill included Hush (whom Angus had dubbed 'The Blue Suede Thongs' and would soon score a major hit with a cover of the old rocker 'Bony Maronie'), and former Masters Apprentices singer Jim Keays.

The band's on-stage presence was growing rapidly, as the Festival Hall show proved beyond doubt. Malcolm was fast mastering the art of simple yet highly effective rhythm guitar, while Angus's frenzied solo during a marathon 'Baby Please Don't Go' was a highlight. Bon was developing into a lively onstage raconteur. When he introduced 'Can I Sit Next to You Girl', he chuckled at the song's slow chart progress. '[This record] made it to number 100 in Sydney, 200 in Perth—*and 1000 in Melbourne.*'

7

'When you go on stage, you've got to play hard.
The kids want it.'

In January 1975, Malcolm's dream of building a great
rock band moved even closer to reality with a new recruit:
drummer Phil Rudd. Until then, the band had been shuf-
fling between temporary tub-thumpers; the latest, Russell
Coleman, had only ever been a stand-in for his predecessor, Peter Clack. Malcolm knew what the band needed:
someone who admired and was inspired by great rock
drummers such as Ringo Starr, Cream's Ginger Baker, and
Simon Kirke of Free and Bad Company. AC/DC needed
a player who could not just give the skins a fair wallop
but keep rock-steady time—and work in unison with the
Youngs' guitar arsenal.

Melburnian Phil Rudd, who was 21 and had mixed
German/Irish/Lithuanian roots, was just the guy. He'd
played in a group called Buster Brown, a big draw with
the sharpie crowd—unruly mobs with a taste for extreme
violence. The band's lead singer was the chrome-domed
firebrand Gary 'Angry' Anderson. More recently, though,
Rudd had been passing time working in his father's car yard.

Rudd was known to mix it up with some colourful types—allegedly, he had one particular buddy who rarely left home without slipping a pistol into the waistband of his jeans.

Go-Set described Rudd as 'quite the swank young jackeroo. [He wears a] thick grey sheep wool Mexican cardigan despite the heat, [has] pale grey-blue eyes, regular features and [a] neatly proportioned small body fitted snugly into de rigueur crotch-tight jeans. He does, in fact, hail from the upper middle sector of a country town.'

By the time Rudd joined the band, they were locked into a series of regular gigs in and around Melbourne—they'd play the Station Hotel in Prahran (for $150), the Hard Rock and the Matthew Flinders (usually for $200). They'd soon become regulars at the 'Rockin' at the Croc' gigs at the Croxton Park Hotel in Thornbury. A week of dates would typically add around $1200 to the band's coffers, which wasn't bad money.

Yet Browning's idea of a weekly wage only really worked for one band member: Angus, the lone teetotaller amidst a group of heavy imbibers. His indulgences were still smokes, spaghetti and chocolate milk. Most weeks at least one, maybe more band members would approach Angus for a loan to get them through to the next payday. Angus gained a new nickname: The Banker. 'He was the band's resident Milton Drysdale,' said Browning, a nod to a money-hungry character in the 1960s TV comedy *The Beverly Hillbillies*.

'We were always broke,' admitted Malcolm, with Angus being the exception.

'Angus is bloody amazing with money,' said new kid Rudd.

Life at Lansdowne Road proved to be a tad too lively, so the band shifted base to the Freeway Gardens Motel in North

Melbourne, a little way out of town. A frequent visitor was the Rock Doctor, their man in penicillin, who might as well have been on the band's payroll. While residing at Freeway Gardens, Bon Scott wrote a lyric about a close encounter he'd had with a full-figured woman named Rosie. It became an AC/DC classic.

According to Malcolm, he was with Bon when Rosie appeared on the scene one night in Melbourne.

'Listen, Mal,' Bon had told him, 'there's a couple of girls. One's pretty ugly, the other's pretty cute, but she's huge— and they've offered to make us dinner.' The offer of a free meal was all that Malcolm needed to hear, so he and Bon fronted up to Rosie's house.

As Malcolm recalled, 'At the end of the night, after dinner and some drinks, big Rosie grabs Bon and says, "Right, you're mine for the night," and I ran away from the other one. I went home.' (In another version, Malcolm said he excused himself to take a piss and never returned.) 'Bon woke up in the morning squashed against the wall, and he tried to get away, so she grabbed him again and got more payment for the meal.'

Malcolm came to the fore as leader of this motley crew on 26 January, when they were booked to appear after the headliner Deep Purple at the Sunbury Rock Festival, 'Australia's Woodstock', at a site 50 kilometres outside of Melbourne. They'd be playing to an audience of about 15,000. Big brother George agreed to play bass. Also on the bill were Billy Thorpe and the Aztecs (formerly managed by Browning) and Daddy Cool, along with Rudd's old band Buster Brown and Skyhooks, whose *Living in the 70's* LP had started to sell by the warehouse-load.

Hundreds of cardboard Anguses had been distributed among the Sunbury crowd before the band arrived, but there was trouble pretty much from the get-go. The band had only been offered the gig at the last minute, and were humping their gear through the slush—the site was a quagmire—when Deep Purple's Rolls-Royces raced past them, spraying them with mud. As if they needed reminding of who the stars were.

After Deep Purple played their set, AC/DC's roadie Tana Douglas began setting up their onstage gear for a planned 9 p.m. start time, but she was instructed by Deep Purple's crew that the British band wanted to 'break down' their gear before she could set up. This meant that AC/DC would be prevented from playing until about 2 a.m., by which time much of the crowd would have faded away (or passed out). Douglas went backstage and told Malcolm what was going on.

'Fuck them,' he told her. 'Go and do it again.'

It was only a matter of time before a brawl broke out; it was George Young who threw the first punch. In a moment that would go down in Oz rock folklore, George responded to a Deep Purple's roadie's taunt: 'You can't talk to me like that—I'm from New York,' with a simple: 'Fuck you, I'm from Glasgow!' Then George headbutted him. Everyone, Malcolm included, jumped into the fray.

Angus later insisted that some members of the crowd had jumped the barrier separating the audience from the stage and were offering to help AC/DC win the fight. Thankfully it didn't come to that and eventually the warring parties were separated in what Angus described as a 'stand-off'.

Malcolm and the band were given an option by the promoter: play early the next morning or not at all.

'Fuck it,' said Malcolm, and they drove back to Melbourne. It was a very rare occurrence of the band blowing out a gig—but with good reason. It hadn't helped their state of mind when they'd learned that Deep Purple were collecting $60,000 for their night's work. AC/DC were being paid just $300.

A fired-up Angus spoke about the brawl with a reporter from *RAM*. Things didn't start well, Angus admitted, when he and the others learned soon after arriving that all the local bands were sharing one trailer backstage, while Deep Purple 'had everything else, all the other caravans and changing rooms, 'cause they're international, right?' The band didn't regret their decision to leave. 'We cancelled them,' Angus insisted. 'They didn't cancel us.'

It didn't harm the band, however, when their punch-up became the key topic of media analysis the next day—they didn't get to play and yet they still gained more column inches than Deep Purple. A bit of controversy never hurt a young band on the rise. 'More people came to see us after that,' Angus told a reporter.

This conflict was a big moment for the band: it amped up their 'us against the world' mindset, and it also hastened Malcolm's desire to get the hell out of Australia, where he felt too many so-called 'big bands' were given the star treatment by starstruck (or just plain greedy) promoters at the expense of local acts.

As far as Malcolm was concerned, AC/DC was more than equal to any of these overseas bands, a point he drove home when he spoke with *Juke* magazine. 'Music's the same all over the world,' he insisted. 'There's nothing an Australian group can't do that they're doing [overseas]. The kids want the same things. The audiences are the same.' He may not have been drawing on personal experience—Malcolm hadn't yet travelled outside the country, beyond his trip from Glasgow—but he definitely had the power of conviction.

And the band did have the last laugh. When Deep Purple planned another Oz visit in 1976, the local Musicians' Union, which hadn't forgotten Sunbury, made it clear that the tour 'could lead to considerable unrest'. Feeling threatened, Deep Purple placed money in a fund so that other bands on the 1975 Sunbury bill, who still hadn't been paid by the promoter, received the full artist rate.

But even then, when AC/DC were approached to support Deep Purple, Michael Browning turned them down flat.

★

In March 1975, Malcolm and the band headed back into the Alberts studio to work on their second LP with Vanda and Young. The producers' hot streak was well underway; not only had Stevie Wright's 'Evie' been the biggest local record of 1974, but John Paul Young's 'Yesterday's Hero', another Vanda/Young/Alberts production, was about to reach the Top 10 in the local charts, and a new star—simply known as JPY—was born. (JPY, like Ted Mulry and the Youngs, was very working class: he turned up for his first session at Alberts wearing blue overalls, straight off the factory floor.)

Before the band got to work, as they were filling the studio with beer and Jack Daniels—standard procedure at Alberts—Malcolm spoke with George, asking if they should try to expand their sound. After all, George had done that with The Easybeats.

George's reply was an emphatic 'no.' He knew that AC/DC was lucky. They'd discovered early on what they did best—gut-level, balls-out rock and roll, played live, raw and loud. His job was to capture that in the studio.

'That's your thing,' George said. 'Stick with it.'

It was probably the best advice Malcolm ever received.

Writing in *RAM*, Anthony O'Grady took a stab at characterising that sound, describing AC/DC as a 'street punk band'. 'AC/DC, they play real blitzkrieger rock and roll and you'd better not believe they won't stomp you if you make a wrong move,' he wrote

Nineteen-year-old street-smart bassist Mark Evans, like drummer Rudd a native Melburnian, had just joined the band. (Evans wasn't very tall, either, which helped him get hired.) He was given a couple of key pieces of information before he started, delivered by one of the band's roadies. First: this was Malcolm's band, something that should never, ever be forgotten. And secondly, Malcolm was hell-bent on having the band based in the UK in a year—he'd timed their intended departure to coincide with the final payment date on his Marshall amp. Evans was up for the challenge, but had no real idea if it was achievable.

Journalist O'Grady was struck by the triple threat of Malcolm and the band's new rhythm section; the classic AC/DC line-up was finally in place. 'Rudd, . . . Evans and rhythm guitarist Malcolm Young are acknowledged [as] one of the most powerful rhythm sections ever bred by the uncompromising brutality of Australian pub rock,' he wrote.

Within weeks, new recruit Evans had his chance to witness the Youngs at work in the studio. The process, as he described to Bon Scott biographer Clinton Walker, was as simple as it was effective:

> Malcolm and Angus would come up with riffs and all that, and then we'd go into the studio. Malcolm and George would sit down at the piano and work it out. Malcolm and Angus would have the barest bones of a song, the riff and different bits, and George would hammer it into a tune . . . Once the backing track was done, [Bon] would literally be locked in the kitchen there at Alberts [writing lyrics], and come out with a finished song.

Malcolm knew what they were looking for, 'the same loose feeling like we were on stage still. The studio was just like an extension of the gig'. And above all, to have a blast.

His method was pretty simple. 'If you shut your eyes,' said Malcolm, 'you're in a club, you really are, and that's what the whole band has really been about from day one. Getting back to the stage. That's where it counts.'

The *T.N.T.* sessions ran for two weeks in total, which became standard operating procedure for the band. The first week was spent recording the basic tracks; the second was devoted to Angus's solos and Scott's vocals. Scott's self-proclaimed 'toilet poetry' was hitting an early peak, and the results—anthems of hard living and comic misadventure such as 'It's a Long Way to the Top (If You Wanna Rock 'n' Roll)', 'High Voltage', 'T.N.T.', 'The Jack' and 'Live Wire'— were among Scott and the band's best. These were songs that would remain in their set list for the next 40 years (as of 2016, according to stats at setlist.fm, the band has played the latter four songs in concert something like 5000 times collectively). Three of these tracks—'Long Way to the Top', 'High Voltage' and 'T.N.T.'—would be released as singles.

'The Jack' was inspired, in a manner of speaking, by Malcolm. The band had been playing in Adelaide when Malcolm received a letter from a woman who insisted he'd given her the dreaded 'jack' (gonorrhoea). He went as far as to get tested; the results, to his relief, came back negative (which wasn't always the case). Still, there was plenty of material there for Scott to conjure up one of his funnier commentaries about the hazards of life on the road. (Or, to be frank, the hazards that Scott and the others sometimes posed to their more obliging fans.)

'If I'd known what she was dealin' out,' smirked Scott, stretching both the card-playing and sexual metaphors to breaking point, 'I'd have dealt it back.'

As for Malcolm, virtually every track of the nine on the album featured a riff of his that seemed cast in stone, from 'Rock 'n' Roll Singer' to 'T.N.T.', 'High Voltage' and 'Long Way to the Top'. Malcolm had truly found his voice, and it came in the shape of a Gretsch guitar and a Marshall amp. There were no lead solos from him this time around; Malcolm was strictly rhythm. And it was rock-hard rhythm, tailor-made for the tough suburban beer barns that were fast becoming their stomping ground.

'When you go on stage, you've got to play hard,' Malcolm explained when asked about his rhythm guitar tactics. 'The kids want it.' He'd describe his playing as 'right down the middle of the line'. In short, no bullshit—like the man himself.

'He's the solid thing,' Angus said in 1984, when asked about his brother's playing. 'I don't think anyone can do what he does.'

The evidence of this was all over the band's second album.

'Long Way to the Top' had been brought into the studio once before, but George Young thought it was over-rehearsed, a bit too carefully considered. 'Fuck that off,' he told his brothers. 'You're not some poxy pop band. Play it live until you know how it works.'

Only once it had been properly road-tested did they finally record the song. When the idea for using bagpipes was floated, Bon Scott offered his services. George Young agreed, being under the impression that Scott had been a piper back in Fremantle (he had actually been a drummer in a pipe band with his father, Chick). A set of bagpipes, which cost the band (that is, Alberts) the considerable sum of $435, was quickly procured. But not only could Scott not play them, he also had no idea how to assemble them, as bassist Evans recalled in his memoir, *Dirty Deeds*. 'If you want a good giggle,' Evans wrote, 'get a bunch of Scotsmen with no previous bagpipe experience and ask them to put some bagpipes together.'

The relationships in the studio weren't all smooth sailing, either. One day, Angus and George argued; George told his younger brother to 'stop being such a little fookin' prima-donna' and the dispute spilled out into the hallway, where Angus tried in vain to land a punch.

But this was family, and the dispute faded within minutes. Then they got back to work.

*

While finishing up the *T.N.T.* album, AC/DC's debut LP *High Voltage* entered the Australian album chart, peaking at number 14 and charting for a healthy 39 weeks. 'When stacked up against the melodious pop of Sherbet and the glitter/glam of Skyhooks and Hush,' wrote Ian McFarlane in *The Encyclopedia of Australian Rock and Pop*, 'AC/DC's brand of hard rock was rugged, outrageous and irrepress-ible. AC/DC were the bad boys . . . [they were] not doing anything original at this stage . . . but it was the *way* they did it that got fans excited.'

The number 1 album in Australia in late February 1975, just after *High Voltage* was released, was Skyhooks' *Living in the 70's*, which was beginning its sixteen-week run at the top of the charts. Skyhooks was the most prominent of all the local bands AC/DC had in their sights. Angus liked to give their 'rivals' nicknames, but he didn't have one for Skyhooks. The Youngs believed that Skyhooks were in the way, stealing their audience. Soon enough, they'd eclipse them, in both sales and in controversy.

★

In early 1975, AC/DC were travelling in a beaten-up Greyhound bus nicknamed 'Old Swivel Hips', due to its inability to travel in a straight line. Air conditioning and/ or heating were not its best features, either. On the way to a sold-out gig at Melbourne's Festival Hall—where the head-liners were pop pin-ups Sherbet—the bus broke down and the band was forced to push it to the venue. Not surprisingly, they arrived late. But so what? They weren't the headliners.

On 23 March, Malcolm and the band assembled on the *Countdown* soundstage, preparing to once again perform 'Baby Please Don't Go'. The usual crowd of rowdy teenage girls was gathered at the front of the stage, raring to go. Malcolm wore a long-sleeved white top and white jeans stuffed into his knee-high boots (not his best look); Angus was in his best schoolboy blues. The band was ready. But there was a problem: no Bon Scott.

Producer Kris Noble glanced anxiously at his watch. No one had seen Scott since they had arrived at the studio and rehearsed the song.

Then, with quite literally seconds to go before the cameras rolled, Scott emerged, dressed as the hairiest schoolgirl to ever grace a stage. He wore pigtails, hoop earrings, blue eyeliner, falsies and a skimpy tunic. Almost choking on their own laughter, the band began playing—Bon, clearly at ease, sparked up a ciggie during an instrumental break and drew deeply. Scott then produced an aqua-coloured mallet, which he menaced Angus with as 'Baby' built to a lively climax. It was a great bit of rock-and-roll pantomime, Scott and Angus mugging for the ABC cameras like a pair of cheeky school-kids caught with their pants down. AC/DC, especially the Young brothers, were not the kind of guys to have giggling attacks, but the entire group struggled to keep straight faces throughout the four barnstorming minutes of 'Baby'.

If Malcolm had harboured any doubts about the new line-up, he could now rest easy. Brother George was right: they were a real rock-and-roll band. And so what if their singer was partial to a bit of cross-dressing?

8

'We don't mind being called George's brothers all the
time. Why should we?'

As far as AC/DC's relationship with *Countdown* was
concerned, they gained something extra from their exposure on the show—it gave them a strong visual presence. In
1975, many punters around the country who hadn't yet seen
AC/DC play already knew them as 'the band with the crazy
schoolkid and the bloke with tatts and a sneer'. (And sometimes a dress.) It suited Malcolm perfectly, too. He was no
showman like Angus; he was more than happy to keep out of
the spotlight, let the Bon and Angus show thrive, and stick
with what he did best: pulling killer riffs out of his guitar, his
still-boyish face hidden behind his mane of dark hair, and
watch proudly as the band's star rose.

Countdown also accidentally created a weird schism when
it came to AC/DC's audience: one half of their fans were
screaming teen girls who'd seen them on the telly and quite
fancied the guys in the band, particularly Malcolm. (This
audience initiated a riot of looting and stage demolition
when the band attempted to play a lunchtime show at the
Myer's Miss Melbourne Shop in August 1975.) Their other

audience was the 'suck-more-piss' crowd, usually blokes in their late teens and early twenties out to bang and/or punch heads, who frequented the bacterial beer barns that the band was now regularly filling. Soon enough, the band was asking for, and receiving, $600 per gig. And Angus was demanding to know why it wasn't possible to have chicken wire installed at venues, so he didn't get hit so often by flying projectiles.

Yet back on *Countdown* on 30 March, only a week after Bon's schoolgirl antics, they performed the uncharacteristically schmaltzy 'Love Song'. It was no 'Baby Please Don't Go'; Angus was again in his basic schoolyard blues, his scabby knees on full display, while Bon sported red overalls, without a pigtail in sight. It was neither their best look nor their best song. Still, the producers of *Countdown* had bigger and bolder plans for AC/DC; over time 'Molly' Meldrum would cook up one particularly wild idea that he almost feared running by Malcolm. Meldrum was convinced that there was just no way he'd go for it.

There was also movement on the international front. And things were happening quickly. Michael Browning had arranged to film a performance of 'High Voltage' at a Festival Hall gig, which had been very carefully stage-managed. On the afternoon of the gig, the band had been busy handcrafting banners—one read, 'AC/DC'S GOT BALLS', another screamed, 'ANGUS U SPUNK'—which were handed out to the audience in advance. When they played, a rudimentary lighting rig flashed their name in neon lights. All of this, matched with a typically over-the-top performance from Angus, generated a video that, to anyone new to the band, appeared to indicate that they were superstars at home—the biggest thing since, well, The Easybeats.

Browning's sister Coral was based in London; she worked for Bob Marley's management. Her brother had sent her a copy of the 'High Voltage' clip and loaned her his Fairchild video cassette machine, a sophisticated bit of technology for the time (which the band referred to as his 'Maxwell Smart briefcase'). She met with various London-based record execs, who were equally impressed by the very attractive and persuasive Coral, the Fairchild, and the film clip.

When she played it to Atlantic Records' Senior VP Phil Carson in March 1975, he was sold straightaway. 'Get your brother on the phone,' he told Coral.

Within days, Browning was on a flight to London, where he met with Carlson and Dave Dee, formerly of the group Dave Dee, Dozy, Beaky, Mick & Tich, now the General Manager of Atlantic, which had been the label of choice for such breakout rock bands as Cream and Led Zeppelin. In fact, Dee told Browning that to him 'AC/DC sounds like a cross between Led Zeppelin and Slade' (which he chose not to share with Malcolm, who would have been underwhelmed). Atlantic quickly put an offer on the table. It was boilerplate stuff: an advance of $25,000 and a royalty rate on record sales of twelve per cent. (When Led Zeppelin signed with Atlantic in 1968, their advance was a whopping $200,000.)

'It may not have been the most lucrative record deal ever made,' Browning wrote in his book *Dog Eat Dog*, 'but it was still a deal.'

It didn't take long for Carlson and Atlantic to work out who was in charge of AC/DC; clearly, there was more to the band than the manic schoolboy guitarist. In one of their earliest press releases, this was said of Malcolm: 'Not only is he a great guitarist and songwriter, but also a person with vision—he is the planner in AC/DC. He is also the quiet one, deep and intensely aware.'

*

Mark Evans once wrote that 'AC/DC was all about momentum', and the proof was in the distance they covered. In April 1975 alone they played something like two dozen gigs, in Victoria and New South Wales. That was a typical month for the band. In one mammoth round trip they covered almost 2000 kilometres, playing a gig at Wyong on the New South Wales Central Coast on 20 April at the local Memorial Hall before heading south for a show in the Melbourne suburb of Broadmeadows on the 22nd. A few weeks later they undertook an overnighter of some 800 kilometres, in order to play shows on successive nights in South Australia and Victoria.

Malcolm saw the band as his livelihood; he wasn't in it to be a rock star. If there was a gig to be played, he was there, plugged in, ready to go, regardless of the location. 'This is a nine-to-five sort of gig,' he would much later tell *Rolling Stone* magazine. (The emphasis was on 'sort of'; Malcolm travelled by day and worked at night.) His working-man's attitude, he explained, 'comes from working in the factories, that world. You don't forget it.'

At least he'd taken *something* away from his stint at the lingerie factory.

Angus backed this up in a comment he made about what many would see as the endless grind of touring. It was the only world he and Malcolm knew. 'If we don't play,' Angus figured, reasonably enough, 'we don't eat.'

It wasn't as though he and Malcolm had a fallback plan. They were in it for the long haul. And in 1975 they did quite literally have to play to eat.

One of their stranger gigs during April '75 was a Year 12 dance at Ivanhoe Grammar School. As a gesture of good-will—and probably to save a few bob—the band gave their crew the night off and let the students run the lights and sound. The school got them at a good price, too; they'd booked them before *Countdown* came calling.

'It cost about $240 to book them to play at the dance,' Ivanhoe old boy Doug Golden told Melbourne's *Herald-Sun,* 'and they held the price.'

In typical AC/DC style, when a photo shoot was booked with *Go-Set* photographer Philip Morris in May, they fitted it in around a series of Sydney dates. The old 'stand-em-up-against-a-wall-and-shoot-away' approach was not the preference of either Morris or AC/DC—so instead they planned a guerilla-style shoot on the street at night.

Malcolm and the band reached Morris's studio at about six in the evening, well prepared: they brought with them a slab of beer, a supply of green ginger wine and cans of spray paint. Then they piled into the band's van for the drive to Lavender Bay, where Morris shot the group staging a mock arrest and scuffle with the 'cops'. Then someone tagged 'We Luv AC/DC' on a wall. Manager Browning and roadie Pat Pickett helped out, dressed as cops.

'We spent about an hour doing different poses,' Morris recalled. 'Bon was drinking out of a bottle in a paper bag and arguing with the "police".'

Malcolm typically wore a poker face, even in his early twenties. Those who didn't know him well sometimes found him dour, stern, or quiet to the point of silence. But his smile was a mile wide during this shoot and their burst of spontaneous tagging; he grinned madly as he slugged from a tinnie. He knew how to have a good time.

As for Bon Scott, sometimes he took the high life a little too seriously. In late April, during a Melbourne Festival Hall show with avant-garde New Zealanders Split Enz—a classic line-up mismatch if there ever was one—Scott, dressed in a leopard-skin outfit, swung out over the 5000-strong crowd on a specially installed rope, like rock and roll's very own Tarzan. It was all good fun until he got tangled up and crashed into the PA; he ended the show covered in bruises.

One day in May, when the band were to play a lunchtime show at the Hard Rock, Scott slept through his alarm, and punters were treated to the very rare spectacle of Malcolm and Angus sharing vocals.

Whenever they returned to Sydney, Malcolm and Angus would bunk at the family home in Burwood. It was a rare chance for the brothers to reconnect with their family; their lives seemed to be spent in constant motion. One Sydney stop in 1975 was a four-night residency at the Bondi Lifesaver, a notorious beachside venue frequented by music lovers and industry types, a place to get trashed, rock out, get laid and perhaps score a record deal. They were booked to play four 45-minute sets each night. At the end of their sparsely attended first set on the night of 5 May, the venue's owner confronted the band, swearing and cursing like a crazy person. They'd been playing so loudly that they'd killed all the fish in the venue's aquarium—and the fish had been her pride and joy.

Things improved as their residency continued; there were near full houses by the end of their run. On the day of their final Lifesaver gig, 'Baby Please Don't Go' entered the Australian singles chart at number 38; it spent seven weeks in the charts and peaked at number 19. It wasn't a smash, but it was a solid enough start. And Malcolm knew they had better songs in the can.

Malcolm and the others sat down with *Juke*'s Ed Nimmervoll in early June 1975 for the first lengthy press coverage of the band (they were given a full page). Malcolm took the chance to speak both about his older brother George—his boyhood idol—as well as Angus.

'We don't mind being called George's brothers all the time,' Malcolm stated. 'Why should we? He's helped us a lot.' (Bon referred to George as 'like a father to the group'.) As for Malcolm's memories of the days of Easyfever, he said he didn't have that many, apart from one biggie. 'We remember the women,' he admitted, with a smirk. How could he have missed them? He'd often come home to Burwood to find them inside his house.

Then talk turned to Angus. Malcolm remembered how Angus 'used to just stand there, playing guitar', but things swiftly changed. (Although he didn't mention it to Nimmervoll, Malcolm had helped bring out the performer in Angus, advising him: 'Just go fucking crazy!') There was also the huge influence of Chuck Berry: on Angus's playing, on his performance and on the brothers' writing. 'Chuck Berry and his duckwalk will go over better [with the audience] every time,' said Angus. As for Berry's peer, Little Richard, 'there's never been another rock voice like [his]', Malcolm insisted.

And what about the band's name? Malcolm was asked. Has that caused any problems? It clearly did for Bon Scott, who told writer Nimmervoll that when he first heard the group back in Adelaide, 'I thought, "bunch of pooftahs". Now I'm singing with them.'

Malcolm pleaded ignorance. 'We didn't know what the name meant. We just liked the sound of it.'

A few weeks later, they were back on the pages of *Juke*, in the strangest possible way. It was in the peculiar story of a Japanese tourist named Izumi Tanaka, who after experiencing AC/DC while visiting Australia, was inspired to write a letter to the group. 'I never forget about AC/DC,' she wrote. 'You are one of the greatest groups in the world. I believe you're international and I wish you come to Japan.'

It looked as though Malcolm's plan to go global was kicking in, one convert at a time.

9

'So . . . we climb over the back fence and we screw . . .
having relations if you want to be polite about it,
on the loungeroom floor.'

Violence was always on the fringes of AC/DC's world, and had been ever since the night Malcolm wielded a pipe to chase off his likely attackers in the back alley near Chequers. But now it was an even more regular part of a night with AC/DC, especially when the band was confronted with the yobbo sector of their audience (although, admittedly, those screaming teens could also get a tad feisty). As 1975 progressed, the band found themselves entangled in a number of very physical encounters, punishing for both band and fans.

Sometimes it was all part of the fun, as one punter recalled of a lively show in the Victorian town of Bendigo, where Angus played while wearing a Zorro costume. 'Fantastic,' he gushed, 'even though I lost a tooth.'

But there were other nights, especially playing rooms such as Melbourne's Manhattan Hotel, when things got way out of control. One night in August, with the venue full to the brim, the madness kicked in even before they started playing. One of their roadies came backstage and tried to warn them off playing: 'You are all out of your minds if you go out there.' He'd seen beer glasses and punches flying in all directions. Blowing out a gig wasn't part of the Youngs' mindset, but when the band did take the stage, Angus was hit by a flying glass. Badly cut and bleeding, he stormed off the stage—a rare occasion when safety took precedence over converting the masses. Malcolm and the others followed him backstage, warily eyeing the restless natives as they departed.

Then it erupted. The entire venue seemed to be immersed in a massive all-in brawl; one unfortunate punter was hurled from the venue's upper tier onto the floor below. Glass crunched underfoot. Even when the police arrived, in numbers, followed by a flotilla of ambulances, the band were given a directive by the publican: stay backstage. Do not try to leave. It was hours before they could safely pack up their gear and drive back to the Freeway Gardens.

'We'd have to fight our way into the venues to play,' Malcolm later said of this period of the band's career. That night was a rare case of almost having to fight their way out.

Things got even uglier in late August when they played the Matthew Flinders Hotel in suburban Chadstone; the room was filled with the usual assortment of rough-heads and yobbos. Angus waded into the crowd to perform his nightly Dying Bug during 'Baby Please Don't Go'. Typically, an audience would part and let him do his sweaty thing, but not tonight. As Angus spun wildly on the ground, a punter started kicking into him and a melee quickly broke out. Drummer Phil Rudd, who could look after himself in a skirmish, leapt out from behind his kit and jumped into the melee. Unfortunately, his first punch connected with someone's rock-solid noggin and the drummer's thumb made a loud cracking sound. Mark Evans also joined the fray but was king-hit by a bouncer who didn't recognise him without his bass. With their lead guitarist and rhythm section out of action, Malcolm and Bon were left on stage, wondering what the hell to do next.

When the dust finally settled, Rudd was told he'd broken his thumb and required surgery. From then on, the drummer would be known as 'Left Hook Rudd'. Angus continued with his Dying Bug, but always with a watchful eye on the crowd around him.

There was also a gig in rural Victoria, where the band genuinely feared for their lives. Before going on, the local promoter had a quiet word with Malcolm and Angus, who were wondering why there were such a strong police presence outside the hall.

'Just so you know,' the promoter whispered to the brothers, 'there's a maniac loose in the audience with a meat cleaver. But you'll be fine. Just start playing and we'll get him.'

Angus turned to Malcolm. He looked genuinely fearful.

'I don't think I should go out there, especially in this,' he said, tugging at his school uniform. Surely, if there was a mass murder, he'd be the first to go.

'It's nothing,' Malcolm replied. 'You'll be fine.'

Then he pushed his brother towards the stage and the show went on.

At a return gig in another mining town, Mount Gambier in South Australia, some locals without tickets discovered that the back door of the Kings Theatre had been left unlocked. They let themselves in and joined the fray.

When the band played at the Sandgroper Hotel in Perth,

Angus got into a verbal stoush with some drunken punters down the front of the stage.

'Fuck, you're ugly,' someone yelled at Angus.

'Have a fuckin' look at yourself,' Angus snapped back, and kept on playing. Malcolm nodded his approval from his side of the stage and he too got back to work.

Angus compared the scene at gigs like these to life in the trenches during World War I. 'You pick up the guitar and just dig in. Those outback places in Australia are the toughest audiences in the world. You have to give them blood.'

During another show at the Matthew Flinders, the local boys in blue cooked up a 'sting' to snare Angus, presuming that he was under-age. The plan was for plain-clothes police to mingle with the crowd and arrest Angus when the band's set started. But before any of that could occur, roadie Tana Douglas had started chatting with the cops. One offered to buy her a drink, which she gladly accepted, the cop not realising Douglas was the one who was under-age. The 'sting' came to nothing, of course—Angus was a twenty-year-old teetotaller.

★

By early September, the cumulative impact of *Countdown*, the band's relentless touring and their *High Voltage* LP had led to AC/DC's first big headlining show, a free, 2SM-sponsored blast at Victoria Park in Sydney, just a few blocks down Broadway from Chequers. The high-rating Top 40 station 2SM had become AC/DC advocates, despite being owned by the Catholic Church, who surely wouldn't have endorsed such a bunch of reprobates. But their progress was aided and abetted by Alberts, who bought airtime to promote the group.

'AC/DC is not a nice band,' the radio ad declared.

It was perfect.

Also on the bill at Victoria Park were Stevie Wright— whose latest single, 'Black Eyed Bruiser', featured Angus on guitar—and singer-songwriter Ross Ryan, who'd had a local hit with 'I Am Pegasus', which was precisely the kind of touchy-feely song that had inspired Malcolm to form a loud and hairy rock band.

During their eleven-song set, which began with 'Live Wire', continued with 'Long Way to the Top' and 'T.N.T.' and closed with the usual 'Baby Please Don't Go', Angus took full advantage of the scope of the gig. At one point he shimmied up a ladder and played perched on top of the PA. Bon did likewise on the opposite side of the stage. Angus also waded into the crowd mid-solo, manager Browning and various roadies clearing a path for him through the thousands of fans who had gathered. No one put the boot into him this time; instead, the crowd headbanged furiously, caught up in the moment. Photographer Philip Morris chased Angus up and down the ladder while shooting this era-defining gig.

Off stage, producer Harry Vanda looked on proudly, his son in his arms. The child wore one of Angus's schoolboy caps, the letter 'A' emblazoned upon it.

Interestingly, Malcolm played the show in his white pants and knee-high boots, the last remnants of his glam-rock obsession. Both would soon be long gone; in their place would be the denim-and-singlet combo that he'd make his own.

The Victoria Park show's impact was immediate. Within a week 'High Voltage' had entered the Australian Top 40 at number 26; it would hang about the charts for twelve weeks. 2SM played the track repeatedly. The song had come about thanks to an idea of George Young's. During the *T.N.T.* sessions, he'd suggested to his brothers that it would be a neat trick to write a song using the chord progression A-C-D-C. Malcolm and Angus got to work, and a great song was born.

The band were fast becoming press favourites, too; they were pretty dependable when it came to a juicy quote or a wild story from the road. In mid-September, during a discussion with *RAM*, Malcolm disclosed perhaps a little too much, as part of an article entitled 'The Lusts of AC/DC: Band Bids for Supreme Punkdom'. He told a story about two eager 'chicks' inviting him and Scott 'back to Granny's place', an offer they readily accepted.

'So . . . we climb over the back fence and we screw . . . having relations if you want to be polite about it, on the loungeroom floor.' Scott, meanwhile, raced around the house naked, 'turning somersaults', according to Malcolm, which must have been quite a sight. The pair's fun ended when Granny returned unexpectedly. As Malcolm recalled, 'The chick throws me off, pushes me out the window . . . and throws my clothes after me. And then Bon lands beside me.'

Malcolm told reporter Bob Granger that he longed for a lifestyle more like that of The Rolling Stones. '[They] have a plane and the stewardesses give blow jobs while they're eight miles high—and we're being thrown out of places when Granny comes home.'

*

As the band readied themselves for a run of dates in rural New South Wales, their *T.N.T.* LP was released on 1 December 1975. To help promote the album with the local media, early copies were sent out with a special bonus gift: a pair of women's underpants. The album featured a stellar selection of tracks, many of which—'Long Way to the Top', 'T.N.T.', 'Live Wire' and 'High Voltage'—fast became AC/DC standards, stone cold career-builders. One track, however, didn't quite cut the mustard, a stomper called 'Rocker', for reasons beyond the band's control. 'Rocker' abruptly cut out a few seconds shy of the three-minute mark, just as Angus let rip on guitar—most likely because they ran out of tape. A similar situation occurred with 'High Voltage', which segued into a cover of Chuck Berry's 'School Days' to close the album.

Reviewing *T.N.T.* for *The Canberra Times*, writer Tony Catterall didn't quite know what to make of AC/DC. He stated that 'it's not hard to reach the conclusion that AC/DC is the best punk-rock band in Australia'—a description the band would have dismissed in a heartbeat. (Malcolm always insisted they were a 'rock-and-roll band', not punk in any way. This would become a big problem when they reached the UK.)

Yet Catterall seemed unsure if the album was actually any good. 'It's really hard to know how to take *T.N.T.* I mean, do you condemn it for its brutalising tendencies or praise it as authentic representation of a segment of society?' Weirdly, he criticised the Youngs' guitars, finding them 'too clean and pure for the overall sound'.

It's probably the last time *that* was said about Malcolm and Angus's playing.

★

As the album gradually climbed the local charts—it would peak at number 2, only held off the top spot by Swedish superstars ABBA, and chart for 30 weeks—Malcolm and the band ended the year as they'd started it: on the road. Their tour of rural New South Wales, which consumed much of December, took them to Gunnedah, country music heartland Tamworth and onwards to Wyong, Newcastle, Taree, Port Macquarie, Kempsey, Coffs Harbour (the home of the Big Banana), Grafton, Moree and Inverell, where they filled the Town Hall on 14 December. They also rocked the same venue—the Amoco Hall in Orange—where The Easybeats had played during their final tour back in 1969. AC/DC packed the place. It was sweet revenge for Malcolm and Angus, because The Easybeats had played to a near-empty room.

In between dates, Scott took the time to write to his ex-wife Irene Thornton, with whom he remained close. His words would prove to be remarkably prophetic. 'I reckon we'd have to be the hottest band in the country at the moment. Not bad for a 29-year-old, 3rd-time-around has-been.'

On Christmas Eve, the band were back in Sydney, the big smoke, for a show at the Hordern Pavilion. The headliners were arch rivals Skyhooks. Wanting to cash in on AC/DC's 'bad boy' reputation, manager Browning cooked up an idea, which Malcolm endorsed, to start an onstage fight during AC/DC's set. Waiting in the wings would be Browning and a few others dressed as cops (the same outfits they'd used for their Lavender Bay photo shoot), who would dash on stage and end the commotion by 'arresting' the band and frog-marching them into the wings. That was bound to get some headlines, maybe even one-up the headline act.

Unfortunately, before a punch could be thrown in jest, bassist Evans gave Bon Scott a playful shove and the singer toppled off the stage and into the audience. That wasn't scripted. Evans then jumped on Angus, as planned, and they began wrestling onstage. Chaos ensued until, finally, a barely conscious Scott was rescued from the clutches of the audience and was dragged backstage, followed by the rest of the band.

Waiting there was Malcolm and Angus's big sister, Margaret, who hadn't been informed of the faux fight. (Margaret cared for Malcolm and Angus like they were her children, a trait she'd inherited when she began, in Malcolm's words, 'running the show' at home due to their mother's problems with rheumatism.) And she wasn't happy, warning Evans to keep his mitts off her little brother. But that wasn't the end of it. An angry roadie then burst into the dressing room, screaming blue murder about some equipment that had been damaged in the chaos. The roadie grabbed a cassette tape of the bagpipe solo from 'It's a Long Way to the Top', which they'd been using during shows, and destroyed it while the startled band looked on.

It had been quite the gig.

If that wasn't lively enough, a few nights later, back in rural Victoria, members of the audience antagonised Angus to the point where he and the band's crew decided to track the culprits down afterwards and dispense a bit of rough justice. They found them in a milk bar—it was a small town—but were unaware that the local police station was right next door. Soon after the inevitable fight started, a copper allegedly arrested Angus and left him to cool his heels for a night in the cells.

Malcolm and the band closed down the liveliest year yet for AC/DC with a late gig in Adelaide, their last of more than 200 shows for the year, coming on stage at 11.30 p.m. The electricity cut out after two songs, and the crowd began chanting, 'Turn on the power!' The lights came back on to reveal that someone had started a fire in the middle of the dance floor.

Gig done, and the new year seen in, the band then jumped in the van and drove more than 850 kilometres for a New Year's Day show at Inverloch in Victoria. It was a blessing that he and Angus were so young—Malcolm was 23, Angus just 21—because the pace of their life was so hectic. After a frantic year of dues paid in blood, sweat and beer, the band barely stopped for a breath. There were more shows to play, another album to record. And Malcolm only had a few more payments to go on his amp.

And after that, anything was possible.

10

'We ain't a punk band, we're rock 'n' roll.'

Early in the new year, *Countdown* host Molly Meldrum
finally had the chance to speak with Malcolm about the idea
he'd been cooking up with ABC producer Paul Drane.

'What if,' Meldrum asked in his typically nervy manner,
'we put you guys on the back of a truck and filmed you
rolling down Swanston Street during peak hour?'

By now, Meldrum had convinced himself that Malcolm
would hate the idea. No way would he go for it. It was a crazy
scheme, totally nuts. So he was taken aback by Malcolm's
reaction.

'Sounds great,' Malcolm said. Simple as that.

On 23 February 1976, the band—along with three
members of pipe band The Rats of Tobruk—assembled
in the early morning and squeezed onto a flatbed truck.
Manager Browning positioned himself next to the vehicle,
alongside the film crew. There was no talk of paperwork or
council permits; they simply set up and got to work.

As the truck slowly moved down Swanston Street, making
the first of three circuits, a crowd of curious onlookers started

to gather; one especially supportive fan stealthily passed a joint to Bon Scott, just off camera, as 'A Long Way to the Top' roared from the speakers.

On the truck, Malcolm was resplendent in a white 'Concert for Bangladesh' T-shirt and blue jeans—a working bloke's clothes—and he poured himself into one of his soon-to-be-classic riffs, his hair blowing in the breeze. Angus played so hard that his schoolboy cap went flying, while the pipers wrestled with their instruments, squeezed onto the rear of the truck, facing the band as they wailed away. Some additional footage of the band performing in the city centre was also shot, Malcolm still sporting his Concert for Bangladesh T-shirt. Costume changes were for posers.

Countdown managed to capture a band fast coming into its prime, playing what was probably their first great rock-and-roll song—certainly Bon Scott's first great lyric. It was a series of reflections about life on the road plucked directly from his own experiences: 'Gettin' robbed/Gettin' stoned/Getting' beat up/Broken bones'. Clinton Walker, in his definitive biography of Scott, suggests it resembled an epitaph: 'It's as if Bon acknowledges he's living on borrowed time, and luckily at that. But even then, or perhaps for that very reason, the song remains celebratory.'

Angus, as he liked to do, retooled the lyrics to 'It's a long way to the shop if you want a sausage roll', duly launching hundreds of other (usually X-rated) versions of the lyric.

A great moment in Australian rock and roll had been realised, though not many of those looking on from the street would have known it at the time. The film clip certainly helped the song's progress—it had been released as a single in December 1975, two months before the filming—and it reached number 9, remaining on the charts for almost three months. It was their first big hit.

★

A few weeks before the clip was filmed, the band had returned to Sydney, playing a three-night-stand at the Bondi Lifesaver (having been forgiven for killing the owner's fish). The 250-square-metre dance floor was jam-packed each night. Covering the craziness for *RAM*, Anthony O'Grady noted how varied AC/DC's audience had become: skinheads and sharpies were headbanging alongside yobs, drunks and eager female fans.

'There's a skinhead front of the stage,' wrote O'Grady, 'in a denim shirt with sleeves ripped off, tatts down his arms, whose howling, dervish dance grants him wary space.'

Backstage, Scott grumbled to O'Grady about his lack of success with the ladies. He insisted it was 'the other three'—Malcolm, Evans and Rudd—who fared best. 'They do the least moving about on stage and they still pull more chicks than Angus or me. Bloody unfair it is. Being a singer ain't what it used to be, not in this band, anyway.'

While in Sydney, Malcolm and the band put the finishing touches on their next album, *Dirty Deeds Done Dirt Cheap*. The name of the album, and of its title track, was another Angus brainwave; it was borrowed from one of his favourite cartoons, *Beany and Cecil*. In one episode, the show's baddie, Dishonest John, hands around a card that lists his services as 'Dirty deeds done dirt cheap'. Inspiration could strike from the strangest places. Malcolm's right hand went into overdrive as he added another of his titanium-strength riffs, and 'Dirty Deeds Done Dirt Cheap' came to loud and vivid life.

The album, like their previous two LPs, was made on the run, between December 1975 and March 1976, on days (and nights) when they had time off from playing live. Sometimes they'd even record after gigs, as Malcolm recalled when he looked back on its recording.

'We didn't have much time to do that album,' he remembered. 'After *High Voltage* we seemed to be touring constantly. Then we signed the record deal to go over to England and just as we'd completed the tour, [Alberts] told us we had to do another album. All we did was go straight into the studio after doing the night's gig and knock up some new ideas.'

It may have been an album made in a hurry, but *Dirty Deeds* had no shortage of terrific rock songs. Among them was 'Problem Child', which provided an introduction to AC/DC for a Midwestern American teenager William Bruce Bailey, something of a problem child himself, who'd become better known as Axl Rose. 'One day,' Rose promised himself, 'I'm going to play in that band.'

'Ride On' was a highly effective slow blues, another standout of the album, given life by Malcolm's subtle but effective rhythm guitar. Many players felt that Malcolm's Gretsch guitar was better suited for blues than rock—Rory Gallagher had used a Gretsch, as had Eric Clapton in his early days with the Yardbirds—and here was the stark, soulful evidence.

What Malcolm saw as Scott's obsession with his testicles hadn't abated; when one more track was needed to complete the record, Scott glanced downwards and came up with the oh-so-subtle 'Big Balls'. 'It was just a bit of a joke, a bit of fun,' said Malcolm. 'We needed to fill up the album, someone came up with a rumba or a tango, and Bon started writing these hilarious words. Bon loved an innuendo.' He also loved celebrating his nuts in song.

Alberts hosted a reception for the band (and for Vanda and Young) in Melbourne, where they were presented with gold records for *High Voltage* and *T.N.T.* Even with various family members in attendance, nothing was toned down; the event was typical AC/DC. A sexy young woman emerged from a cake, clutching one of the gold records, while a belly dancer somehow lost her bra while shaking it up on the dance floor. Bon gave a juicy, expletive-laden acceptance speech, although Angus kept it simple: 'I'd just like to thank me,' he said, grinning madly.

Malcolm said little, but was clearly thrilled, even though he knew this was just one step further down the road. 'Having a big in album in Oz is like having a big seller in Guernsey,' he'd admit to a journalist. 'It doesn't pay the rent.' He was right, of course.

The entire band was totally focused on Malcolm's larger goal—getting to London. The Atlantic deal was now firmly in place. They also had a departure date, 1 April, which would be just days after Malcolm was due to make his final payment on his amp. There was a UK tour booked, and they had the new album in the can. Their latest single, 'T.N.T.', was doing well in the Australian charts (it would peak at number 15).

What could go wrong?

★

In March, the ABC stumped up a bit of cash—probably no more than a few hundred dollars—to produce a clip for the song 'Jailbreak', again exclusively for *Countdown*. The site chosen was a quarry in the Melbourne suburb of Sunshine. In keeping with the song's on-the-lam theme, a façade of prison walls was built on the site. In the paper-thin script for the shoot, Bon and Angus were to race through the gates, with Malcolm and Mark Evans dressed as convict-era coppers on their tail, firing away with actual handguns— six-shot revolvers—loaded (thank Christ) with blanks. It was perhaps the most fun Malcolm had yet had while in the band—when had he ever had the chance to muck about with real weapons?

Safety officers were thin on the ground in 1976, so it was pretty much anything goes on the shoot. The homemade explosives came in large orange juice containers, the type typically used as bongs, which were filled with petrol and then loaded into a metal tube and fired like a cannon. Not exactly up to military standards, but effective enough for *Countdown*'s needs.

For the live portion of the clip, the band was required to play while perched atop boulders. Scott almost fell off his rocky perch when the first drink bottle cannon was detonated behind him. (The look on his face clearly says: 'What the *fuck* was that?') The cannons radiated both heat and noise and the band members flinched every time one exploded.

The grand finale, such as it was, was the moment when the prison gates were set alight and the big chase took place, Malcolm and Evans firing blanks at Bon and Angus running full tilt. The bombs exploded—'shit went everywhere', Evans recalled—and Angus, who had swapped his schoolboy gear for convict pyjamas (popular evening wear at the time), burst through the flaming gates at high speed, only just avoiding being set alight himself.

It was low-budget, sure, and rough-as-guts—and pretty damned risky at times—but 'Jailbreak' did the trick. AC/DC had another great clip, Malcolm got to play with some fire-arms, and *Countdown* had both bragging rights and a video they swiftly put on repeat play.

★

The UK tour that Atlantic Records had set in place seemed perfect, especially for Malcolm and Angus: a run of dates with labelmates Back Street Crawler, whose frizzy-haired guitarist, Paul Kossoff, had played in Free. They'd been one of Malcolm and Angus's favourite bands, who injected a fair dose of the blues into bar-room-basic rock and roll. The brothers had seen Free play at the Sydney Showgrounds in 1971 and been highly impressed; Kossoff exerted a strong influence on Angus's playing. Malcolm's old band Velvet Underground had renamed themselves Pony after the Free song, 'Ride on Pony'. Add the fact that Kossoff was as verti-cally challenged as the Youngs, and it was clear they had plenty in common. The tour was set to begin in early April, within days of AC/DC arriving in London. What better way to launch your overseas assault than a run of dates with one of your guitar heroes?

But on 19 March, news reached the band: the tour wasn't going to happen. Kossoff was dead, yet another rock-and-roll casualty. He died on a transatlantic flight from New York to London, from a pulmonary embolism; the fact that he was also addicted to heroin clearly hadn't helped. Kossoff hadn't even reached 27, the cursed age at which Jim Morrison, Janis Joplin and Brian Jones had died. He was just 25.

When Bon Scott heard about Kossoff's untimely death, he took the news to heart. 'That cunt Kossoff fucked up our first tour,' Scott told a reporter from *RAM*. 'Wait'll Angus gets hold of him.'

The band's plans were too far advanced to change, so they'd now leave for London as intended, get settled and then see what opportunities arose—hopefully in a hurry, because they'd be living off savings until they got some work.

On 1 April, just before boarding their Garuda Airlines flight to the UK, the entire band sat down with Molly Meldrum in a lounge at Sydney Airport. Everyone, bar Angus, was sipping drinks, the first of many for the long haul ahead. Angus, at the time sporting a pudding-bowl haircut, was sucking down yet another smoke. While the others bantered with Meldrum, cracking jokes, Malcolm, who seemed to be in the same T-shirt and jeans he'd been wearing ever since he'd ditched his knee-high boots and satin pants, was far more serious.

'What's coming out in the UK?' Meldrum asked.

'It's a combination of the *High Voltage* and *T.N.T.* albums,' Malcolm replied. 'One album called *High Voltage*.'

And a single?

'"Long Way to the Top"; it's released in England today.'

Serious discussion, however, wasn't foremost on their minds. Malcolm—and all of the band, in fact—was obviously thrilled to be taking on the rest of the world; there was a flight to catch, they were raring to go. ('We're confident,' Angus insisted when asked about their immediate future, 'but not overconfident.') When Malcolm was asked to appear in a quick grab to promote *Countdown,* he simply couldn't get his lines right.

'Hi there. This is the boyz,' Malcolm said to camera, accidentally pointing at the cue card as he spoke. 'We're just reminding ya that you're tuned to *Countdown,* Australia's top rock show.' Then he paused, looking away. 'Blew it!' he laughed, and decided to leave the role to Phil Rudd, who spoke with all the ease of a man who'd rather be playing the drums.

When Malcolm's former bandmate, Ted Mulry, gate-crashed the interview, everyone seemed relieved by the interruption. It was an interesting moment for Malcolm; he'd come a long way in a relatively short time since striking out on his own because he didn't want to be part of Mulry's backing band. Clearly, he'd made the right decision. Ted Mulry Gang hadn't fared too badly—a few months back, their single 'Jump in My Car' had been a nationwide number 1 smash, even pushing ABBA off the top of the charts—but Malcolm's plans for AC/DC were too big for Australia alone.

As Meldrum and his crew packed up their gear, Bon, Mark Evans and Angus hiked Mulry up on their shoulders and everyone belted out a raucous, impromptu version of 'Long Way to the Top', sounding more like a footy team than a rock-and-roll band. It was something not often witnessed in the Sydney Airport lounge.

All they had to do now was find a way to endure the 36-hour haul to Heathrow. The in-flight drinks would help.

★

Malcolm hated punk rock. Couldn't stand it. Yet he and the band were heading straight into London's summer of punk. The abrasive music that punk bands hammered out didn't inspire Malcolm—it lacked the swing he loved, for one thing—nor did he share their disdain for such 'dinosaur' acts as The Rolling Stones, whom Malcolm still rated highly. But Malcolm would soon find himself being asked to define AC/DC: were they punks? Were they the new Sex Pistols, the next Saints? Was Angus going to trade the school uniform for bondage pants and safety pins?

'We ain't a punk band, we're rock 'n' roll,' Malcolm said firmly. There was something else, too; he felt that punks were wimps who wouldn't last a minute in the Aussie bloodhouses that had helped define AC/DC and their sound.

'[We're] tougher than any of those punks,' Malcolm continued. 'We used to sit there laughing at these guys who were supposed to be able to bite your head off, thinking, we could just rip the safety pin out of his nose and knock the shit out of him.'

But well before they hit the UK, the term 'punk' had already been bandied around in discussions of AC/DC— Anthony O'Grady's 1975 *RAM* article featured a huge banner headline that read: 'AC/DC: Australia Has Punk Rock Bands Too Y'know.' 'High Voltage Punk Rock,' screamed a tour poster from the same year, accompanied by an image of Angus in full cry.

This wasn't how Malcolm perceived the band. As far as he was concerned, there was only one positive thing to come out of punk rock: 'It was good that it came along and changed the face of music for a while and wiped out all the hippie shit.' Here he echoed Sex Pistol Johnny Rotten, who'd recently snarled to a reporter from *Sounds:* 'I hate hippies and what they stand for.' So they did have one thing in common.

Yet as the band settled into rented digs at 49 Inverness Terrace in Bayswater, a few Tube stops away from the centre of London, what they were hearing on the radio was vastly different to what was happening in such clubs as the Nashville Rooms—where the Sex Pistols played on 3 April— and the 100 Club, soon to host Buzzcocks and The Clash and The Damned. If you didn't pogo yourself into a frenzy at these clubs or hang out at Malcolm McLaren and Vivienne Westwood's SEX boutique on the King's Road, you wouldn't know that punk existed—well not yet, anyway.

The record-buying public of England was binging on sugary pop, judging by the charts of early April 1976. The number 1 single was Brotherhood of Man's 'Save Your Kisses for Me', with ABBA's 'Fernando' and Billy Ocean's 'Love Really Hurts Without You' not far behind. Also lingering in the charts were acts such as the Bellamy Brothers, Sailor, and Gallagher & Lyle, who all peddled exactly the kind of music that Malcolm had been rebelling against when he formed AC/DC. Even Rod Stewart, not so long ago a member of the Faces—a good-time rock band that Malcolm respected— had gone solo and soft with 'Tonight's the Night'.

If that wasn't enough to contend with, there was also the matter of Bon Scott's teeth. Soon after their arrival, killing time while waiting for news of some work, Scott dropped by a pub in suburban Finchley that he had frequented back in his days with Fraternity. Within minutes of finding his favourite bar stool, Scott was king-hit with a beer mug. He stumbled back to Bayswater nursing a dislocated jaw and missing several teeth, swearing blind (when he could swear) that he was the victim of collateral damage. 'It wasn't even my fight,' Scott insisted. Admittedly, Scott could have used some dental work anyway, but this wasn't quite what he'd had in mind. Paying for his new set of chompers set the band back the equivalent of $2000—hardly the best way to begin their UK assault, particularly with no new money coming in.

Finally, on 23 April, almost three weeks after landing in London, the band made their UK debut, at a venue called the Red Cow. The Red Cow was a West London pub with a band room at the rear; at a squeeze 250 punters would fill the room, although on a good night many more would climb in through the toilet window to avoid the cover charge. They were to play two sets, all for a princely fee of £35. A sign outside the pub read, simply: 'AC/DC—from Australia!'

The room was empty when the band arrived, apart from the publican's Dobermans, who snapped at them as they got ready. Yet, from the opener 'Live Wire' onwards, AC/DC played as though it was another big gig back in Oz. Angus even dropped to the floor and performed a stellar Dying Bug routine during 'Baby Please Don't Go', much to the shock of the few people in the room.

Those few onlookers faded away after the first set, leaving Malcolm and the others to wonder how much worse things could get. But in fact those few punters called everyone they knew, demanding they get down to the Red Cow as quickly as they could.

As their second set began, the room swiftly filled to the brim. In the audience was Silver Smith, a woman with whom Bon Scott had an affair in 1971. They'd go home together that night and soon enough move in together. (The rest of the band remained resolutely single.)

Angus busted out all his signature moves to a now jam-packed back room. At one stage, mid-solo, he dashed out the door of the pub and down Hammersmith Road, a roadie close behind him, while the band played on.

AC/DC's UK booking agent, Richard Griffiths, who ran Headline Artists (and would go on to manage boy band One Direction), spoke with the band at the end of the night. He'd never heard anything so loud and mean in his life. He was converted. Now for the rest of England.

11

'We want the audience to go home with laryngitis;
that's the idea.'

It wasn't just pasty-faced scenesters in bondage pants that
Malcolm and the band had to contend with in the London
summer of 1976. There was also the annoyingly fickle local
media, who took great delight in putting the boot into a
bunch of scruffy Aussie upstarts—especially an outfit as
wilfully unfashionable as AC/DC. If AC/DC had a musical
peer among the UK's current breed, it was pub rockers Dr
Feelgood, one of the acts on the shitlist of Johnny Rotten
and his punk peers.

When the music press did bother covering AC/DC, it
brought out the usual sarcasm and colonial-bashing. The
lousy puns were bad enough—the *New Musical Express*
referred to Angus as 'the human kangaroo', while another rag
snickered 'Chunder Down Under'—but the actual observa-
tions on the band were even worse.

On 8 May, writing in the *New Musical Express*, Phil
McNeill wondered what business the band had appearing
'in the middle of the Great British Punk Rock Explosion'.
The *Record Mirror* mentioned koala bears, kangaroos, the

'duck bill platypus', boomerangs, cold lager, Rolf Harris and billabongs—and that was just in their intro.

Over at *Melody Maker*, writer Caroline Coon made references to 'outback rednecks' and 'macho chunder bar-proppers' (whatever the hell they were). Most writers paused to give human livewire Angus some praise—he was called a 'virtuoso' and the proud owner of 'the fastest knees in the west'—but the others were not so fortunate.

'AC/DC are nothing new,' wrote Coon. 'The legs astride, uncompromisingly male stance of Malcolm Young (rhythm guitar), Phillip Rudd (drums) and Mark Evans (bass) . . . their faded denims and sweat-soaked T-shirts are a familiar sight in the rock 'n' roll arena.'

'They stand for everything I disagree with about our chauvinist view of the woman's role,' boomed *Sounds*, laying on the 'high and mighty' with a trowel.

Bon was smart, though, and he seized upon the British tabloid fondness for sleazy titillation, regaling journalists with lurid tales of his sexual conquests. He told a writer from *Sounds* how he once caught the dreaded 'jack'. 'This girl wanted fucking and she was so ugly; I figured, shit . . . when we'd finished she went next door to Phil and gave it to him.'

Scott, when asked, also came up with a quote that perfectly defined his role in the band. 'They say to me, are you AC or DC and I say, "Neither. I'm the lightning flash in the middle."'

Jokes and barbs aside, there was one key thing that Malcolm (and Bon) understood. The music press could be influential, but it wasn't writers who bought tickets and albums; it was the kids in the audience. That's who they'd need to win over—not the critics. Fraternity had been much fancied by the Aussie music press, appearing on the cover of *Go-Set*, but they had barely sold a record. Malcolm underwent the same experience in his pre-AC/DC life. Good reviews didn't always put denim-clad bums on seats.

It'd take several months before the band was given the chance to tackle this with the press, but when Scott spoke with the *New Musical Express*, he didn't hold back. 'The music press is totally out of touch with what the kids actually want to listen to,' he said firmly. 'These kids might be working in a shitty factory, or they might be on the dole—come the weekend, they just want to have a good time, get drunk and go wild. We give them the opportunity to do that.'

Perhaps Scott was biting the hand that fed him—and the band—by savaging the music press, but it was fair payback for the lousy way they'd been treated. Only *Sounds*, one of the four music weeklies in the UK, eventually came to grasp what the band was all about. And Scott was right; they were a band of the people, not the critics.

Malcolm, meanwhile, said little, but the statement on the T-shirt he wore while playing at the Nashville Rooms in late May summed up his attitude: 'No Wuckin Furries'. Winning over the masses was far more important to him than seducing the media. What he wanted was 'the whole audience going wild. We want the audience to go home with laryngitis; that's the idea'.

*

The band's HQ in Bayswater was perfect. In fact it was so spacious that Malcolm, Angus and Bon (until he moved in with Silver Smith) each had their own room. There was ample room downstairs for the epic, all-night card games that consumed much of their free time. There was also enough room for the band to plug in and have a 'blow'—a jam—in the hallway.

Not too long after they settled in, *Countdown* sourced a London-based crew and a reporter named Doug Crawford to speak with the band in Covent Garden.

All Bon wore was a pair of dangerously tight shorts; he had tucked a banana into his waistband. Phil Rudd sported a Hawaiian shirt, a garish new addition to his wardrobe. Angus could have been mistaken for a barber's pole in his striped top. Malcolm wore the blue jeans that he probably slept in.

Crawford asked how their trip had been going.

'When the people come to see us,' Bon explained, 'we just give them the show we give the Australian people, you know?'

'Are you rich, though?' the interviewer asked. 'Are you making the bread?'

'We just bought Big Ben,' Angus deadpanned, his hands on his hips, barely suppressing a smirk.

Little did he know that barely five years down the line he and Malcolm would be millionaires.

*

Despite their resistance, Malcolm and the band seemingly couldn't escape the dreaded 'punk' tag. Malcolm maintained his line that there were two kinds of rock bands: 'Good and bad. We're the good.' He didn't need to clarify who he felt was 'the bad'. Angus laughed off punk rock acts as 'shite': 'They can't play. They can't sing.'

So when their free Nashville Rooms gig on 26 April was inaccurately billed as 'An Antipodean Punk Extravaganza', it's unlikely that Malcolm and Angus were thrilled. A group named Captain Video opened for them; their manager, Bryan Taylor, was standing behind the mixing desk when Malcolm Young struck his first power chord and the band ripped into 'Live Wire'.

'From then on,' Taylor would write of the experience, 'I was on another planet! This was raw energy; loud, proud, vibrant.'

Finally, on 30 April, the 'international' version of *High Voltage*, which Malcolm had mentioned in their farewell chat with Molly Meldrum, was released in the UK. Interestingly, Angus was the only band member to appear on the cover of this version; he was caught mid-solo as a lightning bolt hit him; it's clear who Atlantic Records believed to be the star of the band. The others didn't seem to mind; they'd started using the London office of Atlantic as a surrogate boozer, dropping by on 'business' and leaving with drinks swiped from the label's private stock.

Critical response to the record was mixed, as expected. It didn't chart in the UK; neither did 'Long Way to the Top', which was released as a single. The *New Musical Express* didn't bother to review the album, while *Melody Maker* dismissed it as 'the same old boogie'. *Sounds'* Geoff Barton, however, gave *High Voltage* a big thumbs up, calling it 'a tonic in the midst of the all-too-serious, poker-faced groups of today. If there ever was a good time band, this is it'. At least one scribe was getting the message.

High Voltage was panned by US *Rolling Stone* upon its North American release. 'Those concerned with the future of hard rock,' wrote Billy Altman, 'may take solace in knowing that with the release of the first US album by these Australian gross-out champions, the genre has unquestionably hit its all-time low. Things can only get better (at least I hope so) . . .

'Stupidity bothers me,' Altman huffed in conclusion. 'Calculated stupidity offends me.'

High Voltage may have only reached a 'peak' of number 146 on the *Billboard* 200 chart, but over time it went on to sell more than three million copies in the US alone. Australia's 'gross-out champions' would have the last laugh.

★

London venue the Marquee was little more than a shoebox, but it had real rock history, having hosted residencies by such legends as The Who, The Rolling Stones, Yardbirds, Led Zeppelin, Jimi Hendrix and Pink Floyd—mostly at key moments in each band's career, just as their stars began to rise. It was a hangout for fellow musos and record industry people, as well as the man (and woman) in the street. It was an influential venue; a great gig at the Marquee always gained the right kind of attention.

AC/DC were booked for a two-night stand at the Marquee on 11 and 12 May, the dates set in place by Richard Griffiths. The first night they were to open for a Paul Kossoff-less Back Street Crawler. Gig-hardened Marquee punters thought they'd seen everything that rock and roll had to offer, from Hendrix setting his guitar alight to

The Who trashing their gear, but experiencing Angus leaping from one table to the next, scattering drinks and ashtrays (and onlookers) in all directions, was a totally new sensation. And Malcolm's riffing, which ignited such fire-starters as 'High Voltage', 'T.N.T.' and 'Long Way to the Top', had the many musos in the room nodding their approval. There was a lot of muscle in that diminutive frame, and some real magic in his right hand. The Marquee's owner, Jack Barrie, was sufficiently impressed to invite them back for further gigs.

The band, with the exception of homebody Angus, celebrated by seeing The Rolling Stones play at Earls Court in London two weeks later. It was the first time that Malcolm—who'd covered loads of Stones songs in both Velvet Underground and the early days of AC/DC—had seen the band since 1973. The production might have been a bit flashier, and Mick Jagger's hip-wiggling a tad more contrived, but as far as Malcolm was concerned, there were still only two 'real' rock-and-roll acts: 'The Stones and us'. And what of other contenders? 'They don't understand the feel, the movement, you know, the *jungle* of it all.'

★

Angus appeared solo on the *Sounds* cover on 12 June, giving the camera a fearful stare. The cover line asked the question, 'Would you give a job to this school leaver?'

Angus had convinced the music press that he was fifteen years old, sixteen at most, despite the fact he was actually 21. Even the reputable BBC was fooled, introducing him as 'only sixteen years old, a schoolboy' when the band played a set on the BBC's *In Concert* series. Bon Scott wasn't the only one who enjoyed messing with the local media.

Scott was also acquiring his fair share of admirers, many of them male, as Malcolm would explain during a VH1 documentary. 'Bon was becoming a real hero among the tougher guys in the audience. They all wanted Bon, the wild life. They loved him.' Scott enjoyed providing these punters with an endless stream of laughs, as he regularly toyed with his lyrics on stage. He'd introduce 'Can I Sit Next to You Girl' as 'Can I Shit Next to You Girl'—'as John Lydon would say'—or 'Can I Sit on Your Face Girl'. He also riffed on the lyrics of 'The Jack', stretching out the line 'I curdled her cream' like a seasoned comic. On stage at Leith Theatre in Edinburgh, Scott asked the audience if anyone would admit to ever having the dreaded 'jack'. 'Put your hands up. And keep your hands up if you've still got it.' When some in the theatre came clean, Scott laughed. 'You dirty bastards!'

Manager Browning, meanwhile, had arranged a deal that would vastly improve the onstage lives of Malcolm and Angus. He'd met with the legendary Jim Marshall, creator of the eponymous line of amplifiers—the weapon of choice for such greats as Eric Clapton and Jimi Hendrix and much fancied by Malcolm—and he'd agreed to supply the band with new, state-of-the-art gear. The brothers were so eager to plug in and let rip that they did just that one lunchtime at home, but disgruntled neighbours slipped notes under their door, demanding they keep the noise down. That was okay; requests for gigs had started pouring in, and Malcolm and the band were set to spend most of their time on the road. *Sounds* sponsored a tour that kept them out of the house throughout much of June and July 1976, playing to increasingly bigger and rowdier crowds.

★

Malcolm admired Marc Bolan of T. Rex, even to the extent of sticking a poster of the man who created 'Jeepster' and 'Hot Love' on his bedroom wall back in Burwood. ('A small poster, admittedly,' his friend Herm Kovac clarified.) When an offer arose to appear on the *Rollin' Bolan* TV special, which was being filmed at the Wimbledon Theatre in mid-July, Malcolm couldn't accept quickly enough.

AC/DC looked and sounded great as they rocked 'Jailbreak', 'Live Wire' and especially 'Can I Sit Next to You Girl', where Malcolm and Angus stood side by side, riffing furiously, their heads bobbing in unison, truly brothers in arms. Vanda and Young, visiting from Australia, proudly watched from the wings. Bon wore a leopard-skin vest and a suggestive leer; Malcolm was in his usual working-man's clobber, T-shirt and jeans, while Angus donned his schoolboy blues. Although forced to use unfamiliar gear, the band absolutely blazed.

By contrast, Marc Bolan was overweight, stumbling on high heels, his make-up running under the lights. 'I was waiting for him to go arse-up,' bassist Evans admitted in his memoir *Dirty Deeds,* adding that Bolan 'had the look of a guy who was rapidly nearing his use-by date'. (Bolan died in a car crash a little over a year later.)

Watching Bolan from off stage, Malcolm thought it best not to mention his own obsession with T. Rex. Lesson learned: sometimes, he realised, it's best not to get too close to your heroes.

Typically, the AC/DC machine kept on rolling. In mid-July, in one of the stranger arrangements of the band's career, a 'swap' was put in place with Swedish promoter Thomas Johansson, who represented ABBA. AC/DC would play their first set of European dates in Swedish hotspots such as Falkenberg, Malmo, Stockholm, Vaxjo and Anderstorp, and in exchange Johansson could book an Australian tour for ABBA. ABBA travelled like royalty, with an entourage of more than 100, in a Boeing 727 hired especially for the tour, and played for 160,000-plus people, shooting *ABBA: The Movie* as they traversed the country. It was the height of ABBA-mania.

As for AC/DC, they crossed the Channel in a clapped-out tour bus that sometimes doubled as sleeping quarters, and fed British coins into vending machines that coughed up croquettes and cigarettes. Angus, as was his wont, moaned to manager Browning, 'What the fuck are we doing in Sweden?'

Their first Swedish concert was at an old-school dance hall; only 40 people showed up. Not many more turned out in Stockholm. A punter swiped Angus's cap at the Falkenberg show but returned it when he discovered it didn't fit.

Malcolm would admit that while the crowds were disappointing, they did get the chance to familiarise themselves with the friendlier Swedish natives, though perhaps not the pick of the bunch. 'In Sweden,' he said, 'there are 90 per cent beautiful women and 10 per cent ugly—guess which ones we got?'

★

Things were picking up, however, back in London. Marquee owner Jack Barrie invited the band to stage an eight-week/

eight-gig residency at the club. Barrie said that AC/DC was 'the best band to appear at the Marquee since Led Zeppelin'.

The first night of their residency was sparsely attended, but word spread about the band and they swiftly broke the venue's attendance record. At some Marquee gigs, 1000 fans were shoehorned into the venue, at least 300 more than its capacity.

Most nights Angus did his onstage striptease, usually culminating in a bared bum—the ol' 'brown-eye', a move partly inspired by Malcolm's mate Herm Kovac (who'd been 'pantsed' once on stage, accidentally baring his bum, while Angus and Malcolm looked on from the wings). 'I think they thought I was some kind of male stripper at one point,' Angus laughed.

He wasn't the only one to shed clothes during these gigs. Bon Scott told a reporter from the Melbourne *Herald* that 'the place looked like a nudist colony by the time we finished'.

'The heat is beyond belief,' wrote *Sounds'* Phil Sutcliffe. 'The humidity is just a little lower than in the deep end at the municipal baths.' In the words of manager Browning, 'the [Marquee's] walls were like waterfalls of sweat'.

True believer Molly Meldrum flew out from Melbourne to document the band's rise for *Countdown*. One punter grabbed Meldrum's arm and, gasping for air and for words, gestured towards Angus. 'He's the best thing I've seen since Pete Townshend!'

During their residency, an impressive array of stars checked out these Aussie rockers. Deep Purple's Ritchie Blackmore, clearly having gotten over their dust-up back at Sunbury, was so taken that he requested a jam with AC/DC, but there was some confusion, and he was left standing alone on stage.

'We didn't know he was there,' Malcolm later insisted. 'We just went home.'

Creedence Clearwater Revival's Doug Clifford and Stu Cook caught their act at the Marquee and were so impressed they offered to produce the band, an offer Malcolm politely refused. The band already had Vanda and Young; what was the point?

On 11 August, with the band well into their residency, photographer Michael Putland squeezed into the dingy, heavily graffitied backstage area, snapping the band in various stages of undress. In one shot, Malcolm reclines on the Marquee's ratty couch, nursing a beer that is far bigger than his right hand. The smile on his face says plenty: AC/DC had arrived.

12

'We're a scandal. Mums dragging their kids away from
us on the street. Oh look—THEM!'

Malcolm could be dour and deadly serious, especially
when it came to the band. AC/DC was his baby, his reason
for being, and anyone who didn't share his passion was
simply in the way. He tended to keep his bandmates, with
the exception of Angus, at arm's length. As bassist Evans
wrote in *Dirty Deeds*, 'Malcolm was the driven one . . . the
planner, the schemer, the behind the scenes guy, ruthless
and astute.' If that meant some people saw Malcolm as
humourless, so be it. He didn't care; he was too absorbed
in the world of AC/DC to worry too much about what
others thought.

But he did have a sense of mirth. Sometimes it could be
pretty puerile, such as the occasion that a reporter asked
Angus if he was the 'Joan Collins of rock and roll' and
Malcolm felt compelled to intervene. 'He can't get his ankles
behind his ears,' Malcolm snickered, looking towards his
younger brother, as the others fell about in hysterics.

There were times when he could be good-spirited, too.
When the band shifted to a new HQ in Barnes, just over

the Hammersmith Bridge, another house with room in the hallway for jam sessions, they befriended the local dustmen—the garbos—many of whom lived in nearby council housing.

One morning, when he could hear the garbage truck rumbling by outside, Malcolm stuck his head out the window and burst into song, bellowing the lyrics to 'My Old Man's a Dustman', the old Lonnie Donegan chestnut, to the men at work in the street below.

'That's how I knew the garbage men were cool in the collective eyes of the band,' wrote Mark Evans. 'For Mal, that was a real statement.'

But sometimes Malcolm's world could get deadly serious, such as the time the band went out on the road with metal masters Black Sabbath.

In April 1977, they began a month-long European tour with the notorious Ozzy Osbourne and his group, Black Sabbath, whom they'd opened for back in Australia three years back. The two bands, despite their different styles, shared strong working-class roots—the Birmingham-born Osbourne referred to himself as the 'plumber of darkness' (like Malcolm, he had failed to complete his trade). Most nights, as the tour rolled through Switzerland, Denmark, France and Germany, Malcolm and the others would gather side stage as Sabbath's bass player, Geezer Butler—another Birmingham native—launched into what Malcolm and the others saw as a completely pointless bass solo. And, just as predictably, every night Butler would hit a bum note, sending five antipodean rockers into peals of laughter. Butler would shoot them a dirty look, clearly annoyed by these cocky upstarts.

After a show in Belgium, Geezer Butler was in the hotel bar, moaning about life on the road. 'Wait until you guys have been around ten years,' he grumbled to Malcolm, who was sitting nearby. 'You'll feel just like us.'

'I don't think so,' Malcolm cheekily replied.

With that, Butler produced a flick knife and started waving it about, which came as quite a shock for Malcolm. Ozzy Osbourne then walked into the bar.

'You fuckin' idiot, Butler,' he snapped. 'Get to bed.'

Butler, not surprisingly, had a different take on events, as he told *Classic Rock* magazine in 2016. 'We were having a drink together and I was just playing about with the knife . . . I was having a drink, flicking my knife—like you do—and he came over and said: "You must think you're big, having a flick-knife." I said, "What are you talking about?" And that was it. Nobody got hurt.'

Whatever the truth actually was, it was perhaps the first time that Ozzy Osbourne prevented chaos rather than creating it. Never one to miss a party, Osbourne did, however, settle in and see out the night with Malcolm and the others once Butler had trudged off to his room. Ozzy became tight with the band.

★

The Sabbath tour, despite this flare-up, was a welcome break from recent events in the UK. After their trailblazing success at the Marquee, Jack Barrie had invited the band to play at the Reading Festival on 29 August 1976. This was a massive two-day affair, a key event in the British rock calendar, but AC/DC's Reading debut was a very public disaster. It was the first major setback for Malcolm and the band since they had relocated from Melbourne (with all due respect to the demise of 'that cunt Kossoff').

The 1976 Reading line-up was the usual mix of progressive rock acts—Camel, Phil Manzanera, Van der Graaf Generator, Manfred Mann's Earth Band—with the more primal, in the shape of Black Oak Arkansas and American wild man Ted Nugent, a fan of both guitar blitzkriegs and firearms.

Quite an entourage accompanied AC/DC to the site, including Browning and his sister Coral, Harry Vanda and George Young, Atlantic's Phil Carson, and their booking agent, Richard Griffiths. Expectations were high. En route they stopped at Griffith's family estate for cucumber sandwiches and a few games of croquet, which was a new, rather gentrified experience for Malcolm and the others.

The band fully understood how important the Reading festival gig was: a blistering set would almost guarantee an upswing in sales for *High Voltage,* which was not exactly burning up the UK charts (a failure that was causing some concern in the US, where Atlantic were dithering about releasing the album at all, perhaps even dropping the band from their roster).

Malcolm, usually the calmest man in the band pre-gig, was nervous, pacing around backstage. Once on stage, Bon tried his hardest to get the crowd inspired. 'Hello there,' he yelled. 'With all this rain we're having, the best thing to do about it is to cause some heat amongst ya to make it evaporate before it fucking hits ya, alright?'

The silence from the crowd was deafening—and the gig went steadily downhill from there.

The general consensus was that a mid-afternoon set didn't suit AC/DC, who worked better with a late-night crowd fired up by booze and adrenaline and testosterone. Another theory was that the split-stage arrangement at Reading, which enabled one band to set up while another played, thereby keeping the show rolling, restricted their ability to project to the entire audience. Whatever the reason, the response was apathetic and the band knew they'd blown a big opportunity.

According to Malcolm, there was also some confusion regarding influential DJ John Peel, one of the band's few supporters in radio, who'd tried to watch their set from up close but was turned away. This didn't help. 'Peel came up to see us there, but unfortunately one of the security blokes chucked him off when we were playing. So he wrote in the newspaper, "That's the last time I play one of these guys' fucking records." We didn't know anything about it. We didn't even have a roadie, let alone a security guy.'

Back at the band's Barnes hub, a hasty and heated post-mortem ensued. George Young accused bassist Evans of 'looking surly' on stage; then a full-on brawl erupted, with Malcolm, Angus and George all throwing punches. Evans tried to intervene and he, too, was dragged into the melee. (Angus and Evans had clashed after another show, and Angus had punched him in the face, so there was already tension between the two.)

Then there were the hassles brought on by the band's necessary return to Australia at the end of 1976, which was only weeks after the UK release of the *Dirty Deeds Done Dirt Cheap* LP. They were booked to cut a new record with Vanda and Young, now an annual ritual, and they needed to top up their coffers through playing bigger, more lucrative shows than they were booking in the UK. They also had to promote *Dirty Deeds*, which had been released in Oz during September and had just slipped out of the Top 10. But Malcolm wasn't crazy about returning to Australia; he felt the band was making great progress in the UK, despite the Reading disaster.

The rest of the band agreed. *Sounds* had just crowned AC/DC number 1 in their New Order Top 20 list, beating out the Sex Pistols, the Ramones and The Damned, which must have pleased Malcolm hugely, given his disdain for punk rock. Even the reluctant *Melody Maker*, in their wrap of 1976, conceded that AC/DC were 'one of the most popular bands currently shooting'. To Malcolm, returning to Australia felt like he'd be treading water, perhaps even taking a backwards step.

Still, the band were slaves to their work schedule, and they flew into Sydney Airport on 26 November, landing in a country currently in thrall to ABBA and their latest number 1, 'Money Money Money'. After making their way around a small but vocal contingent of female fans, the band spoke with local radio station 2SM.

At the press conference, Malcolm—who'd grown his hair even longer than usual, well below his shoulders—nursed a beer, as did Rudd, Scott and Evans, who was sporting a T-shirt plugging Neil Young's *Harvest* album (a curious choice, given Malcolm and Angus's resistance to all things West Coast and mellow). Angus slugged a milkshake and boasted about troubles back in the UK—he'd almost been arrested during shows in Glasgow and Liverpool for baring his backside. (A shot of his pimply bum featured in a *Sounds* article, under the heading 'Have You Seen This Man?')

If only Angus knew how big a problem his backside was about to become for the band.

★

Press conference done, Malcolm and Angus headed back to Burwood; they hadn't seen their family in months. The others settled into the Hyatt Kingsgate in Kings Cross, but only for a few days, as the 24-date tour was to commence in Perth on 2 December.

The band had an idea, which they shared with tour promoters Ray Evans and Michael Gudinski. They'd come up with a name for the tour.

'Let's call it "The Little Cunts Have Done It".'

Oddly, it was rejected. Instead they reluctantly agreed to the vaguely suggestive 'A Giant Dose of Rock 'n' Roll'.

The tour started well enough, especially for Malcolm. During a secret warm-up show in Melbourne, at the Tiger Lounge in Richmond's Royal Oaks Hotel, rather than run through their standard set list, the band ripped up some old classics, many of them favourites of Malcolm and Angus. They tore into 'Roll Over Beethoven', 'Whole Lotta Shakin' Goin' On', 'Jailhouse Rock' and more, songs they hadn't played since the earliest days of the band. Malcolm was still very fond of what he called the 'roots of [rock and roll], the excitement that rock and roll used to generate, with Elvis, and Little Richard jumping on his piano, the whole audience just going wild.'

The Myer Music Bowl show on 5 December *was* wild; it was the first time that AC/DC had generated real fan hysteria. The noise of the crowd almost exceeded the volume of the band. Something like 5000 fans packed into the amphitheatre, with just as many looking on from the other side of the cyclone fence that separated ticket holders from freeloaders. The band played an encore, despite a threat to cut the power if they did, and then they kept playing for another ten minutes, with the promoters nervously glancing at their watches as the show ran way overtime.

'AC/DC creates another rock concert riot,' announced *TV Week.*

A few nights later, as the band started playing gigs in rural centres, problems emerged. AC/DC may have thrived on controversy, but not the type that the tour generated. This seemed more like a case of tall-poppy syndrome. Mid-set, Angus dropped his pants during shows at Shepparton in Victoria, and Albury and Newcastle in New South Wales. By the middle of December, local councils began issuing threats to the band: if Angus's pants came down, the house lights would come up, and there might even be arrests. Police presence was increased at their shows—at least a dozen grim-faced coppers stood at stage front when they played in Orange. The band was forced to pay bonds as high as $5000 just to ensure gigs could go ahead. Fans turned up with posters that read, 'DROP 'EM ANGUS', which didn't help matters (he could be easily persuaded). When Angus dropped his strides during a press conference, a female reporter stormed out in a huff.

An editorial in *The Border Mail* demanded to know why Angus felt the need to expose 'his pimply white buttocks'. 'It's a sad commentary on his faith in the drawing power of the band's music ability,' the paper's editor sniffed.

Angus simply replied, 'Because my arse is better looking than my face.' But no one seemed to find this funny anymore.

Then a story ran in Melbourne's *Truth* newspaper, under
the headline, 'Pop Hit Makes Widow's Phone Run Hot'. It
was reported that 'a wealthy widow was shocked and upset
when she began to receive obscene telephone calls'. It turned
out that she shared the same 36-24-36 number as the character in 'Dirty Deeds' and fans had been hitting the phones,
calling her at all hours and requesting certain dirty deeds
at a discount. It was another bad omen. Their Melbourne
hotel was raided by police in search of someone's wayward
daughter. Angus was told that the girl's father had formed 'a
sort of posse'.

'They had guns and they were after us, especially Bon,'
he recalled.

Malcolm had had enough. 'We're a scandal,' he scoffed.
'Mums dragging their kids away from us on the street. Oh
look—THEM!'

There were also problems stateside. Manager Browning
was deep in negotiations with Atlantic Records in the US,
who made it clear they didn't intend to pick up their 'option'
on the band and release their music. Phil Carson from the
UK office, who'd signed the band, dug in when he heard
the news from the US. He advised them: 'I think you're
making a very big mistake.' When this went unheeded, he
met with Neshui Ertegun, the co-owner of the label, and
showed him sales figures for *High Voltage*. On the label's
US$25,000 investment, the record had sold about 40,000
copies globally; clearly, Atlantic had earned back their
money. They finally agreed to release the record, but this
reaction from Atlantic was hardly a vote of confidence, nor
was it helpful news for the band in the midst of such a difficult homecoming.

The band decided to re-christen the tour. It was now 'A Giant Pain in the Arse'.

Perhaps the band's pent-up frustration—this was a homecoming, after all, and look how it was turning out—came out when Bon spoke with Christie Eliezer from *RAM*, just before a show at the Civic Theatre in Newcastle, New South Wales. He took aim at their so-called punk 'rivals'. Just like Malcolm, Scott had no time for these pretenders; he said he'd spent the first few weeks of their London sortie checking out the opposition—when he wasn't getting his teeth put back together—and what he saw didn't impress him. It was all a big pose. 'They come on stage swearing and spitting and telling everyone to go fuck themselves,' he laughed, 'but at least the Small Faces and Rolling Stones were musically competent . . . some of these idiots could not even tune a guitar.'

★

The band limped into Tamworth, the country musical capital of Australia, on 16 December, only to learn that their show had been cancelled by the local council, fearing a flash of Angus's arse. A crew from Channel 9's *A Current Affair* had begun stalking the band as the Giant Dose controversies stacked up, and the show's host, Mike Willesee, flew by chopper to Tamworth, hoping to sniff out a story. But the band holed up in their motel room, said nothing, and the next day drove to Toowoomba in Queensland to play the Harristown High School hall. Then a few weeks later, in January 1977, another gig was cancelled, this time in the Victorian town of Warrnambool, and Angus duly blew his top.

'It will take only a couple more hassles from the authorities and we will leave Australia,' he told a reporter. The next day, a local newspaper headline screamed: 'ROCK BAND THREATENS TO LEAVE COUNTRY!'

Over at the venerable *The Australian Women's Weekly*, a letter writer offered her feelings about the band. 'I feel sorry for people who classify as good rock music the sounds AC/DC produce. They have taken rock music to its lowest point ever . . . Anyone who idolises these tattooed idiots must be lacking in the old grey matter.'

Back in Sydney, radio station 2SM, which had been a fervent supporter of the band, banned all AC/DC records. 'Members of the Australian group AC/DC must decide if they are strippers or musicians,' declared the station's general manager, Garvin Rutherford. 'Until they do, the station will not associate with them in any way.'

There was one moment of respite in the form of Ted Albert, who—along with Vanda and Young—had continued to champion the band, despite the mounting controversies (which, it should be said, usually helped sales). While the band was in Sydney, Albert gave each member a royalty cheque for $3,957.29. 'On behalf of the whole company,' Albert wrote in an attached note, 'our thanks for your efforts overseas and our best wishes for the coming year.'

The final Giant Dose concert took place at the Perth Entertainment Centre on 15 February, and provided one more chance for Bon Scott to check in with his parents, Chick and Isa, with whom he'd remained very close.

But all the drama and controversies and bans had taken a hefty toll. AC/DC headed back to the UK and wouldn't tour Australia again in Bon Scott's lifetime.

13

'We wanted to get a rawer sound and cut out those
commercial choruses.'

In late July 1977 the band's new album, *Let There Be Rock*,
was released internationally. Malcolm had a very clear vision
for the record when he and the band reconnected with Vanda
and Young in the midst of the Giant Dose tour drama. He'd
witnessed enough lengthy solos and rock-and-roll theatrics
from acts such as Queen and Alice Cooper, both huge acts
at the time, to realise that AC/DC, *his* band, needed to stick
with the basics. No bullshit. No pretension. 'We wanted to
get a rawer sound,' he said, 'and cut out those commercial
choruses like "T.N.T.".'

Malcolm knew what the band needed to do. There was
no need for them to change direction, the way big brother
George's Easybeats had felt compelled to do in the wake of
'Friday on My Mind'. (And duly lost their way.) Malcolm
believed they simply needed to fine-tune their existing style.
As he would one day tell *Q* magazine, 'It's best just to stay
where you're at; you're going to come back there anyway, so
why leave in the first place?'

George asked his brothers what type of record they hoped

to make. 'It would be great if we could just make a lot of guitar riffs,' said Angus, 'because we're fired up after doing all this touring.'

Malcolm picked up on this when he spoke about the creation of their early albums, how they would hit the studio straight after gigs. 'George and Harry would have a couple of dozen [beer] cans in and a few bottles of Jack Daniels and we'd all get in and have a party and rip it up, get the fast tracks . . . done right so it was the same loose feeling like we were on stage still. The studio was just like an extension of the gig.'

There were three new songs that Malcolm believed would give the album an extra boost; the first was 'Whole Lotta Rosie'. 'We knew it was going to be a surefire winner,' Malcolm said years later. 'If anything, for "Whole Lotta Rosie" we were looking for a feel like Little Richard, a good steamin' rock feel, and see what we could lay on top with the guitars. It evoked that, but you're just looking for the vibe, what's exciting, and that's what we were listening to. Simple to put together, but still around like a classic.'

'Bad Boy Boogie' and 'Let There Be Rock' were the other two songs that Malcolm felt 'would go the distance on stage'. He was right, of course; they'd end up becoming AC/DC live staples for the next few decades—according to the stats at setlist.fm, the band played 'Boogie' 767 times between its release and 2003, while 'Let There Be Rock', still in AC/DC's 2016 set list, checked in at a sizeable 1534 plays.

The recording of 'Let There Be Rock' would become part of AC/DC folklore. As he was recording his solo on this Biblical-style ode to the rock-and-roll life, Angus noticed that his amplifier was shooting out sparks and smoke. He hesitated, fearing a studio fire, but George gestured frantically at him through the control room glass to keep playing.

Angus complied and his gear just made it to the end of the take, but then spluttered out in what he described as 'a smouldering puddle of wiring and valves'. The take, fortunately, was gold.

'There was no way,' George later told US *Rolling Stone,* 'we were going to stop a shit-hot performance for a technical reason like amps blowing up.'

AC/DC's Alberts labelmates The Angels were recording in the same fifth-floor studio, doing what was known as 'hot-bedding'—when one band ended their session, the next set up and got cracking, which meant that the Alberts studio was in operation around the clock. Angels drummer Graham 'Buzz' Bidstrup would never forget his first close encounter with AC/DC.

'The lift was a bit slow,' he said, 'and as it climbed the floors the dull rumble of the band became more audible—until the doors finally opened and the crash of drums, guitar and bass in full fury became omnipresent. [It] was not uncommon to see Angus climbing over his amp or spinning on the floor as a take was being recorded.' And you couldn't escape the action at Alberts, because the lift doors opened directly into the studio.

Let There Be Rock would be stage one of a creative hot streak for Malcolm and the band that would extend all the way to 1980's huge smash-hit LP *Back in Black*. Vanda and Young were in the midst of their own purple patch, too, having scored major chart success with Ted Mulry Gang ('Jump in My Car' and a rockin' rework of the old jazz song 'The

Darktown Strutters Ball'), John Paul Young ('Yesterday's Hero' and 'I Hate the Music') and Stevie Wright. They were Australia's hottest production team, hitmakers who were now in control of what was known within the industry as 'the house of hits': the Alberts studio.

Just as *Dirty Deeds* had turned the head of American teenager Axl Rose, *Let There Be Rock* converted at least two other young hopefuls to a life in rock. Danish-born Lars Ulrich heard the song 'Overdose' and was sold on the spot. 'When the two guitars lock in, it's just the fucking heaviest thing ever,' said Ulrich, the drummer who would later form Metallica with James Hetfield.

'Overdose' had a similar impact on Dave Mustaine, Metallica's original guitarist and co-founder of Megadeth. 'The first couple of notes just blew my mind.' He maintained that hearing the record was a 'defining moment in my life, when I made my mind up that I was gonna do this, no matter what'.

Malcolm and the band, of course, still had a big hurdle to overcome, as 1977 rolled along. They needed to win over America.

★

Manager Michael Browning understood that the best way to sell the band to their US label was to get them to see AC/DC live, especially given that Atlantic didn't seem too impressed by their recorded product. First invitee was Doug Thaler, an influential American booking agent, who came over to the UK to catch a show, then Atlantic's Jerry Greenberg and John Kalodner, who flew to AC/DC's Hamburg gig at the Ernst Merck Hall in April 1977, one of the dates on the Black Sabbath tour.

It was the perfect gig to impress the Americans, because German audiences in particular had really taken to AC/DC, as Malcolm told a writer from *Rock Star* magazine. 'We [go over] a bomb in Germany,' Malcolm said, perhaps not choosing his words too carefully. 'They just like basic, good time rock 'n' roll, which is what we're about.' (Malcolm never forgot this support. Years later, during another show in Germany, Malcolm apologised to an uber-fan for not being able to get her into the show. 'Why don't you fly home?' he suggested, handing her £500.)

The entire party ended up in the Reeperbahn, Hamburg's red-light district, where they witnessed live sex acts and other assorted debauchery. At one club, a couple bonked madly on a tabletop right alongside the band and their entourage. Public masturbation, while not part of the act, wasn't frowned upon either, judging by the reaction of at least one member of the crowd. The AC/DC party wasn't sure which way to look. Their big night out must have done the trick, because their debut US tour was booked to begin on 27 July.

It was a slightly new-look AC/DC that checked into the first of many Red Roof Inns, a budget chain hotel that dotted the highways and byways of the US, in late July. (The band were back to travelling on the cheap.) Bassist Evans had been replaced by Englishman Cliff Williams. When he was sacked in June, Evans had been told by Malcolm that they needed a bassist who could sing, but the more likely reason was that he'd clashed once too often with Angus and had to go.

'If Angus had one crucial problem with people,' Evans would write of the experience, 'it was those who didn't share his utter commitment to the band and music; you had to be in 100% or you weren't worth bothering about . . . I believe it frustrated him when others, me included, didn't perform to his expectations.'

AC/DC's timing was spot on. KISS were about to head out on their Alive II tour, which would include a three-night stand at the 15,000-plus capacity Madison Square Garden. AC/DC would support them on a number of shows. Riding high on the US Top 40 were Steve Miller's 'Jet Airliner' and Foreigner's 'Feels Like the First Time', songs with a bit of grunt—even the Eagles were rocking out with 'Life in the Fast Lane', having hired The James Gang's Joe Walsh as guitarist and resident madman. (The guy was a dab hand with a chainsaw, especially during those long, boring nights on the road—and a future Malcolm Young fan.) Boston, Alice Cooper and Heart were also in the charts. It was a good time to be a rock band on the rise.

The first room AC/DC played in the US—the fabulously named Armadillo World Headquarters in Austin, Texas—was far more to Malcolm's taste than Angus's. It was owned by cosmic cowboy Willie Nelson, and many of the 1500 patrons took their cue from Nelson and sparked up joints while the band played. As a pot smoker, Malcolm had no issue with this, whereas Angus—who still thought drug takers were 'hippie cunts'—wasn't thrilled by the smog-like conditions inside the room. (It was also hotter than hell.) When Angus did a lap of the venue on Bon Scott's shoulders, he experienced an unwelcome contact high. In a curious coincidence, the gig's promoter, Jack Orbin, like Malcolm, had some history with Black Sabbath—Orbin had once bailed Ozzy out of prison for pissing on the Alamo Cenotaph in San Antonio.

This first US tour found the band keeping some interesting company, opening for acts that were sometimes simpatico with AC/DC, and other times left you wondering whether the promoter had actually ever heard Malcolm and the band play. In the latter group were The Charlie Daniels Band (of 'The Devil Went Down to Georgia' fame) and melodramatic rockers REO Speedwagon. They even shared a bill with Latino-rock legends Santana. Not that AC/DC had much say in it, of course; they were starting at the bottom all over again.

But, as always, Malcolm and the band left an impression. When they played an impromptu set at legendary New York punk hole-in-the-wall CBGB, the home of Blondie and the Ramones and Talking Heads—hardly a scene in which AC/DC felt comfortable—Andy Shernoff, the founder of punk band The Dictators, looked on with shock and awe as the band went about their business. Malcolm and Angus just about took his head off. 'It's amazing,' he said after the show. 'How can short guys make a sound like that? It's almost technically impossible.'

Southern rockers Lynyrd Skynyrd also became converts. They caught the band in action at a gig in Jacksonville, Florida, where local DJ Bill Bartlett had been championing AC/DC, and were hooked.

There were other tour highlights for the band, such as playing a Mafia-run venue during an Atlantic Records convention in Florida, and being given the keys to the city of North Miami (it helped that city mayor Michael Colodny was a relative of an Atlantic staffer). Malcolm wasn't the type of guy to smile on demand for the camera, but even he couldn't supress a mile-wide grin when Mayor Colodny handed them an oversized key.

What the fuck does this thing open? he might have thought
to himself.

Proving that just about anything was possible in the US,
while in New York, on their way to a baseball game, Malcolm
spotted John Lennon and Yoko Ono, the city's most famous
rock-and-roll couple, crossing the street in the opposite direction. Holy shit: a Beatle! Malcolm couldn't believe his eyes.

In Los Angeles for a three-night run at the Whisky a Go
Go, where KISS's Gene Simmons introduced himself backstage, the band stayed at the notorious Hyatt House—aka
the Riot House—the site of Keith Richards' first experi-
ments with the aerodynamics of TV sets, and where Led
Zeppelin's John Bonham would ride his Harley up and
down the hallways. The decadence was impressive, even to a
road-hardened bunch like AC/DC. In particular, all of the
band loved the US groupies, who made their intentions very
clear. 'In America,' Angus confided to a reporter, 'the chicks
who come backstage all want to screw you.'

There were improvements on the technical front, too.
While in LA, thanks to Atlantic staffer Michael Klenfner,
the group were introduced to Ken Schaffer, a trailblazer in
the high-tech world of wireless guitars and microphones—
Malcolm described him as a 'wacko rocket scientist'. Schaffer
gave Angus a wireless transmitter (the Schaffer–Vega
Diversity System, valued at around US$3300) and Bon a
wireless mic. Malcolm and the others were dumbstruck. 'We
were amazed,' he said. 'Shit! No cord!'

Schaffer told Angus, 'Once you've used this, you'll never
want to play with a lead again.'

He was dead right. AC/DC's roadies breathed a hefty
sigh of relief, too; no longer would they have to trail behind

Angus, running cable, when he decided to 'go rogue' and mix it with the crowd.

All up, the run of sixteen US dates from 27 July to 24 August, which covered a good chunk of the country, grossed almost US$19,000. Just as importantly, it snagged the band new fans and influential supporters, despite slow record sales. Within a few months they'd be back for an even longer tour—22 dates across five weeks—in bigger venues, teaming up with much more compatible acts such as Aerosmith and Cheap Trick (who'd both became huge AC/DC fans) and the Blue Öyster Cult. Enthusiasm for the band grew, as the group's collective focus shifted from the UK and Europe to the US. Even The Beatles had admitted that they didn't feel as though they'd conquered the world until they'd won over America, which was, in John Lennon's words, 'the toppermost of the poppermost'. Malcolm didn't have Lennon's verbal gifts, but he agreed: America was the rock-and-roll pot of gold.

Just like they had in the UK, and in Australia before that, the band found their biggest following in the trenches, among the working-class fans, especially in blue-collar, industrial domains such as Detroit and Cleveland and much of the Midwest. American critics, however, didn't quite know what to make of the band.

Creem magazine's Rick Johnson just couldn't grasp what the fuss was about when he reviewed *Let There Be Rock*. 'These guys suck,' he wrote. 'Somewhere in the granite mudpies of hard rock, there's got to be a distinction between boogie and plod, and AC/DC falls into the latter category.'

Sometimes even live shows, the band's calling card, drew unfavourable press. 'AC/DC [rely] on a lot of athletic prancing around by its lead guitarist, who strips from a Little Lord Fauntleroy outfit down to shorts, and does a lot of falling down while continuing to perform,' wrote a reporter for a newspaper in Louisville, Kentucky, where they opened for KISS. And then this, in a closing statement the writer would come to regret: 'It's hard to see where groups like KISS and AC/DC can go from here.'

Another review of that same show, which ran in *The Lexington Leader,* was a doozy. 'One final bit of advice,' said writer Ellen Aman. 'Unless you are addicted to this sort of music, you can skip the opening act, a 45-minute set by something called AC/DC . . . AC/DC's concept of "good music" seems to be the ability to play the guitar while running. And I don't think they're any too strict about the caliber of guitar playing, either.'

It would take several years, and a fair deal of revisionist thinking, for the US press to finally get behind AC/DC—and significantly, it came about because of the band's fans. When US *Rolling Stone* conducted a reader's poll listing their 10 Best AC/DC Songs, 'Let There Be Rock' checked in at number 10. As the magazine noted, 'The title track to AC/DC's 1977 LP has a very simple concept: what would the Bible have sounded like had it been written by AC/DC?'

Malcolm's plans for AC/DC were always big, but even he would have said this was a touch over-the-top. Not that he had too much time for contemplation as 1977 ticked over into the new year. He and the band were about to reconvene with Vanda and Young to make a record: one that, to Malcolm's ears, would be among AC/DC's best ever.

14

'We knew [the US] was a big country and it was going
to be lot of touring so we thought, "Screw it", and just
went for it—everywhere, even in the middle of winter.'

Powerage, the band's fifth album, began with a setback.
Newish bassist Cliff Williams had troubles both with his
visa and with the hard-to-please Australian Musicians
Union, who, in order to grant him working papers, needed
to be convinced that Englishman Williams could do what an
Australian musician could not. (The irony would not have
been lost on the recently sacked Mark Evans.) Eventually,
after management completed enough paperwork to denude
a small forest, Williams was given the okay and joined the
rest of the group, who were already back in Australia, in late
January 1978.

Unlike previous productions with Vanda and Young,
which were typically built around their summer touring
commitments, Malcolm insisted that the band focus all
their attention and energy on the new album. There'd be no
touring this time around—it was unintentionally convenient
that Williams had paperwork hassles, because they couldn't
tour without him. And who needed a re-run of the dramas
they'd experienced during the Giant Dose ordeal? Enough

with the uptight local councils and burghers of small-town Australia. So instead of recording between gigs, the band spent an eight-week stretch inside Alberts during the early months of 1978. This was in addition to some earlier sessions with Vanda and Young in London during the summer of 1977. In AC/DC terms, it was an absolute marathon.

Engineer Mark Opitz was at the starting point of his own stellar career—which would include projects with Cold Chisel, INXS, KISS and even Bob Dylan—when he was hired to help Vanda and Young. Opitz immediately understood that AC/DC was Malcolm's band. 'Malcolm definitely held sway,' he'd tell writer Murray Engleheart. 'I don't think a lot of people realise that . . . most people look at it and think it's Angus's band . . . Malcolm's very intense.' (Future AC/DC tour manager Ian Jeffery had a similar take. 'Malcolm was the decision maker,' he told *Classic Rock* magazine. 'Even if Angus had strong points, Malcolm would be, "Fuck off, mate, we're not doing that".')

If Malcolm didn't appreciate something that was being tried out in the studio, he'd make his feelings very clear. 'That's fucked,' he'd snap, and the rest of the band knew it wasn't a matter for debate—it was hardly diplomatic, but to Malcolm the studio wasn't a place for niceties. It was a place of business. Malcolm also had a habit of working himself into a right mood while in the studio, grouching about other bands, other people—whatever got under his skin. According to Opitz, Malcolm's diatribes typically ran along the lines of 'Fuckin' this, fuckin' that,' as he sucked down cigarette after cigarette. This got him into the perfect pissed-off mindset to make some blood-and-guts rock and roll—and George Young knew the exact moment to stop the gabbing and start recording.

Moments of respite were few in those sessions, apart from one morning when Malcolm, Opitz and Rudd commandeered a runabout, a slab of beer and some fishing gear and took to the water on Sydney Harbour. They shocked commuters making their way to work on the morning ferry.

Mind you, Opitz found George Young to be every bit as focused as Malcolm. '[George] could look at an ashtray and make it move just by thinking about it,' he said. 'He's got that determination . . . The intensity from the Youngs was just insane.'

That intensity is on full display throughout the finished album, from the instant that Malcolm's right hand kicks 'Rock 'n' Roll Damnation' into gear, all the way through to the fierce closer, 'Kicked in the Teeth'. Live, the Bon and Angus show might have become the big crowd-puller, as they commanded the stage (and various parts of the venues they now filled), but on record, it was Malcolm's riffs that were rolled gold. From 'Riff Raff', which built and built almost to breaking point—at least until Angus took over with a killer hook of his own—to the thunderous, ominous chords of 'Sin City' and 'Gone Shootin', Malcolm's riffs were breathing fire.

The album even received the seal of approval from The Human Riff himself, Keith Richards. 'You can hear it,' said the Rolling Stone, not one to randomly shower others with praise. 'It has the spirit.' Others with considerably lower profiles would also heap praise on *Powerage*, something Malcolm observed over time as he spoke with fans about the record. 'I know a lot of people respect it,' he said, 'a lot of real rock and roll AC/DC fans, the real pure rock and roll guys.'

If *Powerage* was missing anything, it was novelty songs like 'Rosie' or 'The Jack'. Bon Scott had little time for his balls or his sexual health this time around; clearly, this was serious rock-and-roll business. It was there in the song titles: 'Rock 'n' Roll Damnation', 'Down Payment Blues', 'Gimme a Bullet'—*Powerage* was the real deal, and Scott sang every note, every single word, with the same steely determination you can hear in Malcolm and Angus's guitar playing. And it was a key record for the band; if the album didn't connect globally, it'd be back to the bra factory for Malcolm.

Yet the reaction from their record label after a first listen was not what Malcolm had hoped for. In fact, it was down-right disastrous. Phil Carson from Atlantic in the UK—the man who'd signed the band back in 1975—couldn't hear an obvious track for radio. He wasn't entirely wrong; the finished songs melded together better than anything the band had recorded before, and each packed a red-hot intensity, but there was nothing with the *Countdown*-ready catchiness of 'T.N.T.' or 'Dirty Deeds'. There was a reason for this: when the band was in the studio, Malcolm had insisted they 'cut out those commercial choruses'. Now the record company was asking them to get cracking and come up with one, or *Powerage* wouldn't see the light of day.

Malcolm, not surprisingly, bristled at the idea, but he was also a pragmatist: what option did they have if the record company wasn't getting behind the record even before it was released? So first he got pissed off; then he got back to work. The band returned to the Alberts studio in March to record 'Rock 'n' Roll Damnation'. But it wasn't a typical AC/DC track—it lacked an Angus solo, for one thing, and there was a lot more percussion on it than on anything they'd recorded before. It actually sounded like a heavier version of The Easybeats. Still, it rocked like a hurricane, with yet another killer Malcolm riff at its heart, and the entire band played it, not surprisingly, as though their careers depended on it.

While in Australia finishing 'Damnation', Scott sought out a tarot reader. 'You will meet a blonde,' she told him, 'get divorced, meet a dark-haired girl, and have a short life.' He shared the revelations with some friends in Melbourne before heading back to the UK: 'I'll be dead by 1980.'

★

'Damnation' wasn't a typical AC/DC song by any stretch, but it was deemed commercial enough to be *Powerage's* first single, released to coincide with the LP's May 1978 release. (Maybe Carson really was onto something, because it was the only single lifted from the album.) 'Damnation' was a big mover for the band in the UK, their first single to graze the Top 20, reaching a peak of number 24, yet in Australia it barely broke the Top 100—perhaps the victim of some residual fallout from their Giant Dose disaster, and the band's lack of live presence in the country. Or perhaps it just didn't sit comfortably alongside the likes of the Bee Gees, Kate Bush and Boney M., who were dominating the charts in 1978.

AC/DC's US label, however, did give the album some support, producing a radio ad for the local market. And it was a beauty. As grabs of the album played in the background, there was the sound of an explosion, followed by a newsreader-style voice over. The message was clear: 'Nuclear energy is dead. The neutron bomb can kiss my [bleep]. AC/DC's newest blast has arrived: *Powerage. Powerage.* The ultimate AC/DC album.'

Perfect.

Reviewing the album for *The Canberra Times*, Luis Feliu felt the noise—so much so it blew up one of the speakers on his home stereo. 'Ahhhhh, welcome to some juicy rock and roll, the sweaty, loud sort and yes, from Australia's best-ever rock export . . . *Powerage* is nothing more or nothing less than open-throttle rock 'n' roll . . . A damn good party rage record.'

But yet again, the influential US *Rolling Stone* wasn't sold, giving the album a flaccid two-and-a-half-star review, despite the fact that, over time, the album would sell one million copies in the USA. Yet it only reached number 133 on the *Billboard* 200 chart on release. The US was proving to be a much harder market to conquer than the UK and Europe.

★

It was a surprisingly conservative-looking Malcolm who stepped out with the band to play 'Damnation' on UK TV's *Top of the Pops* on 8 June 1978. His hair had been shorn back considerably—all of the band looked as though they'd taken a trip to the same no-frills barber. His new 'do' made Malcolm look considerably younger than his 25 years. Bon Scott, bizarrely, wearing a red sweater, looked more like a slumming accountant than a rock-and-roller, with a watch on his left wrist—once very much a no-go, as decreed by manager Browning.

It took some sleight of hand for the band to appear on the show at all. A British union rule stated that for a song to be performed on *TOTP*, it had to have been recorded in the UK, which was clearly not the case with 'Damnation'. So a staffer from Atlantic, along with a rep from the UK Musicians' Union, spent a day in a studio with the band 're-recording' the song, even though the Atlantic staffer made sure that at the end of the session, the original recording was swapped for the 'new' version. The union rep didn't notice and the band was finally given the okay to appear. Very crafty.

Having a charting single in the UK was a great boost, but Malcolm's eyes were clearly still on the US, and the band began yet another American sortie some two weeks later. They'd remain in the States until the end of September. When it came to work ethic, AC/DC were unbeatable. As far as Malcolm was concerned, it simply wasn't up for debate: they were a working band. That's what they did.

'We knew it was a big country and it was going to be lot of touring so we thought, "Screw it," and just went for it— everywhere, even in the middle of winter,' Malcolm said of their early tours of the US. 'One gig we were the only people who got there because there was a blizzard and the snow was three feet deep and the audience didn't make it through, so we went back and did it again. It was tough—different states had different things going on with music—but there were areas like Jacksonville, Austin, Columbus, Ohio where we were playing to bigger crowds than in England.'

Bon Scott, however, was starting to feel his age, even if he was only 32. In a letter that he wrote to his sister Valerie, during a stop in Pittsburgh in August, his weariness was obvious. 'I'm always travelling or drunk or hungover or . . . today I'm shaking so much I can hardly write.'

Once again, AC/DC were sharing bills with acts either on the rise or well and truly established (Alice Cooper, the Blue Öyster Cult, Aerosmith, KISS, Thin Lizzy), playing venues with capacities as large as 15,000. Many of the acts with whom they shared bills were quickly converted to the cut-the-crap ways of AC/DC—Aerosmith's Steve Tyler jumped at the chance to introduce the band when they appeared on influential TV show *The Midnight Special* in early September, where they played 'Sin City'. Tyler didn't even seem to mind when Aerosmith shared a bill with them in Indiana and the crowd began cheering for AC/DC— while Aerosmith was playing.

Cheap Trick guitarist Rick Nielsen, a player every bit as flamboyant and eccentric as Angus, became equally evangelical about these Aussie upstarts when his band co-headlined a series of shows with AC/DC on the 1978 tour. 'They were just great,' he remembered. 'They were the only band that I stayed every night to watch.' Nielsen even took the time to introduce the band to Mexican food—a departure from the usual greasy junk they wolfed down while on the road. Cheap Trick's drummer, Bun E. Carlos, spoke for the entire band when he made it clear who called the shots: 'Malcolm was the main man in the band.'

Ginger-haired rocker Sammy Hagar, later to front Van Halen, caught the band in Oakland and he too became a rusted-on fan.

Aerosmith weren't the only band to learn that AC/DC was proving to be a hard act to follow. They were booked to play the huge Day on the Green festival at Oakland Coliseum on 23 July, an annual event put together by legendary promoter Bill Graham. AC/DC were the first act to play, as part of a bill that included Foreigner, Aerosmith and Van Halen. Despite plugging in at the ridiculous time of 10.40 a.m., they made one hell of a ruckus. Sitting in his trailer backstage, Eddie Van Halen—no slouch with a guitar himself—heard Malcolm's trusty riff kickstart their usual opener 'Live Wire' into furious action and decided to check out the spectacle for himself. He'd describe the scene to *Guitar Player* magazine.

> I went up there and saw 60,000 people bopping up and down at the same time. Angus did his incredible wind-me-up-and-let-me-go dance and Bon . . . he sounded exactly like the record. I remember standing on the side of the stage thinking, 'We have to follow these mother-fuckers' . . . AC/DC was probably one of the most powerful bands I've seen in my life.

Van Halen would later describe Malcolm as 'the heart and soul of AC/DC'.

One story from the tour, most likely apocryphal, emerged from a set at Boston's Paradise Theater on 21 August, which was broadcast live on radio station WBCN. As the band locked into the marathon jam of 'Rocker', which typically allowed the now wireless Bon and Angus to roam about the crowd, Angus took matters one step further. Allegedly he left the venue, jumped in a cab and disembarked soon after at the radio station's downtown HQ, all the while playing the same solo. Sometimes AC/DC stories were so good that it didn't matter if they were true or not.

Bon Scott's old buddy from The Valentines era, Vince Lovegrove, caught up with the band during the tour and interviewed them for a program called *Australian Music to the World*. This was a moment in time when Australians were all over the charts in the US, with everyone from the Bee Gees to Olivia Newton-John and Little River Band selling records by the millions. But the band didn't see themselves as part of some 'Aussie invasion'—anything but. (If there was one band that ascribed to Groucho Marx's old maxim of 'not wanting to belong to a club that would have me for a member,' it was AC/DC.)

Scott seemed a bit confused by Lovegrove's question: what 'Aussie invasion'? 'We're the only ones that are invading anywhere,' he insisted.

Angus also laughed at the idea. 'We're like Martians.'

Scott, however, could see the benefits of their relentless work regime, even if he seemed exhausted in the letter he wrote to his girlfriend. 'The more we work, the more we tour, we get more ideas,' he said. 'It's going to get better and better. I can't see it ever coming to an end—it's like infinity rock and roll.'

Gradually making their way up the rock-and-roll ladder provided an interesting life lesson for Malcolm: success had a strange way of blurring reality. 'Especially if you're just an ordinary working-class bloke,' he explained. 'Your privacy's gone. You lose the number of places you can go and your life becomes a lot more sheltered, especially if you're instantly recognised like Bon was. He found it difficult to escape.'

More often than not, Scott would disappear into the warm embrace of the Heathen Girls, a consortium of American groupies who'd taken a particular shine to him.

As far as Malcolm was concerned, playing in the band was still like a nine-to-five gig; it just came with strange hours. He was no star. He was simply a bloke from the 'burbs who played guitar for a living. His only indulgences at the time—if you could call them that—were a new pair of Cuban-heeled boots and a sky-blue Triumph T-shirt, which he wore seemingly every time he played.

From the band's earliest days, Malcolm and Angus had shared a simple philosophy: 'If we don't play, we don't eat.' Even in late 1978, as the venues they filled grew bigger, nothing much had changed.

15

'You've got to get us the fuck out of this situation.
The guy's hopeless.'

For the previous few years, AC/DC's life had been pretty well arranged: every Christmas they'd return home, check in with family, make a new record with Vanda and Young, tour Australia—Angus's bum permitting—and then head back out onto the global stage until it was time to do it all over again. But now, as another year of rock beckoned, the band was confronted with a new drama, one in which Malcolm would become well and truly embroiled. This time it was family.

As good a record as *Powerage* was, and despite their ever-expanding reputation as the type of live act no one fancied following on stage, the album hadn't set the US charts on fire. Frankly, they weren't even smouldering. The band were now four studio albums deep into their deal with Atlantic and hadn't broken through commercially. There was also a live LP, 1978's *If You Want Blood*—a favourite of Malcolm's, who said it was the sound of a band 'that was young, fresh, vital and kicking ass'—released at a time when live albums such as KISS's *Alive!* and (Peter) *Frampton Comes Alive!* were all the rage. But it too didn't sell.

There'd been a huge commercial upswing for many of
the bands they'd recently toured with, who'd started shifting
records by the warehouse-load: Aerosmith's 1976 LP *Rocks* was
on its way to sales of four million, while between 1976 and
1978 KISS earned a massive US$17.7 million from royalties
and publishing, to which you could add a hefty pile of cash
earned from touring. Cheap Trick had just been to Japan and
the frenzied live record they brought home, *Cheap Trick At
Budokan,* was set to sell three million copies in the US alone.
Van Halen's self-titled debut album from 1978 would eventually eclipse sales of ten million. Ten freaking million!

And AC/DC? *Powerage* had fizzled out in the US charts
and slipped away into oblivion. Atlantic decided, with some
justification, that it was time for a sit-down.

★

In December 1978, Atlantic's Michael Klenfner, a big man
whose support of the band was equalled only by his girth,
flew to Sydney for an awkward meeting with manager
Michael Browning, and Alberts staff and band mentors
Vanda and Young. The key subject of discussion was the
production of their next album. Atlantic was convinced that
the band needed to change producers; they felt that they
needed to work with someone who had more of a feel for
what worked on radio in the US.

Klenfner only had one name on his list: 36-year-old South
African–born Eddie Kramer, who had worked with everyone
from Jimi Hendrix (he'd helped establish Hendrix's Electric
Lady Studio) to David Bowie and Led Zeppelin. He was
fresh from engineering Peter Frampton's massively successful

Frampton Comes Alive! record, which would rack up sales of fourteen million copies, so he had an inkling of what connected with FM radio and the record-buying masses.

As much as Klenfner admired the band—and he truly did—he made it clear that if they didn't agree to the change, they'd probably be dropped by Atlantic. When the news was delivered to Malcolm and Angus, their reaction was understandable: they were devastated and angered in equal measure. George and Harry were family—quite literally in George's case—and had been their biggest advocates from the moment Malcolm decided to bring the band together in 1973. They were as much part of AC/DC as its players—and George had been a player too, on stage and in the studio. And now their record company wanted them sidelined. Malcolm felt disrespected: why hadn't he been consulted on this?

But plans for their sacking were already in action and early in the new year, Kramer flew to Sydney to meet with Browning and the Alberts team. Vanda and Young, for their part, responded surprisingly well to their dismissal. As far as they were concerned, the band came first: always had, always would.

Vanda and Young were also sufficiently astute to understand what Atlantic had in mind, and knew that they weren't the guys for the job. The band's US label was seeking a cleaner, more polished sound, but what Vanda and Young had always attempted to do with AC/DC was to capture the band live and raw: sticky carpet, sweat stains, spilt beer and all. 'We wanted to try and get the energy and danger that you got in a pub,' Vanda explained to writer John Tait. 'And it worked wonderfully for AC/DC up to a point. They were popular [live] in America already. But the question was,

"How are we going to make them palatable across the whole spectrum?"'

Vanda may have been very understanding, but Malcolm and Angus were gutted: cutting George adrift was tantamount to losing the sixth member of the band. During an interview with Sydney radio station 2JJ, Malcolm hinted pretty strongly that the band's hand has been forced. He was pissed off, and not in a mindset to welcome Eddie Kramer, with whom sessions were scheduled in Miami for early 1979, with anything but a snarl.

At least the location chosen for their new album sessions was a treat: they were to work at Criteria Studios in sun-kissed Florida. This was the studio that fellow expats the Bee Gees had used for their many disco hits. Eric Clapton, too, had prospered in Criteria, recording the classic 'Layla' there as part of Derek and the Dominos. The Eagles had recorded some of their West Coast classic *Hotel California* at Criteria. But Criteria was no happy hunting ground for AC/DC. The sessions had barely begun when Malcolm called manager Browning.

'You've got to get us the fuck out of this situation,' Malcolm demanded. 'The guy's hopeless.'

Working with Eddie Kramer was a disaster. Kramer's approach was in stark contrast to the method that Malcolm and Angus had grown very comfortable with at Alberts, where their partly formed riffs and ideas were transformed into songs inside the studio. Kramer was nowhere near as collaborative. Allegedly he was urging the band to record a cover of The Spencer Davis Group's 'Gimme Some Lovin''— hardly the act of a producer brimming with confidence and ideas. Malcolm was having none of it.

Kramer wasn't sold on Bon Scott, either; he felt that his drinking was starting to intrude on their recording sessions. 'Can your guy sing?' he asked Malcolm, eyeing Bon suspiciously.

It didn't help matters that Malcolm was surreptitiously sending rough recordings to George back in Sydney, gauging his opinion of their work in progress.

Malcolm, typically, didn't hold back when he spoke about the disastrous sessions. '[Kramer] would interfere and suggest things that were miles from what the band was,' he told *Guitar Legends* magazine. 'He was a bit of a prat . . . He might've sat behind the knobs for Hendrix, but he's certainly not Hendrix, I can tell you that much.'

Miami didn't agree with the band, either. 'Horrible place,' said Bon Scott, 'full of rich old crocks who flock there for the winter.'

'I went there, hung out with them, tried to do some demos,' Kramer countered, when he spoke with music website Louder in November 2013, 'and realised that there was an obvious difficulty with the singer . . . He had the most incredible voice but trying to keep him in check from his drinking was a very tough call. But I think more than anything, the band resented me being foisted onto them. It was like sticking a pin into them.'

Browning was in New York when he got Malcolm's SOS and he agreed to extricate the band from the arrangement with Kramer. He had been speaking with manager Clive Calder, who looked after various record producers, to try to entice Calder's up-and-coming client Robert 'Mutt' Lange to produce AC/DC. (Lange's biggest hit to date was The Boomtown Rats' 'Rat Trap'; he'd also worked with Graham

Parker and City Boy, though neither were big-selling acts.) Browning assured Malcolm that it'd work—Malcolm had never heard of Lange, but was up for anything that would get him free of Kramer—and then he broke the news to Klenfner.

But before there could be any change of producer, Lange had to actually hear what the band was trying to record. In 1979, Malcolm spoke with *RAM* and gave his version of what happened next. 'Three weeks in Miami and we hadn't written a thing with Kramer. So one day we told him we were going to have a day off and not to bother coming in. This was Saturday, and we snuck into the studio and on that one day we put down six songs, sent the tape to Lange and said, "Will you work with us?"'

One positive to emerge from Miami was the bare bones of the track 'Highway to Hell'. Angus had a guitar part; Malcolm, meanwhile, sat in on drums. Malcolm asked Angus if he had a title for the song. 'No,' he replied, then he ducked out for a toilet break and a ciggie. On his return Angus said, 'It's called "Highway to Hell".' Simple as that.

Despite the label's resistance—they fired Klenfner— plans were set in place for the group to work with Lange at London's Roundhouse Studios. Working with Scott was also a challenge for producer Lange, but one he came to embrace. (Scott had heard that Lange had described his voice as a 'weasel in heat'. 'Can you work with that?' he asked Lange. 'I think so,' Lange replied with a smile.) As Ian Jeffery, the band's tour manager, would relate to music website Louder, there was a flashpoint when the band was recording 'If You Want Blood'. '[Bon] starts doing it and he's struggling, you know? There's more fucking breath than voice coming out.

Lange says to him, "Listen, you've got to co-ordinate your breathing". Bon was like, "You're so fucking good, cunt, you do it!" Mutt sat in his seat and did it without standing up! That was when they all went, "What the fucking hell are we dealing with here?"'

Scott later said this of Lange: 'He really injected new life into us and brought out things we didn't know we were capable of. We were really trying to be acceptable for American radio without sounding drippy like those stupid American bands. And it works, too.'

Lange's meticulous, step-by-laborious-step approach was not Malcolm's style by any measure; he preferred the 'get it while it's hot' technique of Vanda and Young. Lange was also a teetotaller and a vegetarian, so he and Malcolm didn't have a whole lot in common beyond music. But as the fifteen-hour days (and nights) passed by, Malcolm came to see what Lange was all about: getting their sound absolutely perfect and heavier than hell itself. There was no way US radio could reject the band this time, particularly with such a powerful set of songs.

Malcolm spoke about this with writer Mark Blake. 'Mutt [Lange] seemed to know music, and he looked after the commercial side while we took care of the riffs, and somehow we managed to meet in the middle without sounding as though we'd compromised ourselves. In fact, there was no way we'd back down on anything'—including the album title, which led to a stoush with Atlantic; the label feared a conservative backlash. 'We were a pretty tough band for any producer to work for.'

Interestingly, Lange insisted that Angus record his solos while standing alongside him at the recording desk, rather than throwing himself around the studio as he'd always done at Alberts. It worked—the evidence was all over the finished record—but still Angus was more concerned as to how Malcolm had responded to his work. Was it a good solo, Mal? Did it fly?

According to Angus, 'Mutt Lange . . . says to me, "That's a great piece of guitar there," [and] I thought, *I'm not worried what he says, I'm worried what Malcolm says.* If Malcolm went, "Yeah, that's good", I knew there was something there.'

For Malcolm, there were two standouts on the finished record: 'Touch Too Much,' the first single; and the epic title track, a classic of hard living and hard rocking to rival 'Long Way to the Top'. The band had first recorded 'Touch Too Much' in 1977, but it was radically rearranged for the new album. And Scott was at his lyrical best throughout *Highway to Hell,* dropping ropey double entendres ('Beating Around the Bush'), and boasting about the high life ('Get It Hot') and/or pure lust ('Girls Got Rhythm', which was probably not about a female drummer). He even gave a nod to the hit TV show *Mork & Mindy* on the closer, 'Night Prowler', when he nicked Robin Williams's tag line: 'Shazbot, na-nu na-nu'.

These were the last words Bon Scott ever uttered on an AC/DC record.

★

While it had been a hugely rewarding production with Lange, Malcolm still held onto some residual anger brought about by his brother's sacking. Family, to Malcolm, was the one thing that rated as highly as his band, and someone had to pay for George's firing. He held no grudge towards Lange, who, despite his methodical approach to recording, Malcolm felt was a 'great bloke, polite, mannered, no airs and graces'. But Malcolm's resentment did finally bubble to the surface during their next run of US dates, and he got to vent his anger at a couple of different targets.

First he took issue with some of the acts AC/DC opened for in the US, whose sets seemed to last forever. This, to Malcolm, was as tiresome as the endless takes Mutt Lange insisted upon in the studio.

'I can't stand those bands that take two hours to warm a crowd up,' he said to a reporter when the Highway to Hell tour reached Indiana. 'We got all the time we need when we play second to the headliner . . . We feel we don't need to start slow and build up our set, so we just go on without any soundchecks or warm-ups and play as loud and hard as we can.'

But Malcolm also had a target who was much closer to home. Since signing on as manager in 1975, Michael Browning had done great things. He'd helped transform the once broke and disorganised band into a well-oiled machine. He'd bailed them out when they were flat-out on the bones of their backsides after their cross-country disaster in 1974, found them a base in Melbourne, helped secure the deal with Atlantic, and then quietly put the pieces into place that had helped get them to where they were in 1979: poised on the verge of an international breakthrough.

But Malcolm didn't see a lot of Browning, who bounced between New York, London and Australia, putting deals in place. Aerosmith's manager Peter Mensch, meanwhile, had been quietly insinuating his way into the band's inner circle. And there had been some big problems of late: the sacking of George, obviously, but also the firing of Atlantic's Michael Klenfner, whom the band rated very highly. He'd been sacked by the label as a result of agreeing with Malcolm to get rid of Eddie Kramer, Atlantic's producer of choice for *Highway to Hell*. There was the frustration of a planned Japanese tour for *Powerage* that fell apart, essentially because of Bon Scott's drug arrest record. Then there was Browning's decision to bring Cedric Kushner, Mutt Lange's manager and someone that Malcolm didn't like, into the management fold. Malcolm also didn't respond well when he learned that Johnny Van Zant, brother of the late Ronnie Van Zant from Lynyrd Skynyrd, had reached out to Browning about possibly managing his band. Nothing had come of it, but to Malcolm the mere idea that Browning would even speak with another act without consulting him smacked of disloyalty. Treachery, even.

All this built-up tension erupted after a gig at the Tennessee Theatre in Nashville on 22 May 1979. Malcolm and Angus walked off the stage and, barely pausing to light a post-gig ciggie, got stuck into Browning backstage, airing all their grievances. Even Phil Rudd and Bon Scott threw in some random criticisms, leaving their about-to-become-ex-manager completely snookered. As Browning would write of the encounter, 'It was right then I knew I was screwed . . . I was on the AC/DC shitlist, no doubt about it. But I felt I deserved some credit for where I'd taken the band and in such a relatively short time.'

Browning soon learned that a story had made its way back to the band via Ian Jeffery—who was soon to be elevated within the AC/DC ranks—that Browning had misappropriated thousands of dollars via airline tickets. 'This just wasn't the case,' Browning wrote; he said he actually purchased round-the-world tickets that, while they weren't all used, saved the band a significant pile of cash.

Malcolm could be ruthless. When he wanted someone gone—as had happened with Dave Evans, with Mark Evans and now with Browning—they were gone forever. Forgotten.

Browning endured a silent bus ride with the group back to their hotel in Nashville, and never spoke with Malcolm or the band again.

16

'If certain people had got their way, though, it wouldn't have been called *Highway to Hell*, because the bible belt was very strong.'

Momentum was always crucial for Malcolm and the band, and despite the inevitable disruption brought on by Browning's sacking, they just kept on rolling—their US tour would be the bubble in which they existed until the middle of August 1979. It was a three-and-a-bit-month-long run with very few nights off. They travelled, they played, they slept a bit and then they kept moving.

The band was constantly in motion, essentially, bouncing between stages and cities and hotels. If they were asked where they were from, they'd say, 'Australia'—apart from Englishman Williams—but they rarely saw the place. When asked if he had somewhere to call home, Angus told *Sounds* reporter Phil Sutcliffe that Bon was 'of no fixed abode, and I'm in the flat below'.

They were rock-and-roll gypsies, essentially.

And while the word 'bonhomie' was not bandied about too much when talked turned to the often-wary Youngs, they did form the occasional road bond. Their connection with Midwestern rockers Cheap Trick now stretched across shared gigs, tours and thousands of miles. During the 1979 tour, that connection deepened when Malcolm uncharacteristically agreed to a jam.

It happened on 7 July, a steamy summer's night, as the roadshow reached Sioux Falls in South Dakota, where they filled an 8000-seat venue. As Cheap Trick reached the end of their set, Malcolm, as well as Angus and Bon, joined the band for a raucous rip-and-tear through Chuck Berry's 'Johnny B. Goode'. It was hardly a stellar performance—Malcolm spent most of the time trying to locate the amp into which his guitar, borrowed from singer Robin Zander, was plugged. 'I couldn't figure out where my sound was coming from,' he admitted afterwards. It turned out that a black scrim covered the amp, which was placed under the drum riser. Even when jamming, Malcolm was driven to get it right.

But Malcolm's gesture was more important than the end result. He didn't suffer fools and he didn't jump on stage with just anyone. He wouldn't jam with another band for 24 years—and that band would be none other than The Rolling Stones.

★

A few weeks later, *Highway to Hell* was finally released. Looking back, Malcolm came to accept that moving on from Vanda and Young—the compromise he had so reluctantly agreed to—proved to be a lifeline for the band.

'That was a definitive change for AC/DC,' he later said of *Highway to Hell*. 'Atlantic Records in America were unhappy because they couldn't get the band on the radio, and they were desperate for us to come up with something more accessible.

We'd had our own way for a few albums so we figured, let's give them what they want and keep everyone happy.'

There was one big problem, though: the album title. Atlantic hated it, and feared a backlash in conservative US markets. But Malcolm refused to budge; one compromise per album was more than enough. According to Malcolm, 'If certain people had got their way, though, it wouldn't have been called *Highway to Hell*, because the bible belt was very strong in America at the time, and they made a fuss once the record came out. But even though we were under pressure, we stuck to our guns.'

Angus agreed with his brother. As far as he was concerned, after all their globetrotting, there was no more apt name for the record, as he told *Guitar World* magazine. 'You crawl off the bus at four o'clock in the morning, and some journalist's doing a story and he says, "What would you call an AC/DC tour?" Well, it *was* a highway to hell. It really was. When you're sleeping with the singer's socks two inches from your nose, that's pretty close to hell.'

Not only did Malcolm get his way, but a promotional poster was created using the album's front cover, which became an iconic work of AC/DC art. Devil's horns protruded from the cap of a snarling Angus, while the others in the band were either chuckling (Bon), scowling (Malcolm) or caught somewhere in between (Williams and Rudd). 'AC/DC,' the poster announced, 'burning a Highway to Hell.'

*

The album became their first to crack the US Top 100, peaking at number 17 on 10 November 1979, during a pretty fertile time commercially for rock bands, with albums from Foreigner (*Head Games*), Led Zeppelin (*In Through the Out Door)* and The Knack (*Get the Knack)* all charting strongly in the US. (At time of writing, *Highway to Hell'*s sales sit at around seven million, a handy return on Atlantic's investment, which was more substantial for *Highway to Hell* due to the change of producer.)

In the UK, while the album became a hit, peaking at number 8 and charting for 40 weeks, a sector of the British press still couldn't bring themselves to treat AC/DC seriously. 'The greatest album ever made,' declared a headline in *NME,* under which was printed, in much smaller type, '(in Australia)'. If Malcolm needed further proof that they were a band of the people and not of the critics, there it was.

When Bon Scott sat down with a writer from the *Record Mirror,* he took the time to reflect on their slow climb in the US. 'We're beginning to make an impact . . . at last, [but] I reckon we'll still have to push a bit harder to get to the top of the hill.'

In short, more touring.

★

With their star rising globally, AC/DC were now being hand-picked for big shows in the UK and Europe—and suddenly they were being billed as 'guest stars', rather than just another name in a long list of acts. On 18 August 1979 they made their 'guest star' debut at Wembley Arena, as part of a huge event—the return of The Who, playing their biggest show since the demise of their drummer Keith 'The Loon' Moon, dead from an overdose of prescription drugs at the age of 32.

Also on the oddly balanced bill were punk act The Stranglers and American singer/guitarist Nils Lofgren. The audience was, by some reports, as large as 80,000, certainly the biggest that Malcolm and the band had ever fronted.

'Only AC/DC really manage[s] to move the audience,' reported Harry Doherty, writing for *Melody Maker*. 'The audience left no doubt as to their partiality for AC/DC. This could be just the break the band needed to finally push their point home to Britain.'

But it was hard work for the group. As they tore into 'Whole Lotta Rosie', the PA suddenly cut out, which elicited a rowdy response from the crowd—it seemed that many were there just to see AC/DC, a slap in the face for the resurrected The Who. The band continued playing, but they could barely be heard beyond the first few rows. 'Turn the fucking thing on!' screamed one punter. The PA finally roared back into life during 'Rocker', the crowd yelled its approval and a very pissed-off AC/DC powered on to a huge finale.

That malfunction launched a juicy rumour: were AC/DC the victims of sabotage? Could an envious headliner's crew be to blame? The truth was never disclosed. Despite the hitch, 'they were awesome', according to The Stranglers' J.J. Burnel. 'And it was solid packed.'

After their set, Bon Scott sat down with the band's former roadie, Tana Douglas, who was working elsewhere that day at Wembley, and admitted that he was feeling much older than his 33 years.

★

A French film crew began trailing the band in December, prior to a sold-out show at the Pavilion, shooting footage for the concert film *Let There Be Rock,* which would surface in 1980. Film-makers Eric Dionysius and Eric Mistler provided an unusually candid portrait of Malcolm and Angus—'the notorious Young brothers', grinned Angus.

How's Malcolm as a brother? he was asked.

'Good, fine, upstanding. Likes a drink. And I can look him in the eye.'

The two were filmed backstage, ciggies and guitars in hand. Swathed in smoke, the pair appeared lost in their pre-show tuning, oblivious to the world around them—camera crew, eager audience, the lot. There was a show to play; it was time to get to work.

Despite the usual whiff of superiority that elder sibling Malcolm exhibited towards his 'kid' brother—and Angus would always be the kid, no matter how old he actually was—Malcolm was beginning to pay Angus due credit. 'Sometimes,' Malcolm told a reporter, 'because of the volume on stage, you don't hear the stuff Angus is doing solo-wise . . . He's a hot player. One day they'll see it in their entirety and go, "Fuck, he's one of the best of them all." And that'll be true.'

In a sequence from *Let There Be Rock* that would prove tragically prophetic, a cameraman followed Bon as he walked along a street in Paris.

'I'm a special drunkard,' Bon laughed, when asked why the others in the band referred to him as 'special'. 'I drink too much.'

Did he consider himself a star?

'No,' Bon chuckled. 'But I see stars sometimes.'

Malcolm had his own 'solo' sequence in the film, where he got to indulge his love of soccer. Decked out in what looks like an Aberdeen FC strip, he booted a ball around an empty paddock, celebrated a 'goal' with a drink and then fell into the embrace of his girlfriend, O'linda, who was looking on. She was an employee at Alberts and a close friend of Fifa Riccobono, a long-time employee at Alberts (and eventually its CEO), and a close confidante of the band. O'linda was Malcolm's first serious girlfriend in years; so serious, in fact, that they'd marry just prior to Christmas 1979, and would remain wed for the rest of his life. Angus, too, was in a serious relationship, with a tall blonde Dutchwoman named Ellen, who towered over him protectively whenever they were seen together. They'd wed in February 1980. The 'notorious Young brothers' were settling down.

But not so Bon Scott. He'd overindulged a few times during gigs on their most recent US visit—boozing was fine after, but not during, a show—and was socialising with lively characters such as Pete Way from the British band UFO, a drinking buddy of Scott's. The two bands had toured together in the States. 'Bon was brilliant,' said Way. 'You'd see him first thing in the morning, and he'd been with the barmaid or something, and he'd go: "Had a good workout last night." He'd get out of the elevator, he'd clap his hands and he'd say: "Large Jack Daniels."'

Ever since the band had begun working with Atlantic in the US, people had whispered in Malcolm's ear that Bon wasn't right for the band: he was too wild, he was too ragged, he screamed too much. Someone even suggested that Malcolm should replace him with David Coverdale from the metal band Whitesnake (who Malcolm dismissed as a 'pop singer'). And, by his own admission, Scott was now starting to entertain the notion of recording a solo album, ideally with some of the southern rockers who he'd befriended in the US. He wasn't leaving the band; he just wanted to stretch his musical wings a bit. But Malcolm rejected any notion of sacking Scott. No fucking way that was going to happen— he and Scott had grown very tight since he joined the band. Bon stayed.

*

The rest of 1979 was spent in motion, with a US tour followed by dates in the UK and Europe. Just before heading back to Australia for Christmas, Scott seemed to be in a more upbeat mood than he had been at Wembley a few months earlier. 'I'm 33,' he told a reporter, '[but] you're never too old to rock and roll.' Back in Sydney he reconnected with family and friends, even jumping on stage at the suburban Sydney venue The Family Inn, jamming Chuck Berry's 'Back in the USA' with the band Swanee, whose singer, John Swan, was a fellow expat Scot who also didn't mind a tipple.

Then there was a whistlestop AC/DC tour of France for a week in January, with gigs in Poitiers, Bordeaux, Toulouse, Rouen, Nantes, Brest and Le Mans, followed by a handful of shows back in the UK. The *Highway to Hell* LP was now well represented in the band's set list; they played 'Shot Down in Flames', 'Highway to Hell' and 'Girls Got Rhythm', along with the usual standards. There was also another appearance on *Top of the Pops,* rocking 'Touch Too Much' on 7 February, followed by a spot on a Spanish TV show two days later.

The translated version of the intro from Spanish host Silvia Tortosa laid it on the line: 'Today on *TV Applauso*, we receive a new group in Spain: AC/DC. They're Australian and are considered one of the best rock bands of the last generation . . . Today, for the first time in Spain, AC/DC!'

But Bon didn't look his best; he seemed tired, pale, drained. The seated audience, an odd assortment of young and old Spaniards, clapped politely after the band played 'Girls Got Rhythm'.

A few days later, Bon returned to the Hammersmith Odeon to cheer on his buddies in UFO when they staged a three-night run at a favourite venue of AC/DC's. Members of UFO would subsequently admit that heroin was among their after-show indulgences, and AC/DC's manager Peter Mensch was understandably worried about the impact this toxic environment would have on Scott. But Bon was his own man—and no stranger to drugs, of course. As for Malcolm, he may have considered Bon a brother, but he was in no position to question the guy's lifestyle choices, even if there were some incidents that upset him, such as the time Bon had invited Rose Tattoo's Mick Cocks onto the tour bus, even though Malcolm had made it well known he wasn't a fan of the hard-living guitarist. But Malcolm was hardly a saint himself: he loved a drink and a smoke and a big night; he'd be a hypocrite to even suggest some sort of intervention. And would Bon have listened to him anyway?

If there was one thing bugging Malcolm, it was that he felt Bon wasn't receiving due credit for his rare, funny skill with lyrics and his amazing stage presence. The man was the living embodiment of swagger, one of the best frontmen of his generation. George Young had been spot-on five years before when he'd observed that hiring Bon had transformed AC/DC into a real rock-and-roll band. And as far as Malcolm was concerned, Bon still wasn't getting 'the recognition due to him'.

Maybe the next record would change all that.

★

Malcolm's thoughts were soon elsewhere: by early 1980, he was focused on the next album. *Highway to Hell* had given them a firm foothold in America, and they were now making a reasonable living, so the time was right to capitalise on the momentum. Mutt Lange was locked in to produce; as soon as a bunch of new songs were in decent shape, they would be ready to roll.

News had come through from the US that *Highway to Hell* had just tipped over the one million sales mark, so the future couldn't have been brighter. It was a platinum record—their first.

On 15 February, Malcolm and Angus got together to work in a London rehearsal space, tinkering with instrumental sketches that would become the songs 'Have a Drink on Me' and 'Let Me Put My Love Into You'. Bon dropped in unannounced. The first thing that struck Malcolm was that Bon was in good shape. As he'd say later, 'He looked fantastic; he was looking after himself.'

'Do you mind if I play the drums?' Bon said, motioning towards a kit in the corner. It was a request with a bit of a backstory; when Scott had first met the band in 1974, he'd actually asked if he could be their drummer.

'So when do we get started?' Scott asked, as he whacked away at the drums.

'We're just about ready for you, Bon,' Malcolm told him. 'Maybe next week sometime.'

With that, Bon said goodbye and left. Malcolm would never see him again.

17

'You can't explain a death and how it affects you.
Everything is numb, it's as simple as that.'

Bon Scott spent the night of 18 February with a friend,
Alistair Kinnear, drinking at a North London club called
The Music Machine. Their big night over, Kinnear tried
but failed to haul the drunken singer upstairs to his flat, so
he covered Scott with a blanket and left him in the back
seat of a friend's Renault 5, parked in Overhill Road in East
Dulwich, to sleep off his bender.

As Malcolm understood it, it was just another night out
for Bon—nothing more. 'He went out, just for a drink,
maybe to clear his head, and then he was looking forward to
getting into his writing. He had it all ahead of him.'

Sometime during the night, however, Scott vomited and
choked. Kinnear found the singer's lifeless body the next day.
Scott was rushed to King's College Hospital in Camberwell
but was pronounced dead on arrival. Bon's girlfriend at the
time, a Japanese woman named Anna Baba, phoned Angus,
who was shocked beyond belief. He pulled himself together
sufficiently to call Malcolm.

He then contacted tour manager Ian Jeffery with the awful news.

'Are you joking?' Jeffery asked him.

'Would I fucking joke about a thing like that?' Malcolm snapped back.

'I was totally stunned,' recalled Malcolm. 'You can't explain a death and how it affects you. Everything is numb, it's as simple as that.' As for the cause of Scott's death, 'He choked through the night, because of the position he was in' was Malcolm's understanding.

Manager Peter Mensch travelled to the hospital and identified Scott, but Malcolm took it upon himself to phone Scott's parents back in Australia. He felt it was his duty. 'Someone had to call them, and it was better coming from one of the band than from the newspaper,' he'd later explain on VH1's *Behind the Music* documentary on the band. 'Most difficult thing I've ever had to do; hope I never have to do anything like that again.'

Malcolm was incensed by the tabloid headlines. On learning the news, *The Evening Standard* screamed: 'Rock star drinks himself to death.' 'In Britain, they made [Bon's death] a bit of a joke almost, you know. We've never forgiven them for that. All we were concerned about was Bon's parents, they're really nice people, they don't need this shit.'

Malcolm's sense that Scott didn't get enough credit from the critics came into even sharper focus upon his death. 'After *Highway to Hell*, some of the critics started to realise that Bon did have a talent. Then, when he died, *everyone* was suddenly saying what a great performer he'd been. And these were the same guys that two years before had been saying we'd do much better with a singer that didn't scream all the time.'

A shock death is fodder for the rock-and-roll myth-making machine, and Bon Scott's end was no different—rumours as to how he died started circulating almost as soon as the news got out. Was it heroin-related? Did he overdose? Was he really alone? Why was he left out in the winter cold? Was someone covering something up? His death certificate, issued on 22 February, stated quite clearly that Scott died as a result of 'acute alcohol poisoning', a 'death by misadventure'. There was nothing suspicious: he'd binged and tragically paid the ultimate price.

It took some time for both Malcolm and Angus to speak publicly about Scott's death—their loss was just too personal, too close to home. They were both deep in shock. 'I was sad for Bon,' Angus said, when he did speak to a reporter. 'I didn't even think about the band. We'd been with Bon all that time; we'd seen more of him than his family did.'

Back in Australia, the music industry was also in a state of shock. *Countdown* host Molly Meldrum was crushed by the news. He and Scott had been close, despite their vastly different lifestyles—for one thing, Meldrum was gay, whereas Scott couldn't be any straighter if he tried—but they had history dating back to the time of The Valentines, and Meldrum and *Countdown* had been massive supporters of AC/DC. *Countdown* had funded the trailblazing videos for 'Long Way to the Top' and 'Jailbreak', which had helped establish the band across Australia and beyond, and the show had zealously traced their every step in the UK and the US.

'Earlier this week, there was some very, very sad news . . . for the Australian rock scene,' Meldrum announced on the 24 February episode of the show. Scott had been, Meldrum said, 'in my mind, one of the greatest Australian rock and rollers we've had over the past ten years. Not only was he a friend of mine . . . but I think it's a great blow to the Australian industry and especially to AC/DC.'

Meldrum went on to say how close the band was to becoming 'one of *the* world top supergroups . . . His loss'—Meldrum fumbled around for words—'I mean, what can you say? Except that we at *Countdown* owe Bon and the boys a lot.'

Scott's body was embalmed and returned to Fremantle, Western Australia, where he was cremated and his ashes sprinkled in some of his favourite spots in and around his hometown. His grave marker, in Fremantle Cemetery, reads: 'Close to our hearts / He will always stay / Loved and remembered / Every day.'

At the service on 29 February, Malcolm and Angus, both still clearly devastated, spoke with Scott's parents, Chick and Isa. What should they do? they asked—would it be best to end the band, as a mark of respect for Bon? They'd completely understand if Scott's family thought that was best.

But their response was a surprise.

'Keep going,' the Scotts told them. 'That's what Bon would have wanted.'

★

Even with Scott's parents' blessing to continue, Bon's death still weighed heavily on the brothers upon their return to London. 'I don't think we'll ever really get over it,' Malcolm admitted. He was experiencing what he described as an overwhelming sense of 'nothingness . . . no ambition left, just nothing'—a massive admission for someone as driven as Malcolm. Soon enough, though, he had a reality check.

The best way to deal with his loss was to keep making music; that's what Scott would have done if the situation was reversed. Malcolm also had the livelihoods of many others to consider: Angus, Williams and Rudd, as well as the band's crew and management; they were all affected. Their record company was already asking Malcolm about their plans to record the follow-up to *Highway to Hell.*

Malcolm spoke with Angus. 'I'm not going to sit around all fucking year moping,' he said bluntly. 'Do you wanna come back and rehearse?'

Angus agreed and the two returned to the rehearsal space where they'd last jammed with Bon.

Their management quickly put together a list of contenders to take Scott's place, but Malcolm didn't feel up to checking it out. 'We thought, *We can't replace Bon, it's as simple as that.*'

Yet Malcolm knew that eventually he'd have to start auditioning vocalists. It was a massive ask—not only would the new guy (and it was always going to be a guy) have to sing like a demon, but he needed serious stage presence and a whole lot of swagger. A bit of hair on his chest wouldn't hurt, either. And while Malcolm might have crafted some of the best guitar riffs in rock and roll, lyrics were not his forte by any means; that was the singer's job. Bon had set that particular bar very high: who could possibly top such odes to the rock-and-roll life as 'Highway to Hell' and 'Long Way to the Top', or capture the wild spirit of 'Whole Lotta Rosie' and 'Rock 'n' Roll Damnation'? Funny, poignant, dirty, testicle-referencing—Scott's lyrics had the lot.

Malcolm knew they'd been very lucky with Scott, and he knew there would never be another Bon. But the band needed to get back into action, or else the past seven years would have been a complete waste of time, sweat and energy.

There were several contenders on the list prepared by management, some of whom tried out with the band, but Malcolm recalled a singer that Bon had told him about a few years before, a guy Angus also recalled hearing about. 'Bon had always told us the story of when he toured Britain with Brian [Johnson], when he was in Geordie. Bon always told the story of seeing this wild lead singer rolling around the stage howling. Bon always said it was the best performance he ever saw.' Johnson could also do a pretty fair impression of Little Richard's shriek, which also connected with the Youngs, who were huge fans of the pompadoured American rocker, a man who could wail 'a-wop-bop-a-loo-bop-a-wop-bam-boom' and make it sound perfectly natural.

Producer Mutt Lange, too, had mentioned Johnson to Malcolm, whose interest was now truly piqued.

So on 29 March, Grand National Day in the UK, Malcolm reached out to Johnson, who'd left Geordie in 1976, then watched his career pretty much flatline; he now repaired cars for a living. When AC/DC came calling, he was 32, had two school-aged children to support, and was seriously considering giving music away altogether. Still, he had more in common with the band than a fondness for gut-level rock and roll; a native of Newcastle upon Tyne, Johnson was working-class all the way, from his cloth cap to his bootstraps, and his father had worked 'down pit', in the mines. Plus Johnson, by his own admission, was 'a huge fan of Bon Scott's'.

'Would you like to come and have a sing with the boys?' Malcolm asked Johnson over the phone, from London. Johnson agreed in a flash.

His trip south didn't start so well, with a flat tyre just outside of Newcastle. But Johnson eventually reached the London site of the audition, a studio in Pimlico, with enough time to stop for a game of pool with some of the band's roadies, who he knew from Geordie days.

Upstairs, Malcolm and the band were looking at the clock. 'Where's this guy Brian?' they were wondering. He was late.

'Is he a stocky bloke in a cloth cap?' someone asked. 'He's downstairs playing pool with the roadies.'

Malcolm wasn't annoyed—the exact opposite, in fact. *Well, at least he plays pool,* he thought to himself.

When Johnson finally came into the rehearsal space, tears were welling in his eyes. This was a massive moment for the singer.

'He was as sad about Bon as we were,' said Malcolm. Johnson's old band Geordie had covered 'Whole Lotta Rosie'; he was a true fan. Fittingly, 'Rosie' was the first song he sang with the band during his audition.

When it crashed to a close, Malcolm spoke with Angus. 'Fucking hell, this guy is cutting the mustard.'

Then he turned to Johnson. 'Anything else you know? "Nutbush City Limits?" Okay, we can knock that out.'

As Malcolm recalled, 'He sang that great too. It put a little smile on our faces—for the first time since Bon . . . Brian walked in for an audition and we felt comfortable with him—and he could sing his balls out.'

After that second number, Malcolm handed Johnson a bottle of brown ale. 'You must be thirsty,' he said. The gesture, and the beer, went down well.

Afterwards, Malcolm and Angus sat down with Johnson. They were going to offer him the job—although he did have to nervously endure a second audition—but they needed to spell out a few hard truths.

'Do you mind if your feelings get hurt?' Malcolm asked.

Johnson shrugged. 'I don't think so. Why?'

'Because if you join this band,' Malcolm explained, 'you're going to get fucking stick, because we've been slagged off by every fucking reporter since we left Australia.'

Johnson thought this through for a minute before replying. 'Well,' he said, 'I'm going to have to take stick anyway, taking this lad's place.'

It was a fair point. Although their new recruit would be subjected to what Malcolm described as 'this Bon versus Brian debate' in the music press, Johnson would later say that at no time was he made to feel 'like I was standing in a dead man's shoes'—an acknowledgment of his impartial treatment within the band.

There was still a little confusion before Johnson was officially given the gig. Malcolm called the singer at his parents' house in Newcastle. Johnson was just back from a few beers at The Crown, his local.

'We've got an album to do,' Malcolm said. 'We leave in a couple of weeks, so, if you're set for it . . .'

Johnson cut him off.

'Are you telling me I've got the job?'

When Malcolm said yes, Johnson asked him to call back in ten minutes. 'I just want to be sure it's not someone taking the piss.'

Ten minutes later, right on cue, the phone rang.

'Well, are you coming or what?' demanded Malcolm. There was no time for fucking about; the band had an album to make.

When asked, Malcolm made it very clear why Johnson had been hired. 'At the end of the day, Brian had the balls to get up there, and he was the only guy we found who could sing loud enough to be heard over the racket the rest of us were making. He was always going to be our man.' Malcolm also made it very clear to Johnson who was in charge, as tour manager Ian Jeffery told *Classic Rock* magazine. 'When Brian joined, it was Malcolm that told him to shut the fuck up between songs and just stand there and sing. It would always be Malcolm, every direction or turn they took.'

*

AC/DC had always been a band that thrived on momentum, but even by their standards, the weeks and months after Johnson's hiring flew by at lightning speed. Johnson had the luxury of a fortnight to celebrate his new gig (and convince his mates back home that he really *was* joining AC/DC) and then he was on a plane for the Bahamas, where the band reunited with producer Lange to start work on a record that, like its predecessor, already had a title: *Back in Black*.

If riffmaster Malcolm had found his big, dirty groove on every record from *Powerage* onwards, he excelled himself on *Back in Black*. Perhaps it was Bon Scott's lingering spirit that inspired him. Malcolm had been kicking around the monstrous riff for the album's title track since their last tour, and by the time they reached the Compass Point studios he had it down. It was an absolute window-rattler, the perfect foundation for the song.

Johnson was no Bon Scott in matters lyrical—Scott would never have allowed a lyric like 'Working double time/

On the seduction line' to make it onto a record—but that shortcoming was offset by Malcolm and Angus, who were in dynamic form.

When Malcolm presented Johnson with the track that closed the album, describing it to him as 'something called "Rock and Roll Ain't Noise Pollution",' Johnson's immediate reaction was a touch sarcastic. 'There's a great one to rhyme with,' but again it didn't overly matter, because Malcolm and Angus had unleashed another headbanging monster.

While in the studio, Malcolm proved just how good an 'ear' he had, as they gathered to listen to a playback. He'd learned a lot from Vanda and Young.

'What is that noise?' Malcolm asked.

No one had a clue what he was talking about; they couldn't hear anything beyond the roar of the band.

'No, there's a noise there,' Malcolm insisted, and he asked for the track to be played again. Still convinced there was something wrong, he then requested that each track be turned off, one at a time, until all that remained was the bass drum.

Suddenly, everyone else in the room could hear the sound, too.

One of the engineers walked over and removed the blanket that covered Rudd's bass drum. There, curled up in a corner, was a sand crab. Every time Rudd thumped his drums the crab had moved just enough to make the noise that Malcolm heard.

Almost as one, everyone in the room turned to Malcolm and asked, 'How did you know?'

'Malcolm never missed a trick,' Brian Johnson said years later when he raised the story with *Rolling Stone*. 'He paid attention to everything.'

Just like *Highway to Hell,* there was no room for debate about the album's title, or the plain black sleeve in which it was housed, although the band did compromise slightly by allowing the addition of some white type with their name and the title. (Which made perfect marketing sense; how else would a buyer know whose record it was?) This stark piece of artwork was the band's tribute to Bon Scott, whose essence, if not his voice, could be felt in every song of the finished record, in particular 'Hells Bells', which was chosen as the album's opener. Malcolm, who had a tendency to reflect on albums in terms of his favourite cuts, said this 'was one of the key songs; it reminded us of Bon'. His riff for that track was also massive, earth-quaking; it was so powerful that even the typically understated Malcolm was impressed with his handiwork. He called it 'ominous'; Angus said it was 'mystical'.

'A lot of sweat went into making *Back in Black,*' Malcolm said at the end of their five weeks in the Bahamas plus an additional spell in New York mixing the record. But it was more than sweat on the album's grooves; there was a whole lot of magic there too, as well as real, heartfelt emotion. 'We meant it,' Malcolm summarised. 'It's real. It . . . was made from what we'd all gone through.'

18

'Heavy metal was always trash. Real feel never entered
their vocabulary.'

'Milwaukee,' Brian Johnson roared into the darkness, his
voice hoarse, 'you're fucking brilliant!'

It may have resembled a line from *This is Spinal Tap,* but
Johnson was deadly serious. It was 13 September 1980, and
AC/DC's new recruit was standing on stage on the night of a
full moon, in front of a crowd of more than 6000 screaming,
mad-for-it fans, sweat dripping off him (and them). The band
was six weeks into their latest US adventure and crowds had
been building in both size and volume night by night as *Back
in Black*—released two months earlier—fairly bolted up the
charts. They'd become the hottest rock band on the planet;
Malcolm's goal of world domination was as good as fulfilled.

The album was at number 13 in the US, wedged between
new records from The Cars and The Kinks. It was four
weeks into what would be a remarkable 329 weeks—*more
than six years!*—on the official *Billboard* chart. Angus had
recently joked about the notorious friction between Ray and
Dave Davies of The Kinks, when he was asked if sparks
sometimes flew between him and Malcolm: 'It hasn't quite

got to The Kinks stage,' he laughed. And here they were, sharing chart space with the stroppy British siblings.

Things had changed off stage, as well. Back at the hotel in Milwaukee, Cara, the four-month-old daughter of Malcolm and O'linda, awaited the return of her father from his rock-and-roller duties. Malcolm was still a gypsy—the Back in Black tour would continue until the end of February 1981—but he was a gypsy with a family, with commitments. Another change was the manner in which the band relaxed: at most gigs, an authentic-looking English pub was set up backstage, with beer on tap, a dartboard and all the trimmings. Plus a kettle and plenty of tea bags for Angus, of course. By the time of their next tour it would also feature a pool table and a jukebox.

US *Rolling Stone* had dispatched their writer David Fricke to Milwaukee to capture the madness, and he was immediately drawn to the contrast between the Youngs on stage and off. Malcolm—wielding a wide-body Gretsch White Falcon guitar that Fricke noted was almost as big as he was—may have been a menacing figure while playing, but that changed completely when the house lights went up. 'Malcolm does not look half so mean pushing a baby stroller,' Fricke observed.

And Angus? '[He] is a quiet, reflective sort with a crooked smile, a Scottish accent . . . an attractive Dutch-born wife . . . and an addiction to hot tea with milk.'

A month later, Fricke reviewed the album for *Rolling Stone* and it was clear it had pretty much blown his head clean off his shoulders; he didn't seem to mind, or notice, that the one thing *Back in Black* lacked was Bon Scott's lyrical mischief and canny wordplay. According to Fricke, not only was it 'the best of AC/DC's six American albums', but it was 'the apex of heavy-metal art: the first LP since *Led Zeppelin II* that captures all the blood, sweat and arrogance of the genre'.

He could also see that the band shared little with big-selling heavy rocks acts such as Ted Nugent, Van Halen and Judas Priest—acts that Bon Scott would have referred to as 'tin foil' (as opposed to heavy metal)—despite sharing the odd festival bill and drawing a similar crowd. 'Compared to the boorish, macho plodding of most heavy-metal heathens,' Fricke noted, 'the AC/DC sound is nothing more and nothing less than aggressively catchy song hooks brutalized by a revved-up boogie rhythm, Malcolm's jackhammer riffs, Angus's guitar histrionics and Johnson's bloodcurdling bawl.'

Malcolm was no fan of those spandex-wearing posers either; he rejected them as swiftly as he'd dismissed punk rock when it was in its brief ascendancy. 'Heavy metal was always trash,' Malcolm said. 'Real feel never entered their vocabulary.' It was the Groucho Marx axiom at work again; he had no interest in belonging to a club that would have AC/DC for a member. As far as Malcolm was concerned, bluesman John Lee Hooker, whose fingerpicking style Malcolm admired hugely, was far heavier than that of any of these pretenders. John Lee was the *real* heavy metal. 'That's the boogie man,' he said of Hooker. 'That's a rhythm guitar player.'

In a retrospective four-star review of the album, another US *Rolling Stone* writer, Mark Coleman, was just as enthused as his colleague Fricke. '*Back in Black* proves that noise pollution, when properly deployed, can qualify as rock and roll.'

The band had come a long way from the days when they were written off as 'shamelessly sexist panderers' by the influential music mag. 'I love sex,' Angus had chuckled, when the issue of sexism was raised.

'Anything with the word in it,' added Malcolm.

Malcolm and Angus may have laughed at the tag, but in all honesty it was sometimes deserved. *Back in Black* had its share of questionable lyrical moments, particularly during such tracks as 'Let Me Put My Love Into You', 'You Shook Me All Night Long' and 'What Do You Do For Money Honey'.

Back in Black, while generally praised, did receive the occasional brickbat; arch *Village Voice* critic Robert Christgau, a hard man to please on a good day, noted that Brian Johnson 'sings like there's a cattle prod at his scrotum'.

Malcolm didn't really care—he knew they were a band of the people, a band for the punters who now jostled for spots down the front at each and every gig. New guy Johnson understood this too, telling David Fricke that the band was merely a reflection of their audience. 'The band . . . doesn't look down at them. They know it would be so easy for the roles to be reversed, for Brian Johnson to be in that audience, for Malcolm Young to be in that audience and for those kids to be in Malcolm's or my place.'

Their run of shows in and around the Milwaukee concert proved just how big a sensation they'd become, especially in Middle America. On 14 September they filled the 10,000 capacity Dane County Coliseum in Madison, Wisconsin. Two nights later they took on an 8000-seat venue in the beautifully named Normal, Illinois, and three nights after that it was a 9000-seater in Cedar Rapids, Iowa. ('My hearing has still not recovered,' a fan wrote many years later. 'Great show.') By the time they reached Chicago on 20 September they'd sold out the 14,000-capacity Rosemont Horizon. In Detroit—christened 'Rock City' in a song by KISS and another happy hunting ground for AC/DC—they filled the 11,500-seat Cobo Arena. (Which they'd go on to play twice when they returned in 1981.) Then it was on to the 10,000-capacity St John Arena in Columbus, Ohio, where one first-timer was bowled over by the sheer noise generated by Malcolm and the band. 'I had never heard anything so LOUD!!!' he wrote of the show.

With most tickets going for around US$10 a pop (about US$30 in today's money), the band's coffers weren't just full—they were overflowing. By the end of October, not only had *Back in Black* sold its first million copies, but previous releases *If You Want Blood You've Got It* and *Let There Be Rock* were caught up in its slipstream, each ticking past gold sales (500,000) in the US alone. Then Atlantic in the US cottoned on to the fact that they hadn't yet released the band's first album, *Dirty Deeds Done Dirt Cheap*, an oversight they swiftly rectified in April 1981. It went straight to number 3 on the *Billboard* Top 200 chart. (It has now sold six million copies in the US alone; *Let There Be Rock* sold two million.) The bittersweet aspect of all this was that these were all Bon Scott–era records. Scott was finally receiving his dues; if only he'd been around to enjoy this belated success.

Atlantic's Phil Carson was incensed by these rush releases and lit into the new head of Atlantic in the US, Doug Morris. 'How are you ever going to consider releasing a Bon Scott album when we've just broken our balls introducing the world to Brian Johnson? I think you're crazy,' Carson reputedly told him. Carson went as far as to consider it 'one of the worst money-making decisions ever made by a label executive'. Some insiders felt that this flurry of 'new' material had a negative impact on sales of future AC/DC albums.

As for Brian Johnson, his first royalty cheque was for a handy £30,000; what remained after a long-overdue mortgage payment went on a fancy 'motor', a black-and-white Chevy Blazer. He considered himself the luckiest shouter in rock and roll—so much for giving music away.

When the money really started pouring in, Malcolm and O'linda bought a house in London. Angus and Ellen did likewise in the Netherlands. Bassist Williams found his dream hideaway in Hawaii, while drummer Rudd opted for Sydney. Johnson would eventually move to Florida. After years of living in each other's pockets—'with the singer's socks two inches from your nose', in Angus's words—it was hardly surprising that the band members were spreading themselves far and wide.

Though hardly the kind of person to ponder even the recent past, Malcolm did take the time to reflect on the making of *Back in Black* midway through the tour. He told a journalist that while there'd been problems in the Bahamas—a machete-wielding killer wandering the beach and apocalyptic hurricanes, to name a few—the experience had drawn the band together.

'We became a very close, tight unit,' Malcolm said. 'It wasn't a tropical paradise—it was quite scary sometimes, and at the same time losing Bon and all . . . It was a hard album to make.'

None of this mattered now, as the album stuck like glue to the US chart, alongside such other hits as The Rolling Stones' *Emotional Rescue* and solo records from The Who's Pete Townshend (*Empty Glass*) and Roger Daltrey (the

McVicar soundtrack). But not even Malcolm, AC/DC's biggest advocate, would have dared predict how many copies *Back in Black* would go on to sell.

★

Malcolm knew that the biggest test for this new, mega-selling version of his band would be performing in Australia. They hadn't toured there at any length since the Giant Dose debacle some four years back, and local audiences, who could be way tougher than any prickly critic, were keen to check out this new guy who had taken the place of Bon Scott.

Scott had become more of a cult hero—if that was possible—since his untimely death. He was even the subject of graffiti, as evidenced by the 'Scott Bon Lives' graf that covered a brick wall not far from Sydney's Central Station. Okay, his memorialist had a bit of trouble with word order, but the sentiment was undeniable.

'I was worried,' said Johnson, prior to the tour. 'Like, who am I to try and follow in the footsteps of this great poet?' Johnson realised that while he could scream the paint off a wall, he was no great lyricist.

Neither Malcolm nor Johnson need have worried. From the moment the stage lights dimmed at their first of eight Australian shows, in Perth on 13 February 1981, and their hefty new prop rang out ominously—a 900-kilogram, cast-bronze hell's bell, no less, and an absolute bugger for the crew to handle—the band was in complete control. Johnson, while lacking Bon Scott's macho presence, prowled the stage like a caged tiger, his wiry hair bursting out from under his Andy Capp headwear, while Angus unleashed one electric solo after another as the power trio of Malcolm, Rudd and Williams kept the band in a very straight line. Malcolm, Angus and Williams played in front of a stack of Marshall amps almost twenty metres long; it was another prop, dwarfing their real amps, but it still looked highly imposing. Malcolm had his very own wall of sound.

'Angus and Mal together,' noted one punter at their Brisbane show on 24 February. 'What an ultimate force.'

Malcolm was no fool; he understood that Australian audiences didn't just want to hear *Back in Black*. Accordingly, their set lists included such Scott-era staples as 'Bad Boy Boogie', 'The Jack', 'High Voltage' and 'Problem Child', while 'T.N.T.' and 'Let There Be Rock' brought the curtain down with an eardrum-popping wallop each night. Malcolm played so hard during the latter that most nights he worked his way through two guitar picks—during the one song.

Backstage at their show at the Sydney Showgrounds on 23 February, after Ted Albert presented the band, and erstwhile bassist Mark Evans, with a total of 35 framed records—27 gold and eight platinum—Scott's mother Isa approached the 'new lad'.

'Our Bon would have been proud of you, son,' she said, tears welling in her eyes.

Back in Perth, Johnson had dedicated 'High Voltage' to Isa, a gesture she clearly appreciated.

This was a far more receptive Australia than in 1976—there weren't any angry local burghers trying to have them run out of town, or overly zealous coppers waiting for a sighting of Angus's pimply bum before hustling him off the stage. And Australian radio, particularly the new FM stations such as Sydney's 2MMM, had taken to *Back in Black* like flies to sherbet; no one was banning AC/DC this time around. *Back in Black* peaked at number 1 in Australia and charted for a mightily impressive 74 weeks, while both 'You Shook Me All Night Long' and 'Rock and Roll Ain't Noise Pollution' were Top 10 singles.

Yet no Australian tour, of course, came completely trouble-free. When the band filled Memorial Drive in Adelaide, residents as far as fifteen kilometres away filed complaints, proving that sometimes rock and roll could be noise pollution. The Sydney concert at the showgrounds was postponed twice due to storms of biblical proportions; thirty thousand fans turned up when the show finally went ahead. Thirty people were arrested in Melbourne, which led to some typically hysterical (and alliterative) headlines using the words 'rock' and 'riot'.

Yet the response from the local media was generally supportive, and it sometimes came from the most unlikely sources. The band members' marital status became a matter of discussion in the pages of the thoroughly mainstream *The Australian Women's Weekly*, which noted, with some regret, that only drummer Rudd remained a bachelor: 'He's married to his Ferrari.' Even Angus's onstage antics, which in the past had caused no end of drama for the band, were treated with due respect. 'With those skinny little legs,' noted the *Weekly*, 'he kicks, flails and jumps with limitless energy . . . If he could bottle the secret to his stamina, he'd make a fortune'.

In the wake of the chaotic Giant Dose tour, Malcolm and Angus had begun to doubt whether they even considered themselves an Australian band. ('The fuckers won't let us play here,' was Angus's pithy observation.) And Malcolm wasn't the kind of person who let things like that fade easily. But in 1981, everything changed—it was amazing what could be achieved with a worldwide hit and a major tragedy. AC/DC were now Australia's favourite rock-and-roll urchins.

*

Typically, rather than soak up the adulation and reflect on the journey—perhaps even enjoy spending the money that was finally hitting his bank account—Malcolm got the band back to work within months of their final *Back in Black* date, in Melbourne, on 28 February 1981. 'Downtime' wasn't a word in his vocabulary. But as Malcolm in particular would discover, trying to replicate an album as huge as *Back in Black* could be a joyless task. By the time he'd finally completed the follow-up, Malcolm confessed that he was 'fed up with the whole record'.

Producer Mutt Lange had brought some real sonic oomph to both *Highway to Hell* and *Back in Black;* he'd made the band's sound somehow heavier and yet more palatable for radio. But Lange was a perfectionist, a producer with a Zen-like focus and attention, someone for whom ten takes was just warming up. And that was not how Malcolm and the band had worked when they recorded with Vanda and Young, who instilled in Malcolm an instinct for getting a take when it was hot, rather than when it had been laboured over for days. The band endured Lange's attention to detail while making *Back in Black* because everyone had the sense that it could be their breakthrough record, but the making of what would become *For Those About to Rock We Salute You* felt like an endless struggle.

A harsh reality, too, was that Malcolm and Angus, as songwriters, had been on a hot streak since *Powerage,* a run that had now stretched across three studio albums. Few bands beyond The Beatles had been able to maintain such a creative purple patch. Even Malcolm's heroes, The Rolling Stones, who'd just offered AC/DC a sweet US$1 million dollars for a single support slot on their 1981 tour (only to be knocked back by Malcolm, who'd decided they didn't open for anyone, not even The Stones), coughed up the occasional musical fur ball: in their case pretty much everything from 1976's *Black and Blue* onwards. And the absence of Malcolm and Angus's partner-in-raunch, Bon Scott, that master of 'toilet poetry', was really beginning to show.

19

'Why the fuck are we paying this guy so much money?
We can do it ourselves.'

In the hope of chasing down the same magic as *Back in Black,* it was agreed that the band would again work with Mutt Lange, this time in Paris. But the songs, while ready to record, just weren't as strong as those on *Back in Black.* Even a decade later, Malcolm could only nominate one stand-out on what would become *For Those About to Rock We Salute You:* the way-over-the-top title track, which he'd hoped would become 'another big song to play live, like "Let There Be Rock".' But that was pretty much it. 'There's some good riffs on there,' Malcolm conceded, 'but it doesn't flow properly like an AC/DC album should.'

By the time sessions for the album began late in the northern spring of 1981, the mood within the band wasn't great. They'd just spent a week rehearsing at Montmartre in a dark, cold stone building with little in the way of vibe. There may have been a murderer wandering the Bahaman beaches when they made *Back in Black,* but at least it had been warm. And Malcolm, according to some reports, was still angry about the manner in which Atlantic had hastily rushed out their back catalogue to capitalise on *Back in Black*'s success; he hadn't forgotten the less-than-enthusiastic response *Dirty Deeds* had initially received from Atlantic in 1976.

Producer Lange's meticulous attention to detail kicked in as soon as they began working at EMI's Pathé-Marconi studios in Paris. While Malcolm, Angus and Johnson idled away time on a large sofa, growing increasingly irritable, Lange strove to get the right drum sound from Rudd. Days passed. Malcolm was annoyed by what he felt was Lange's 'fannying around'; Vanda and Young would have recorded the best part of an album by now. The songs were ready, the band was prepared, but it began to feel as though their producer wasn't.

Yet there was a method to Lange's meticulousness, as his engineer Mark Dearnley explained. 'Mutt has a picture of the way he wants to hear it in his head,' he told *Classic Rock*, 'and will keep bashing away until we hit that particular note.' And there was no disputing Lange's role in AC/DC's rise— *Back in Black* was still holding steady in the *Billboard* Hot 200 chart, its sales now well over five million. Lange had recently co-produced Foreigner's *4*, released while he was holed up with AC/DC, and that album was on its way to sales of six million, on the strength of hits such as 'Waiting for a Girl Like You' and 'Urgent'. Lange was the hottest rock producer of the moment, working with the hottest rock band; in theory, it appeared to be the perfect union. (If Malcolm had a crystal ball, though, he might have bailed right there: Lange would take almost three years to produce Def Leppard's *Hysteria*, a huge album in 1987, at a cost of about US$4.5 million.)

Ten days into this ordeal-by-drums, Lange accepted that

he was getting nowhere and the sessions were halted while a new studio was sourced. This consumed another two weeks, only for Lange to decide that the original Montmartre rehearsal studio would do just fine. (Malcolm and the band hated it. They very reluctantly dragged their gear to the icebox of a room and set up.)

Malcolm started longing for simpler times back at Alberts, as he'd later tell *Mojo*. 'We could go in in the old days, set up the kit and the amps, be in there two hours and *bang*, we're knocking out tracks . . . [The new album] was taking too long—[Lange] was trying to outdo *Back in Black* for sound, and it was the sound he was looking for whereas we were thinking of the music—and the performances were starting to suffer.'

If this wasn't stressful enough, Malcolm had agreed to one gig in the second half of 1981: the small matter of a headlining slot at the Monsters of Rock festival at Castle Donington in the UK, where 70,000 tickets had been sold. Some bands may have seen this as an escape from the drudgery of the studio, but for Malcolm it was just another hassle. By August they wouldn't have played live for six months, and were too deeply entangled in the new record to properly rehearse.

The day of 22 August dawned grey and dismal and pretty much stayed that way during sets from the various support acts at Donington. The line-up was another of those mismatches that AC/DC would feature in a lot during the next phase of their career; promoters imagined them as some kind of heavy metal act (which they clearly weren't; Malcolm had made his feelings clear on that subject). Also on the bill at Donington were Slade and metallic rockers Whitesnake, hardly AC/DC's sonic soulmates. If Malcolm thought KISS were 'cartoonish', heaven knows what he made of Noddy Holder and Slade with their daffy haircuts, hats and plat-form heels; guitarist Dave Hill wore snakeskin pants and knee-high white boots. The only act on the bill with any real connection to AC/DC were Americans the Blue Öyster Cult, of '(Don't Fear) The Reaper' fame, who, beyond a bit of facial hair and leather, didn't require too much flash to get their point across.

Malcolm's festival started badly when he was refused entry to the stage by an overzealous security guard because he was carrying the wrong pass (which said a lot about Malcolm's insistence on remaining an ordinary guy, a man of the people—sometimes he was mistaken for one). AC/DC somehow made the rain stop briefly during their set, but they were underprepared and hampered by dodgy sound. The only bright note was the fireworks at the end of their bracket. Then it was back to Paris to continue the grind.

Another issue was starting to eat away at Malcolm. He was beginning to feel as though they'd been 'isolated' by their current manager, who'd recently signed Def Leppard. Who, exactly, was Peter Mensch's priority: a band on the rise, or a band with a massive hit record still in the charts? Where was Mensch while the band was stuck in Paris with the obses-sive Mutt Lange? Five days after their show at Donington, David Krebs, Mensch's partner, relayed a message from the band (i.e. Malcolm): Mensch was fired. Mensch, who has refused to talk about his sacking at any length, says simply, 'I was never told why I was fired.' Tour manager Ian Jeffery, a Mensch supporter, believed that the band felt Mensch 'was only turning up when it was time to give them more float [money], saying: "Why are you not done yet?"'

It wasn't an opinion he shared.

Jeffery tried discussing this with Malcolm. 'I don't think anything has changed with Mensch,' he said.

'It fucking has,' replied Malcolm. Conversation over.

Whatever the reason, it was pretty clear that Malcolm was becoming increasingly annoyed and frustrated by the slow-motion progress of *For Those About to Rock* and needed to vent. Malcolm could still be ruthless; success hadn't changed that side of him. If anything, he now had more to protect and more reason to be wary of people outside of the band. Jeffery effectively took over the day-to-day management from Mensch.

Another huge challenge was inspiration. When writing *Back in Black*, Malcolm and Angus had drawn on the darkest days of the band—the death of Bon Scott; accordingly, there was no shortage of real, raw emotion on the record. The ensuing sales and glory had been mind-boggling—Phil Rudd could now fully indulge his fondness for Ferraris, for one thing, while Malcolm treated himself to a fully equipped boat—but success hardly inspired great music. Songs about living the high life just weren't AC/DC's style, unless you thought Bon Scott's lyric for 'Ain't No Fun (Waiting 'Round to Be a Millionaire)' was meant to be taken seriously. Johnson struggled for lyrical content, resorting to such plain silly song titles as 'Let's Get It Up', 'Inject the Venom' and 'Snowballed'—half-baked ideas that wouldn't have even entered Bon Scott's dirty mind.

And still the album sessions dragged on. It got to the point where the band would jam just to pass the time while

Lange tinkered away; somewhere in the vaults are recordings of Angus bringing his unique vocal stylings to the cabaret standard 'Feelings'. Then Malcolm started to obsess about just how much Lange was being paid—a figure never made public, but it was considerable, with added 'points' on the finished record—which riled him even more.

'Why the fuck are we paying this guy so much money?' he asked. 'We can do it ourselves.' Malcolm had a point: they'd learned plenty from Lange, both good and bad, and given that Malcolm had never quite shaken off his hardscrabble upbringing, the money spent on Lange seemed wildly excessive. Things had to change.

Finally, in September 1981, after four interminable months working with Lange—an absolute marathon by AC/DC standards—the record was done. And Malcolm, for one, had no idea if it was a masterpiece or a disaster. As he said, 'I don't think anyone, neither the band nor the producer, could tell whether it sounded right or wrong. Everyone was fed up with the whole album.'

★

Naturally, the road beckoned AC/DC; the tour in support of *For Those About To Rock We Salute You* began on 14 November 1981 in Detroit, Michigan. But even the tour also came with its own problems; the original start date of 30 September was pushed back due to the delay in finishing the album. As much as Malcolm enjoyed their new stage prop—twelve cannons positioned on either side of the stage, which 'fired' when the band played 'For Those About to Rock (We Salute You)'—the hardware created some hassles.

Police in Hartford, Connecticut, threatened the band with arrest if they used the cannons during their show on 3 December. Malcolm told his roadies to fire them anyway, without knowing that the crew in charge had already been handcuffed. One fan remembered their Detroit show as being 'the loudest show I have ever been to—and we were in the nose bleeds!'

The tour was another epic sprawl, spanning more than a year, but it excluded Australia for reasons that were never made clear. By the time the tour reached the UK in late September 1982, Malcolm was seething. He'd had enough of the album, the road—every bloody thing. Only a handful of *For Those About to Rock* tracks made the tour set list, a clear indicator of the band's feelings about the LP.

An American hard rock band called Y&T were the support act for the UK and European legs of the tour, and from the get-go they were given strict instructions about working with AC/DC, and with Malcolm in particular: tread carefully.

'It was made clear to us that if we did anything that upset Malcolm, we could be tossed off the tour,' said Y&T's Dave Meniketti. 'You definitely didn't want to piss him off. Malcolm was kind of scary to us young, impressionable guys, given the warnings we received from their management and crew.'

Yet as the tour progressed, Meniketti—while still reluctant to approach Malcolm directly—found him reasonably friendly, at least in group settings when the two bands got together backstage (which in itself was uncommon; support acts weren't always invited to 'hang'). AC/DC's English Pub, now named The Bell End Club, was open for business most nights of the tour. Malcolm, despite being more than fond of a tipple, was rarely spotted there, although he did occasionally relent when the call went out for a game of darts.

'Within that group setting, I remember him being very chatty,' said Meniketti. 'Sure he was opinionated, but he was always cordial and also quite funny.' The bands would eat dinner after each show, and Meniketti found the chemistry within AC/DC interesting to observe. 'They were talking and laughing together like a bunch of old friends.'

As for the onstage Malcolm—well, a fan like Meniketti was living out his rock-and-roll dreams. He got to watch the band every night for two months. 'Malcolm's rhythms were as steady and full sounding as any rhythm guitar sound I have ever experienced. Truly impressive the grooves he put down, and the width of his sound. Consistent, every song, every night.'

Malcolm told a reporter from *Sounds* that he sometimes wished the band could rewind to simpler times. He wanted to 'go back to the Red Cow or the Marquee and just play with eight lights and two speaker columns'. That was hardly going to happen; AC/DC was now a brand as much as they were a band. Still, AC/DC's new status meant that Malcolm was keeping some interesting company; while in the States in early 1982, he and Johnson got to meet Blues Brother John Belushi, only weeks before the manic comic overdosed and died. While on the road in Scotland, Malcolm demonstrated that he hadn't altogether lost his sense of humour when he suggested to Johnson that they take a trip up to Loch Ness. 'Let's go see if there is a monster!' After a boozy dinner, Johnson asked Malcolm what he was carrying, as they made their way to the Loch. Malcolm showed Johnson some fireworks he'd bought.

Malcolm explained that if they set them off while searching for 'old Nessy', 'it may just get her attention'.

The pair walked out into the water, fully clothed, laughing like loons while trying to ignite Malcolm's now-soggy fireworks. (And no, the monster didn't show.)

Caught up in *Back in Black's* slipstream, *For Those About to Rock* went to number 3 in the UK and became the band's first US number 1 hit, and their last until 2008. Yet its US sales—four million copies—made it look like a failure in the wake of *Back in Black,* which continued to sell and sell.

US *Rolling Stone* granted the album four stars, at least one more than it warranted. Again, the *Back in Black* factor may have been at play here; it had gained AC/DC some admirers in the US media who were now willing to treat them with respect. *Rolling Stone's* Kurt Loder singled out Malcolm's 'meaty riffs' and the band's 'expert songwriting'.

'The average adolescent male may not know much about critical trends, but he knows bullshit when he hears it,' wrote Loder, 'and he knows he prefers the real thing—which is to say, landslide riffs, stuck-pig vocals and screaming guitar solos that sound like they were recorded in the grip of a *grand mal* seizure.'

Curiously, for a record that had been massaged into meaningless for its creators, Loder felt that some rawness remained. 'The rough edges are the point [of AC/DC],' he said, although Malcolm would have been the first to point out that the rough edges around *For Those About to Rock* were pretty damned hard to locate.

Even the stately *New York Times* treated the band with something approaching deference when they covered their sold-out 2 December show at the prestigious Madison Square Garden. Even though their writer made it clear that in his opinion, AC/DC were not the most original act in rock, it was clear that they understood what worked for their audience. 'More than any other bestselling rock group, AC/DC explicitly equates making music with making war. And at Sunday's concert, it was perfectly clear that such unabashed aggressiveness offered a genuine catharsis for the male dominated teen-age audience.'

The tour was a financial success. Although official numbers were never released, a useful comparison was the 1981 Rolling Stones tour, which grossed US$52 million from 50 shows. AC/DC played twice as many concerts during their run, so the box office was substantial. It was the start of a phase in which touring, not record sales, became the band's main earner. And *For Those About to Rock,* despite its myriad hassles and musical shortcomings, sold its first million copies within months of its release.

But Malcolm was already formulating a new plan for the band, which meant discarding yet another player in the AC/DC story. At the same time, he was drifting deeper and deeper into a problem that would place his role as AC/DC's commander-in-chief in jeopardy.

20

'Nobody was in the mood to spend another year
making a record.'

Over the course of AC/DC's next few albums, and for much
of the subsequent decade, Malcolm would try to chase down
the sound that the band had mastered back in the days of
Vanda and Young: simple, raw and rocking. His first move
was obvious—no more Mutt Lange. Malcolm was done
with the producer's 'fannying about'. Lange wasn't so much
fired as simply never hired again. It no doubt helped that
Lange would soon be knee-deep in the epic, costly production of Def Leppard's *Hysteria;* it's unlikely he would have
been available anyway.

For their next album, 1983's *Flick of the Switch,* not only
did Malcolm go without Lange but he enticed the old guard,
Vanda and Young, to come on board as advisors. Malcolm's
edict—'I want it raw and loud'—was proverbial music to the
ears of Harry and George, who'd spent those early years with
the band trying to recreate the sound of an Aussie pub gig.
Malcolm drove home his point even further by brandishing
a copy of Muddy Waters' 1977 album *Hard Again* in the
studio: that was the vibe Malcolm was seeking—the sound

of musicians playing together in a room, sweaty and live. The band hunkered down in the Bahamas, where *Back in Black* had been recorded, in April 1983.

But once again there were problems; engineer Tony Platt said it was 'an unhappy album to be making'. Phil Rudd had taken to the rock-and-roll high life like, well, a lot of rock-and-roll drummers before him, a tradition dating back to such hard-living types as The Who's Keith Moon and Led Zeppelin's John Bonham. Rudd would later admit that the wild ride from *Back in Black* onwards 'literally drained me'. As usual, Rudd nailed his drum parts in the studio, but something was simmering between Rudd and Malcolm, whose own drinking wasn't doing wonders for his judgement. As band insider Ian Jeffery said of the time, 'Malcolm was pretty heavy on the sauce.' Malcolm and Rudd clashed repeatedly, sometimes coming to blows.

Their conflict had dated back to the Back in Black tour when Rudd turned up two hours late for a show at Long Island's Nassau Coliseum and Malcolm thumped him for his lack of professionalism. But there was more simmering between them than Rudd's tardiness and Malcolm's anger. Though the intensely private Malcolm never revealed the root cause of his problem with Rudd, AC/DC biographer Murray Engleheart referred to it as 'a messy and somewhat mysterious personal situation that involved someone in the Youngs' circle'. All Malcolm had to say, at least on the record, was that '[Rudd] got into drugs and got burned out'.

His work done on *Flick of the Switch*, Rudd was fired by Malcolm and exiled from the band for the next eleven years. He moved to New Zealand and bought into a helicopter company. Something like 700 drummers were auditioned to replace Rudd, including Simon Kirke from the band Free, a favourite act of Malcolm's. Kirke's audition, however, proved he wasn't right for the band, as Malcolm told his friend Herm Kovac. 'He was great on the slow stuff, but couldn't keep up on the fast stuff.' The band finally settled on stocky, dark-haired Englishman Simon Wright.

Rudd's exit meant the band was about to set out on yet another tour, starting in October 1983, in a less-than-upbeat frame of mind. It was a repeat of their lousy mindset when they toured *For Those About to Rock*. This time, while on tour, Malcolm fired long-time tour manager Ian Jeffery. It was another name added to his long list of sackings, winding all the way back to original singer Dave Evans.

As for the album itself, while the sound was less polished than *For Those About to Rock*—as Malcolm had intended—the songs again proved how much the band missed Bon Scott. Song titles such as 'Flick of the Switch', 'Nervous Shakedown' and 'Guns for Hire' read like slogans, lacking the cheek and spark of Scott's best.

Malcolm and Angus sat down with the record company when the record was done and the conversation was hardly encouraging: 'There are no singles here,' they were told. Malcolm stared down the execs and replied, 'That is the way it's going to be. We are not going to be a singles band.' He was right, too; the one single from the album, 'Guns for Hire', flatlined at number 84 on the *Billboard* chart. Def Leppard's 1983 smash album, *Hysteria,* meanwhile, featured no less than seven charting singles, including two *Billboard* number 1s and two more Top 10s. AC/DC had never catered to the mainstream, and now they were very much a band out of step.

US *Rolling Stone's* David Fricke, a vocal advocate of AC/DC, reacted like most listeners—he found *Flick of the Switch* less than thrilling. 'The Youngs' retooling of old riffs for new hits . . . teeters on self-plagiarism at times,' he wrote.

And Malcolm's take on the record? 'We did that one so quickly,' he recalled in 1992, 'and I guess it was a reaction to *For Those About to Rock.* We just thought, "Bugger it, we've had enough of this crap." Nobody was in the mood to spend another year making a record.'

Malcolm's one hit pick from the album was the title song, 'a great live track', which featured a gut-buster of a riff from his own good self and some fireworks from Angus. But that was pretty much it. A few songs from the album—including the title track—made their 1983–84 set list, but during 60-plus dates on the tour, new tracks such as 'Landslide', 'Badlands' and 'Rising Power' were discarded after being played just a few times. Instead they leaned heavily on the classics: 'Rosie', 'Highway to Hell', 'Dirty Deeds', 'The Jack' and 'Let There Be Rock'. In some ways, it was as though Bon Scott had never left the building.

*

In the northern spring of 1985, as the band added the finishing touches to their latest LP, *Fly on the Wall*—another stab at getting back to basics—AC/DC was dragged into two controversies that proved a couple of key things: censors in the US had no sense of humour, and you can't choose your fans. In the latter case, it all came about because of an AC/DC baseball cap.

Richard Ramirez was a truly evil piece of work, a Satanist

who stalked and murdered numerous people in Los Angeles and San Francisco between June 1984 and August 1985, in a variety of horrific ways—he bludgeoned his victims with a hammer, a machete, a tyre iron, whatever was handy. Sometimes he shot them in cold blood. The press dubbed him the 'Night Stalker'. During one of his grisly crimes, in March 1985, Ramirez left behind his AC/DC baseball cap. A boyhood friend, Ray Garcia, confirmed that he was a big fan of the band, especially the Bon Scott–era song 'Night Prowler'. The press jumped onto this and drew a very tenuous connection: one headline declared, 'AC/DC Music Made Me Kill'.

'Did AC/DC drive him onto a personal highway to hell?' asked a stony-faced TV reporter.

A solitary voice of reason was *Billboard* reporter Sam Sutherland. 'That band is about as tongue-through-cheek as you can get.'

Initially Malcolm thought it was a joke. His first response was, 'This is crazy,' as he told VH1's *Behind the Music*. 'Why are we connected?' He was quick to point out that there was no link between the band and the psycho killer; the press didn't even have the song title right. But Malcolm came to understand that he needed to offer some kind of clarification. 'That song is not called "Night Stalker", it's called "Night Prowler" and it's about things you used to do when you were a kid, like sneaking into a girlfriend's bedroom when her parents were asleep.'

Bon Scott may have had trouble in mind, but not the type Ramirez traded in.

Ramirez was eventually caught and given nineteen death sentences, but the association was another problem Malcolm could have lived without. He had his own boozing to contend with, and the band's declining sales, as acts such as Foreigner, U2 and REO Speedwagon dominated record sales. He'd also become a father for the second time; his son, Ross Malcolm Young, was born on 18 October 1984. There was a lot going on in his life.

Around the same time as the Night Stalker imbroglio, the band was drawn into another very public drama. Tipper Gore, the wife of US Vice President Al Gore, was shocked when she arrived home one day and caught her daughter listening to Prince's 'Darling Nikki', which, among various raunchy vignettes, depicted a scene where dear Nikki was 'masturbating with a magazine'. Along with other prominent Washington women, Gore formed the Parents Music Resource Center with the goal of unearthing equally raunchy material and introducing a sort of ratings system, much like that used for movies. The PMRC compiled a 'Filthy 15'— songs they deemed most likely to corrupt the youth of the USA. The list included such obvious choices as Mötley Crüe (although the song on the list, 'Bastard', was hardly their filthiest), Prince (the aforementioned 'Darling Nikki'), W.A.S.P.'s 'Animal (Fuck Like a Beast)', which required little in the way of explanation, Cyndi Lauper's 'She Bop', a witty ditty about female self-pleasuring, and AC/DC's 'Let Me Put My Love Into You'. It seemed that Gore and her colleagues didn't dig especially deep into the AC/DC back catalogue; such Bon Scott–penned gems as 'Crabsody in Blue' or one of his many odes to his testicles were far better suited for a list called the Filthy 15.

This time it was Angus who took on the role of band spokesman, and he managed to mix both the Ramirez issue and the PMRC into one pithy comment, which he shared with *People* magazine. 'People who want to strangle other people's rights are possessed by one of the worst devils around, the Satan in their souls which is called intolerance.' While the band was briefly back in Australia, the host of TV's *Sounds,* Donnie Sutherland, mentioned the PMRC and asked Angus if AC/DC had been a bad influence on teenagers. 'Yeah, we probably have,' he replied with a sly chuckle.

It's impossible to say whether distractions such as Richard Ramirez and Tipper Gore had an impact on AC/DC record sales, but with all the clamour it was easy to overlook that in 1985 the band had a new record in the stores. 'We wanted to pick it up a bit more for this album,' Malcolm said of *Fly on the Wall,* 'so we tried our hand at producing ourselves again. But putting some more time and thought into what we were doing instead of just taping ourselves banging out the songs as we had done on *Flick of the Switch.*'

But like its predecessor, *Fly on the Wall* was no hit, reaching a peak on the US album charts of number 32; it didn't even top the album charts in Australia. Over time it would sell a million copies in the US, but when stacked up against *Back in Black*'s 50-plus-million, it was a dud, relatively speaking. US *Rolling Stone* found little to admire about the record beyond Angus's playing; he was a master, according to writer Tim Holmes, in 'playing the dumbest, most irresistibly repetitive chords in the lexicon'. Tellingly, the review was lumped in with coverage of new albums from hair metal acts Mötley Crüe, Twisted Sister, Ratt and Scorpions—bands that had little in common with AC/DC.

Malcolm tried to make light of the misconception that

they were part of some new wave of heavy metal, but you could sense his simmering frustration. 'There are a lot of pretenders out there,' he said. 'We feel we're timeless. Trends come and go, but we won't ever change. There's nowhere for us to go, believe me!' With good reason he was sticking with his line that 'there are very few rock-and-roll bands', and still insisting that AC/DC belonged to a tradition that dated back to the original rockers of the 1950s. He maintained that only AC/DC and The Rolling Stones had the 'swing' required of a true rock-and-roll band. Malcolm admitted in 1988 that he'd 'never heard' breakout band Guns N' Roses, 'but it's nice if bands like that play our songs'.

Angus baulked at the tag 'heavy metal' when it was raised by Australian *MTV*'s Richard Wilkins. 'We found out long ago that the best thing we did on stage was rock music . . . we knew how to rock. We've been called punk and new wave . . . but we're far away from the heavy metal thing. We can only be ourselves.' And then, in a comment that echoed Malcolm's long-ago observation of Led Zeppelin's Robert Plant: 'We're not a "posey" sort of band.'

★

Throughout this commercially fallow period for the band, Malcolm's drinking problem was always close to the surface. One fellow musician recalled seeing him backstage lugging a bottle of Jack Daniels 'almost as big as he was'; he'd also stumbled about the stage while playing back in 1984 at a Monsters of Rock show. At one point he tumbled into Simon Wright's drums: hardly the act of a disciplined bandleader.

There was also a clash with Mötley Crüe's Nikki Sixx, after the bassist sank his fangs into Angus while fooling around backstage. According to Sixx, quoted on an AC/DC fan's forum, Malcolm told him that biting Angus was bad enough, 'but if you fucking bite me, I'll bite your fucking nose off, you dog-faced faggot'. When Sixx challenged him, Malcolm leapt at the singer, swinging punches. If that wasn't enough drama, Malcolm's father, William, died in 1985, aged 74. Malcolm felt the loss deeply.

By the time they released their next album, 1988's cheekily titled *Blow Up Your Video* (this being the heyday of 'I want my MTV!'), Malcolm's drinking had become a fully blown drama. Malcolm described his boozing habits to a writer from *Q*. 'We'd have two Bloody Marys at the hotel in the morning, then straight to the airport and into the bar. On the plane you go, "I'll have a screwdriver"—and you get two! It hit me big time.'

The album itself was a further attempt to get back to basics; Malcolm described it as a stab at 'capturing that traditional 12-bar rock 'n' roll sound that we had in the beginning'. Malcolm admitted that 'we'd lost our footing by that time and we needed to get the old feeling back again'. Vanda and Young were again brought in to oversee production, which was no great surprise—after all, they'd helped create 'that old feeling' in the first place. They worked at the Studio Miraval in the south of France during August and September 1987.

They did capture that spirit, at least in snatches; songs such as 'That's the Way I Wanna Rock N Roll' had much of the same urgency and energy as their earlier classic recordings. Malcolm particularly liked that song, as well as 'Heatseeker' and 'Meanstreak', 'even though I think [the latter] may have been too funky for some of the fans'. Now that was a first for AC/DC.

As Jim Farber noted in US *Rolling Stone,* despite their self-imposed limitations 'the Young brothers continue to come up with enough inspired riffs to make the tunnel vision justifiable. In fact, the riffs here add up to the band's catchiest work since its classic album *Back in Black'.*

Interestingly, this was the last album to which Brian Johnson contributed lyrics. He'd run short of single entendres, let alone doubles, as the uninspired 'Ruff Stuff' and 'This Means War' proved beyond doubt.

Despite the praise (and the sales, this being their biggest-selling LP since *For Those About to Rock),* Malcolm needed to confront his personal demons. Brother George had witnessed his problems up close while making the album; he told David Fricke from *Rolling Stone* that Malcolm displayed indications of alcoholism during the sessions. 'I saw the signs. Malcolm had a problem.' Straight-talking George advised his brother to 'get his act together'. George was unsure if anything had sunk in, but Malcolm had always respected and admired his big brother, so it's likely his words hit home.

The extensive Blow Up Your Video tour started with Australian shows in February 1988, their first there in almost seven years. By the time the tour reached London's Wembley Arena on 13 April—the fourth Wembley show of the tour—Malcolm knew he had to get some help.

'I'm physically and mentally screwed by the booze,' he told Angus. 'I have to stop. I've lost the plot.'

Angus understood. He didn't want to see his brother end up like Bon Scott.

'Alright,' Malcolm said, 'I'll get myself sorted.'

Malcolm later explained his problem in his usual cut-the-crap manner. 'Just a case of rock and roll,' he said. 'The lifestyle. It just got to me.' He said that drinking brought out the worst parts of his nature, the dark side.

Despite his problems, Malcolm hadn't shut himself off from his fans. On the evening of the Wembley show, Malcolm bumped into some starstruck punters at a nearby hotel. He tried to sign whatever the fans put in front of him, but his pen was out of ink. Rather than apologise and walk away, he disappeared for a few minutes, found a working pen and returned to autograph their shirts.

'You came all the way from Scotland?' Malcolm asked, when the fans told him they shared some roots. Then security came and whisked him off to the show.

Before they began the US leg of the tour in early May, their record company issued a press release stating that Malcolm was taking 'a rest'. As music industry clichés went, it was right up there with 'creative differences'. The reality was that Malcolm had checked into a rehab facility—he even gave up pot while he was at it, which he'd been smoking since he was a teenager. 'I'm not a hippie anymore,' he boasted to his friend Herm Kovac when they caught up.

Stevie Young, his nephew, took over on rhythm guitar. It was a savvy move; first, his recruitment kept things within the family, and there was also the good chance that many in the audience wouldn't spot the difference, because Stevie—only three years younger than his uncle—was a stone-cold Malcolm lookalike. He even played a Gretsch Firebird that had once belonged to Malcolm. Second, Stevie had been down that road before, because his band Starfighters (also the name of Harry Vanda's first band) had supported AC/DC on the *Back in Black* tour. He was given the luxury of ten days to learn his parts before the band returned to the road.

Some months later, out of rehab, Malcolm had the very surreal experience of watching his body double play on stage while he looked on from the wings. Sadly, it wouldn't be the last time Stevie Young stepped in for his uncle.

21

'I don't think we've ever met anyone so genuine and that
you can trust as a person. We owe Ted [Albert] a lot.'

By the mid-1990s, Malcolm and his family had returned to
Australia, settling in the Sydney suburb of Balmain. Several
years earlier he'd bought an impressive sandstone mansion
named Onkaparinga, translated as 'women's river' in the
Indigenous language Kaurna. Malcolm paid $872,000
for the property (its current value is somewhere around
$30 million), but it required substantial renovations over the
course of a year before Malcolm, O'linda and their children
could move in. That's probably why the locals had dubbed
it 'Cockroach Castle' prior to the Youngs taking residency.

Malcolm wasn't often in Balmain, though; well into
the 1990s he was still on the treadmill of recording and
touring that had been his life since the band first formed.
As one neighbour noted, 'Malcolm mostly came [home] at
Christmas time—he would spend a few weeks.' Sometimes
he and Angus could be spotted together on the verandah.
Other times Malcolm could be heard noodling away in the
attic studio that he had custom-built. His neighbours poeti-
cally referred to it as Malcolm's 'studio in the sky'. Sometimes

other music could be heard in the house—his daughter Cara's latest musical obsession was grunge heroes Nirvana, or 'Neeeervana', as Malcolm would say with a chuckle. Other times he would refer to them simply as 'that band'. He was no big fan, even though Nirvana's Kurt Cobain, like so many others, was a serious AC/DC fan, having fallen hard for *Back in Black*.

'It wasn't what you would expect,' noted another neighbour, when asked how it felt to live next door to a rock star (admittedly, one who was now pursuing the quiet life). 'He didn't have wild parties. Most of the time you only knew he was home if you heard him jamming in the studio.'

Malcolm was described as the kind of neighbour who'd stop and say hello—a regular bloke with an irregular job. '[He was] just a normal person, you would see him on the street or heading into town.'

Onkaparinga was proof of just how far Malcolm had come from the days of struggle street Burwood and the Villawood Migrant Hostel. The stately spread, all 1937 square metres of it, was enclosed by a three-metre-high, honey-coloured sandstone wall. The landscaped gardens made it even more of a hideaway for Malcolm and his family when he'd had enough of the rock-and-roll grind. A wraparound verandah encompassed the second floor of the house. There was also a swimming pool—which Malcolm let the neighbours use when he wasn't in town—as well as a tennis court and jacuzzi.

It was one of the largest homes in the area, which was saying something; East Balmain is an area with no shortage of sizeable estates. Onkaparinga took up most of the block. The neighbourhood was also something of an artists' enclave; actors Judy Davis and Colin Friels were long-time residents, likewise Rachel Ward and Bryan Brown. Even Carlotta, the drag queen with whom AC/DC worked (briefly) way back in 1974, was a local. One day, Malcolm braked suddenly to avoid hitting a pedestrian; it was Mark Evans, former AC/DC bassist and still a working musician, who also lived nearby.

Malcolm had a security camera installed, but rather than use it for scoping out invading fans, it was pointed towards the nearby harbour, which he could see from his roof, 'so he can have a live stream of the harbour in his lounge room', according to a local. He'd host New Year's Eve parties for his family; they'd drink in the flawless view of the harbour and the fireworks while Malcolm stood quietly at the back of the room, taking it all in.

*

Loss never seemed too far away from Malcolm even as he settled into this more comfortable, family-oriented lifestyle. Three years after his father's death, his mother, Margaret, died in 1988; she was 75. Stephen, one of his older brothers, a fellow guitarist and another big musical influence on Malcolm, died in 1989, aged just 56. He was the father of Stevie, who'd stood in for Malcolm during that 1988 tour while he was in rehab.

And there was yet another loss during this time that hit Malcolm hard: the death of his first mentor, Ted Albert. Losing Ted Albert was in many ways like losing a family member. Without Albert's advocacy, there might not have even been an AC/DC: he had encouraged Malcolm and Angus even before they formed the band, after that fateful day at Burwood when he overheard them banging away on guitars in their bedroom.

Albert had maintained a watchful eye on the brothers' progress as they became world-beaters; the Alberts company retained control of the band's recordings. But the connection was stronger than purely business—Alberts was their spiritual home (and would be until 2016, when the company was sold off to BMG); it was the one place where Malcolm and Angus, in particular, felt safe. When in Sydney they'd often drop into the Alberts office and check in on such staffers as Fifa Riccobono, a close friend of the band, who'd helped connect Malcolm with his wife O'linda and who was someone the ever-wary Youngs could confide in and trust. 'She was always there,' Malcolm said of Riccobono, 'from the first day, really.' AC/DC's success wasn't in isolation: many other Alberts acts, among them The Angels, Rose Tattoo, Stevie Wright, John Paul Young and the Ted Mulry Gang, became household names—plus, of course, Alberts had its own star producers in Vanda and Young. The tag 'House of Hits' was no idle boast.

On the release of AC/DC's 1990 album *The Razors Edge,* which marked the newly sober Malcolm's return to the band, Ted Albert wrote a letter to Malcolm. He revealed that in expectation of the album he'd had new subwoofers installed in his car, and after just a few listens Albert was so 'blown away' that he felt compelled to write to Malcolm. 'I love it,' he said of the album, wishing Malcolm and the band ongoing success. Albert was every bit the proud father. He promised Malcolm he'd increase the band's royalty rate, again, 'as a way of saying thanks for our long association and the success that you have brought to my company'.

But soon after he wrote that letter, on 11 November 1990, Ted Albert died of a heart attack. He was just 53 years old.

Malcolm was in New York when he got the call about Albert. 'I couldn't believe it,' he said. 'I just couldn't.'

It was a huge loss for Malcolm, the band and the entire Australian music community. Albert was a trailblazer, who of late had established a company called M&A Productions, whose first feature was Baz Luhrmann's *Strictly Ballroom*. Albert didn't live long enough to see the film generate a take of $80 million on its $3 million budget and become an international sensation (just like his rockin' protégés). The central song of the film was 'Love is in the Air', written by Harry Vanda and Malcolm's big brother George, who'd begun their own journey with Albert way back in the mid 1960s. His death marked the end of the company as AC/DC knew it. Alberts could never be the same without Ted Albert.

In the Australian-made documentary *Blood and Thunder: The Sound of Alberts,* Malcolm and Angus were asked about Ted Albert's role in AC/DC's rise. Neither had to think too hard before responding.

'I don't think we've ever met anyone so genuine and that you can trust as a person,' said Malcolm. 'We owe Ted a lot.'

'Ted was instrumental,' agreed Angus, 'a very solid character. He didn't seem to be a person who'd crumble under cannon fire.'

★

Perhaps all this loss inspired some reflection in Malcolm, because around the time of Albert's death he and Angus sat down with a writer from the UK's *Q* magazine and took a long, hard look back at the band's past seventeen years: highs, lows and all the stuff in between. As the writer noted, 'Malcolm is impossibly thin; Angus merely thin', so the good life clearly hadn't made its way to Malcolm's waistline.

Malcolm explained that one of the first things the band learned was to focus on what they were good at, echoing brother George's advice during the early days ('That's your thing. Stick with it.'). Malcolm name-checked The Stones and The Beatles as bands that had dabbled in different styles and sounds but finally got back to what they did best, playing rock and roll. Malcolm's take on this was simple: why bother straying at all?

'We've learned from bands like that that it's best just to stay where you're at; you're going to come back there anyway, so why leave in the first place? Why not simply work better and harder at what you've got?' (Angus had recently half-joked with another reporter that all the band did was 'put out the same album every year with a different cover'.)

Talk turned to matters global; since the Berlin Wall had come down, sales in West Berlin record shops had gone up some 300 per cent and their two biggest sellers were anything from AC/DC, plus the *Dirty Dancing* soundtrack.

Then they moved onto Bon Scott. As far as Malcolm was concerned, 'Bon was the single biggest influence on the band. When Bon came in, it pulled us all together.' It was a big statement from Malcolm, who wasn't one for handing out compliments too readily.

Angus, too, had chosen the quiet life; he and his wife Ellen now lived in the quaint Dutch village of Aalten, where her family had roots. Only 12,000 people lived in Aalten. Theirs, admittedly, was the only three-storey mansion in that particular postcode, but it was hardly a rock-and-roll kind of town. The local blacksmith was down the street; it was run by Ellen's family.

Malcolm's recent drinking problems weren't off limits, either. 'I could feel things were going downhill for me,' he admitted. 'I was losing my enthusiasm for everything, the group, life in general. It was just the drink, dragging me down. I had to pack it in.' Nor had his problems with Mutt Lange at the time of *For Those About to Rock* been forgotten; Malcolm's opinion on that hadn't changed one bit. '[There was] too much time spent fucking around with the sound.'

Eventually, Malcolm got back to the subject at the heart of the band: the unique sibling union that he had with Angus. Again, Malcolm was compelled to speak the truth. 'We have tiffs all the time, but musically we tend to think pretty much the same. I think we battled more before we were in a group, because we didn't have to keep anything together then.'

★

It wasn't as though the band was slowing down—anything but. *The Razors Edge,* which was produced by Canadian Bruce Fairbairn—Malcolm said he was 'a real gentleman'— was a strong return to form; it also introduced new drummer Chris Slade, whose shaved head gave him a passing resemblance to *The Addams Family*'s Uncle Fester. Malcolm and Angus composed all the lyrics; the record was completely their creation.

'We wanted to hear every single instrument on that record and have the overall sound right in your face,' Malcolm said of *The Razors Edge.* 'What we didn't want was one of those American mixes with eight guitar overdubs, but Bruce seemed to give the band a modern sound without watering us down.' The album went on to sell five million copies in the US alone, peaking at number 2 and charting for some eighteen months.

It said something about AC/DC's place in the world that their music was now being reviewed in the very mainstream *Entertainment Weekly*, who loved *The Razors Edge*. 'Hard rock and heavy metal are young people's music,' admitted writer Greg Sandow. 'But often it's the older bands that prove most dependable.' In his less-than-satisfied two-star review for US *Rolling Stone*, John Mendelsohn cited Slade, Black Sabbath and the 'Hitler Youth-rally chorus' of 'Moneytalks' as reference points, before coming to this damning conclusion: 'With *The Razors Edge*, AC/DC sets a new record for the longest career without a single new idea.'

While Malcolm would have laughed this off—fucking journalists!—he did admit that the band knew its limitations, and its strengths, and traded on them accordingly. 'We stick to the same sounds,' he told a writer from *Mojo*. 'We put our amps on the same setting every night and, as Angus said the other day, we put out the same album every year with a different cover. We're not about sitting around climbing up our own arse. Basically we're a two-guitar band with three or four chords, though we might add another one if we're feeling tricky.'

'Thunderstruck', which featured some hugely impressive guitar 'tapping' from Angus, was a real feature of *The Razors Edge* and became their new opening number. 'It's one of those songs that sounded great on stage,' admitted Malcolm. They played the song at virtually all of their 161 shows during 1990 and 1991, and it became a standout of their future shows. Angus was once asked by a journalist to deconstruct the challenging opening of 'Thunderstruck'. He thought it over for a minute and then said, 'Yeah, that gets a bit deadly.' Like Malcolm, he'd always rather play his guitar than discuss technique.

Touring had become the band's bread and butter during the 1990s, but their ever-expanding live show—now a sizeable production, complete with hell's bell, cannons, pyrotechnics and a runway for Angus and Brian Johnson—sometimes also came with serious, even deadly complications.

*

On 18 January 1991 the band were set to play at the Salt Palace Acord Arena in Salt Lake City, Utah, selling all but a few of the 14,000 available tickets. The band had filled the same venue four times before, dating back to July 1978 when they'd opened for Aerosmith. Around 5000 tickets for this gig were sold for the floor, where punters would stand; everyone else was seated.

Angus had barely launched himself into 'Thunderstruck' when there was a commotion at the front of the stage. As one fan standing near the front, 19-year-old Brandi Burton, recalled, 'There was a massive jolt forwards.' Quickly, some 30 people had fallen on Burton and her girlfriend, nineteen-year-old Liz Glausi. 'We were screaming for help,' said Burton, 'but there was no way to pull us up.'

Moshpit crushes were regular occurrences at big rock shows, but this was different, more dangerous—security staff could see hands reaching out from the bottom of the pile that had formed, but despite their best efforts, they couldn't extract the fallen punters. There were prone bodies in front of the stage.

An audio recording of the show, which later surfaced online, made it clear that Brian Johnson, once aware of the drama, did everything he could to stop the band and confront the problem. But perhaps as much as 30 minutes passed before this happened.

'Okay, everybody, hang on,' Johnson barked, 'we've got a bit of a problem down the front . . . Everybody just move back one foot . . . We've got a bit of a problem down the front and we don't want anybody to get hurt.'

Now fully aware of the problem, the band were faced with a serious quandary: did they keep playing, or shut the show down? They decided to stop for fifteen minutes and spoke with local authorities, who told them to play on, for fear of a full-scale riot.

Curtis Child, who was attending his first big rock show, was also in the crush. When he was hauled from the melee he was immediately put on a respirator. Child died, as did fourteen-year-old Jimmie Boyd Jr. Brandi Burton survived, but her friend Liz Glausi died in hospital three days later.

After the show, Malcolm and the band released a statement. They were heartbroken, devastated. In a recent interview, Angus had said, 'It's rock music, it's fun. It doesn't have to be a tragedy.' But now they were deeply immersed in a tragedy over which they had little, if any, control. 'Nothing anyone can say or do will diminish the tragic loss or sense of grief,' read their statement. The band were critical of news reports that said they didn't stop playing when they became aware of the sprawl at the front of the stage. Malcolm couldn't bring himself to ever talk about the night; it hurt too much.

While the tour kept on rolling, the drama of Salt Lake City, which until now had been a favourite spot of the band's, didn't fade away. The three families who'd lost their children filed lawsuits, variously against the band, its management, the company that managed the venue, the concert promoter, J.C. McNeil, and the local radio station and concert sponsor KBER.

The complaint was settled out of court in late 1992, and AC/DC, along with the Salt Lake County, paid an undisclosed amount to the families, believing, understandably, that 'it was the right thing to do'.

The band wouldn't return to Salt Lake City for ten years. It would be the worst concert disaster of AC/DC's lengthy career.

22

'I'd have gone in, but no one fancies a gun to their head.'

Malcolm had a tendency to shut people out of his life and out of the band. Once someone was exiled, they were gone forever (just ask Michael Browning or Mark Evans). But the situation with drummer Phil Rudd, who had been sacked in 1983, was different. As good as his two successors had been, there was something missing when they played—they lacked the 'swing' that Malcolm believed was AC/DC's secret sonic ingredient, and that Rudd had in spades. The Who's Roger Daltrey once said this of Kenney Jones, the drummer who took Keith Moon's place when he died: '[Jones] was a great drummer. But he was completely the wrong drummer for us.' Perhaps Malcolm felt this about Rudd's replacements when the band reconvened to record 1996's *Ballbreaker*, because by this time he'd invited Rudd back into the fold. It was interesting to note, though, that Malcolm's falling out with the drummer had lasted for almost a decade: he could definitely hang onto a grudge.

Their reunion actually dated back to November 1991, when the band was in New Zealand on tour, promoting

The Razors Edge. They reached out to Rudd, asking if he'd like to come to the show, an offer he readily accepted.

'He just seemed like the old Phil,' Malcolm reported after their catch-up. Clearly, the animosity between them had faded; it also appeared that Rudd had toned down his wildness. During that get-together, Rudd made his intentions very clear, telling Malcolm, 'Any time, you know, I'm ready . . .'

Eight years into his isolation from the band, Rudd had stopped playing professionally, preferring only to drum 'when I wanted to rather than when I had to'. The majority of his time was spent on other pursuits—some flashy, some decidedly mundane. 'I raced cars,' he said, 'flew helicopters, became a farmer, planted some crops.' Life in New Zealand's slow lane suited him; it was 'nice and quiet with nobody bothering me'.

But Rudd missed life in AC/DC. He was asked to sign on again formally in late 1993, when the band recorded the 'Big Gun' single for the *Last Action Hero* soundtrack. This single, and the *Who Made Who* album back in 1986—used as the soundtrack of *Maximum Overdrive,* a failed film directed by author (and AC/DC nut) Stephen King—reflected a change of attitude in Malcolm. Until *Who Made Who,* which comprised a few new songs and a bunch of classics (and a title track produced by the old firm of Vanda and Young), Malcolm had been extremely wary of licensing the band's music to films or for use in advertising; in fact he'd always been wary of the entire music business, courtesy of brother George. For Malcolm, licensing the band's music felt as though he was losing control, something he refused to countenance. Whenever Alberts fielded an offer, they'd take a deep breath before running it by Malcolm, because they could predict his answer: No. But he'd now loosened up; it's possible the sheer amount of money typically offered for soundtracks was added motivation. If nothing else, Malcolm was a pragmatist.

As for Rudd's re-hiring, Malcolm, typically, had a very practical explanation: he made the band sound better. He said just that on a Dutch TV show in 2001: 'We've always tried to get drummers who can emulate Phil's style, because that's what the style of the band is, the simpleness of the drums, the swing. We always intended to get Phil back, it was just waiting for the moment. He is the real sound [of AC/DC].'

For his part, Rudd was surprised by how easy and natural it was for him to slip back into the chair. 'In five minutes it was as though I'd popped out for a cup of tea, a pack of cigarettes. That's absolutely true. I love it, it comes out the right way.'

Malcolm agreed to another seemingly unlikely collaboration for the *Ballbreaker* album, opting to work with American Rick Rubin, a producer with a hip-hop and thrash rock background, who'd broken such acts as the Beastie Boys. Rubin was hard to miss—he had a look that was equal parts Allen Ginsberg, Dalai Lama and space cadet. To the untrained eye, Rubin seemed about as un-AC/DC as was humanly possible; the simple idea of him and the staunchly unpretentious Malcolm even being in the same room together bordered on comical. For one thing, Rubin had at least 65 kilograms on Malcolm, maybe even more on Angus—he'd been tagged 'the world's fattest vegan'—and had a beard that almost reached to his nipples (he hadn't shaved since 1986). Rubin also had a real yen for yoga. He'd sometimes work on his downward dog in the studio while Malcolm and the band were tearing a hole in *Ballbreaker* tracks such as 'Hard as a Rock', 'The Honey Roll' and 'Cover You in Oil'.

But then again, part of Rubin's legend was based on working with heavy guitar bands, acts such as The Cult and Danzig. Another metal act, Anthrax, was so inspired by his brainwave of bringing together rockers Aerosmith and hip-hop act Run DMC to record the 1986 crossover hit 'Walk This Way', that they did likewise with Public Enemy (another act with whom Rubin had worked), jamming on the apocalyptic 'Bring the Noise'. (In a not-unrelated coincidence, Anthrax guitarist Scott Ian might well have been Malcolm Young fan numero uno; he learned to play as a kid sitting in his bedroom studying AC/DC records. 'Malcolm's always been my hero since day one because he basically taught me how to play guitar,' Ian said in 2018. Among Ian's many tattoos were the faces of Malcolm and Angus.)

Rick Rubin was also a serious AC/DC devotee. When he first met Malcolm, as they worked on the track 'Big Gun', Rubin told him he'd been an AC/DC fan since he was a kid, and that he used to play 'Highway to Hell' with one of his earliest rap outfits. And despite his lost-in-space demeanour, Rubin was business savvy, having founded Def American (with a later name-change to American Recordings), a label whose roster included acts as diverse as southern US rockers The Black Crowes, X-rated comic Andrew Dice Clay and the Man in Black, Johnny Cash.

But Rubin wasn't the only mogul at work during the *Ballbreaker* sessions, which started in New York and ended up in Los Angeles. In the adjoining studio was an even more eccentric American: the crazy-haired Phil Spector, girl group mastermind, producer of 'River Deep—Mountain High' and 'You've Lost That Lovin' Feeling' and—as history would prove—a man with a violent streak even longer than his string of hits who was known to wave a gun around in the studio as a very unique form of motivation. Malcolm would sometimes press his ear to the wall and listen to whatever it was Spector was cooking up next door.

'I don't know what it was,' he admitted, 'but it sounded great. Like his old girl group sound.' Malcolm was asked if he was tempted to pop in and introduce himself. 'I'd have gone in, but no one fancies a gun to their head.'

Malcolm was only joking—probably—but in April 2009, Phil Spector was found guilty of second-degree murder and sentenced to nineteen years in prison. Malcolm had made a wise decision.

As for Rubin, he favoured the same meticulous studio approach as Mutt Lange (and Phil Spector), and also had a concurrent project with the Red Hot Chili Peppers, working on their *One Hot Minute* album. Over time, this wore the band down—when Rubin was present he'd demand dozens of takes of particular songs, as the sessions dragged on for five months. As Brian Johnson recalled, 'He would come in at night and say, "Hmm we'll try that song a different way tomorrow," and by the time we finished we'd played the song so many different times you'd be sitting there going, Jesus, I'm sick of this bloody thing.' Malcolm likened the studio to prison. (According to a report at the Louder website, something like 50 hours of recordings were made and filed away, never to be used.)

Malcolm had been there before, during the interminable sessions that (very slowly) produced *For Those About to Rock*. He would admit, in a 2000 interview with *Le Monde,* that 'working with [Rubin] was a mistake'. It came as no shock when rumours circulated that Malcolm and Rubin had clashed. They certainly didn't work together again, although Malcolm did give Rubin the gift of a guitar at the end of the recording. 'Well, he is such a big fan,' Malcolm conceded.

Despite the dramas, the commercial reaction to *Ballbreaker* was very upbeat, and Malcolm's rehiring of Phil Rudd was clearly the right move. The initial shipment of the album was 2.5 million copies, and that didn't include Australia (where it debuted at number 1 and sold 35,000 copies the day of its 26 September 1995 release). It reached number 4 on the US chart, number 6 in the UK and the top of various European charts. *Entertainment Weekly* was again on board, fully embracing the band's character flaws, stating that their 'adolescent male fantasies and equally adenoidal riffs are simple pleasures that have stood the test of time'. US *Rolling Stone* wasn't so sure, noting that 'AC/DC still view the world through the mind of a horny 15-year-old'. Again, Bon Scott's absence was deeply felt—at least *his* fantasies, if he was still alive, would have been viewed through the eyes of a horny 49-year-old.

Malcolm usually kept his politics to himself, but he did have something to rebel against with a track on the album called 'Burnin' Alive'. The song was inspired, in part, by the gruesome scenes at the Waco compound of the Branch Davidians, where 76 cult members burned to death after an FBI assault in 1993. But when Malcolm was asked about the song, he steered the conversation in a different direction:

political correctness, especially the anti-smoking movement that was in full force in much of the Western world.

'I don't mind if [political correctness] doesn't interfere with you on the street, but the day they screw around with your cigarettes and everything else—and there's a lot of cigarettes smoked in AC/DC . . . I just don't like being told what to do, basically like anyone.'

Couldn't a guy just have one bad habit and not be made to feel like a leper?

The ensuing *Ballbreaker* world tour was so big it was split into seven individual legs. The 155 shows consumed almost a full year of the band's life—Malcolm saw very little of Onkaparinga during the mid-1990s. As the band's live production values got even bigger—their latest show began with a large wrecking ball bashing away at the stage, forming a hole, from which the band would emerge to play 'Back in Black', as well as a cameo from MTV mall rats Beavis and Butthead—so did their box office takings. The opening 25 shows of the first US leg of the tour grossed somewhere between US$300,000 and US$500,000 every night, with crowds ranging from 10,000 to 20,000. Close to another US$4 million was generated during the month of March 1996 alone, during the second US leg. Almost every night ended with a triple shot of Bon Scott–era rock-and-roll magic: 'Whole Lotta Rosie', 'T.N.T.' and 'Let There Be Rock'.

But as with seemingly every AC/DC tour since *Back in Black,* there was a sacking, when their latest manager, Stewart Young, was fired. Malcolm decided they could look after themselves from now on, with a little help from business manager Alvin Handwerker.

★

The money was fabulous, and Malcolm may have become a member of rock's wealthy elite, but he'd never really escaped his roots—the hand-to-mouth days—as he admitted a few years later in a discussion with Canadian magazine *BW&BK*.

'You don't forget [where you come from]. I get amazed a bit sometimes when you see a lot of young bands who've come up from tough parts of town, especially the rap guys. You see them just buying everything straight away and then six months later they've no more hits, no more money. Scots are thrifty, you know. We're not tight, but we do know what the value of a dollar is.'

Malcolm was asked if he still felt the same onstage spark that he did when he first formed the band:

If it's a good night it's like the first night: same buzz, same excitement. We used to do 15, 16 shows in a week when we first started. We were never fresh: there was a lot of BO going around. The stages have gotten bigger, we fly everywhere, the hotels are nicer, but we still remember getting on stage when there were 20 kids out there and playing like there were 20,000. We always try our hardest, no matter how we feel, that's what keeps us going.

So, was Malcolm ready for the gold watch? By the end of the *Ballbreaker* tour he was almost 44, a middle-aged man playing young men's music. He laughed off the suggestion; after all, what about The Rolling Stones? How old were they? If The Stones could keep touring—and their most recent Voodoo Lounge Tour had grossed a staggering US$320 million—why not Malcolm and AC/DC?

'They're about ten years, fifteen years older than us guys,' Malcolm chuckled, 'so we've still got a long way to go . . . I don't think there is any retirement in the music industry. I don't really know anyone that's retired. If they have, it means nobody wanted them anyway. With most musicians it's like the *Titanic,* they go down with the ship.'

Malcolm's big goal had never changed: he was still chasing that raw, primal sound that his first musical heroes, the first wave of rockers, captured so brilliantly.

'We would love to get something, somewhere near what the guys in the '50s were doing. Not sound-wise, but the quality of the rock and roll. You know back then they had it all, the swing and all that stuff that gets kids up these days. AC/DC play basically what was going on with Chuck Berry, Little Richard, Jerry Lee Lewis—trying to create the excitement and get the mood. We want to keep the flag flyin'.'

But the end of the road was slowly sneaking up on Malcolm Young.

23

'When they said to go, we fucking took off . . .
We ripped the place apart.'

Like the rest of the band, Malcolm wasn't much for red carpets—never had been, never would be. For Malcolm, rock and roll was work; it was about getting the job done. He had no time for flash, for poncing about. As far as he was concerned, a red carpet was a place where you stubbed out cigarette butts when you were in the studio.

But he did make one exception.

There'd been whispers for years that the band was to be inducted into the Rock and Roll Hall of Fame. Of all the musical institutions, this was the only one that Malcolm rated—after all, its original inductees read like a name-check of all his favourite artists: Chuck Berry, Jerry Lee Lewis, Little Richard, Fats Domino, Buddy Holly and Elvis had all been inducted in 1986, the first year of the awards.

In 2002, after the band had completed yet another prosperous lap of the globe, promoting their new record *Stiff Upper Lip*—the tour grossed almost $30 million—they were told that although they'd been on the ballot for the latest inductions, they'd been passed over. (Instead, nods went to the Ramones, Tom Petty and the Heartbreakers, and Talking Heads.) Angus was asked if he was disappointed; after all, they were now the fifth-highest–selling band of all time, behind The Beatles, Pink Floyd, Led Zeppelin and the Eagles, all of whom had already been welcomed into this elite club. Surely they were worthy.

'I've never been a person that worried about prizes,' Angus told *Wall of Sound*, 'because they devalue the currency sometimes . . . With AC/DC, we were never a band to seek out accolades.'

Finally, though, in March 2003, word came through: this time they were in, along with The Clash, Elvis Costello & the Attractions, The Police and The Righteous Brothers. The Hall of Fame blurb that accompanied AC/DC's induction was high-quality hype, despite a few facts slipping past the proofreader (for one thing, Malcolm had formed the band in 1973).

Under the heading 'Consistency, Thy Name is AC/DC', it was made abundantly clear that this may not have been a band interested in variety, but they understood their craft. 'Since 1975 [sic],' read the release, 'the Australian band have churned out album after album full of scorched-earth, metallic hard rock which has rarely deviated from a template of headbanging-inducing guitar riffs, flashy drums and banshee-yell vocals.'

But therein lay the magic of AC/DC, citing such standards as 'Back in Black', 'Highway to Hell' and 'You Shook Me All Night Long' as songs that have inspired budding guitar heroes and fans all around the world.

The late Bon Scott was to be inducted with the band, but bassist Mark Evans, who played on many of their seminal recordings, was not, for reasons that were never made clear. One of Angus's uniforms was enshrined behind glass at the Hall of Fame museum in Cleveland, Ohio, along with Bon Scott's sloppy handwritten lyrics for 'Highway to Hell'.

On Malcolm's request, Steven Tyler from Aerosmith, who'd toured with AC/DC when they were making their earliest US sorties in the mid-1970s, agreed to give the induction speech at the ceremony at New York's Waldorf Astoria. He and Tyler had history, all of it good. Malcolm had never forgotten that it was Tyler who helped get them a spot on the influential TV show *Midnight Special* in 1978. There was also an offstage incident that Malcolm had stored away.

'What really sealed it,' Malcolm told *Billboard*, 'was when we were on a gig with Foreigner, who had a big hit record at the time and it was a big stadium. Aerosmith was on it, too. Foreigner didn't want us on there for one reason or another, and it was Steven Tyler who said, "Well, if you're gonna drop them, we're not playing either." I thought that was brilliant.' This was the same backstage incident that resulted in then-manager Michael Browning almost slugging it out with Bud Prager, who looked after Foreigner.

And as induction speeches went, Tyler's was a doozy.

Shades firmly in place, the seemingly ageless Tyler (he was just about to turn 55) made his point straight away: AC/DC mattered. 'There is no greater purveyor of [the] power chord than AC/DC,' he declared. He cited the 'primal stink' of 'You Shook Me All Night Long', 'the sparks that flew off' *Back in Black* and 'that thunder from Down Under'. Allegedly quoting directly from Angus, Tyler somehow managed to work the terms 'gobful', 'bloody whingers', 'bushpig', 'hard yakka' and 'no worries mate' into the same sentence—no small achievement. As funny as his speech was, Tyler didn't overlook the loss of 'the great singer Bon Scott', 'the worst kind of tragedy imaginable'. He inducted the band 'on behalf of Aerosmith and every kid who has ever rocked his ass off'.

It was impossible to miss Malcolm when he and the band stepped onto the podium. He was the only one wearing a blue singlet and jeans; there'd be no monkey suit for him. Johnson took on the role of band spokesman, but it seemed as though Malcolm might have written his speech, especially the closer: 'Mainly this award is for the fans all around the world who have stuck with us through thick and thin.' No fans, no AC/DC. Simple as that. Malcolm's family looked on proudly from the audience.

Malcolm and the band looked far more comfortable performing, although they'd probably never played to an audience that featured so many suits, ties and evening gowns. They pumped out a thunderous 'Highway to Hell', Johnson screaming himself hoarse. It turned out that the added muscle that went into their performance was a form of venting. While they had been waiting to play, U2's The Edge made a speech in honour of the late Joe Strummer from fellow inductees The Clash. His speech went on, and on, and on, much like one of his guitar solos.

'We were at the side [of the stage], waiting and getting madder and madder,' Malcolm told *Metal Hammer* magazine. 'When they said to go, we fucking took off . . . We ripped the place apart.' A loose-limbed Steve Tyler joined them onstage for a furious 'You Shook Me All Night Long'; he even enticed Angus to bark some backing vocals.

Malcolm, typically, downplayed the significance of the award, pointing out to a writer from *Billboard* that it had been a long time coming. 'We came up for it a few times and we were rejected. So it's a bit of a sweet thing in a way, but to us it's not an honour. We just had to go through with it, in a way; I think it might have been better if we were ignored again!'

The following night Malcolm and the band were in far more comfortable territory, playing a special show for 3000 contest winners at New York's Roseland Ballroom. Steve Tyler hung about for the show; piano man Billy Joel joined him in the wings.

★

It had already been a stellar year for Malcolm. A few weeks before their Hall of Fame induction, Malcolm got a call saying that The Rolling Stones wanted him and Angus to jam with them. The mere idea that this band that he regarded as a touchstone, that he'd first seen all the way back in 1973 at Randwick Racecourse, would call on him to play was a dream fulfilled. This was no support slot; they were being treated as equals, as peers.

In February 2003, The Stones were in Australia in the midst of their Licks Tour, which—aside from the usual monstrous stadium gigs—also included shows at small venues, an attempt on the band's part to keep it a little more real and actually see the faces of the people in their audience.

The last time Keith Richards had fronted a Sydney press conference, he was at his elegantly wasted worst, giving local reporters a hefty serve, snarling as he declared: 'You're known as the most inhospitable country.' But in 2003 it was a mellower Richards; when a reporter mentioned AC/DC, the man known as The Human Riff lit up.

'I love Acca-Dacca,' he declared. 'Angus and Malcolm . . . a great team, man.'

Richards, of course, was a massive fan of their *Powerage* record, the album most often cited by hardcore AC/DC fans as their very best.

When The Stones, who had a show booked at the Enmore Theatre on 19 February, learned that the Youngs were also in Sydney, their guitarist Ronnie Wood reached out to them with a simple message: 'Wanna jam?'

Now, the Youngs weren't going to jam with just anybody; they rarely let anyone share their stage, let alone do the celebrity rock thing with others. But this was The Stones, after all; this was different.

Well into their set at the Enmore, Mick Jagger welcomed the Youngs onto the stage.

Before going on, Malcolm had given everyone a simple direction: 'I'll be standing behind Ronnie [Wood].' And that's exactly where he positioned himself, dressed in his usual street gear, as the ensemble tore into the old BB King blues number 'Rock Me Baby'. The sight of four legendary guitarists—Malcolm, Angus, Richards and Wood—crouched low, rocking hard, was every rock lover's dream come true. The 1600 fans inside the Enmore Theatre couldn't believe their eyes, or their ears.

As the song continued, Angus buddied up with Keith Richards, swapping licks; then, with a gentle shove from Jagger, Angus took centrestage, playing hard and wiggling his bony arse at the crowd. When Jagger also prompted Malcolm to have a turn up front, he demurred. That wasn't his style; he liked to stick to the shadows. Angus could have the spotlight—what Malcolm referred to as the 'dusty end' of the stage. He didn't need it.

Stones drummer Charlie Watts, who normally expressed little emotion while he played, couldn't suppress a grin throughout the jam. (He even reached down from his podium and hugged Malcolm when they did it again in Toronto later in the year.) 'There's no pretence to it,' Watts said afterwards, when asked about the Youngs. 'And they're funny, aren't they?'

The loose and ragged jam was a joy; The Stones were so impressed that they invited the Youngs back to do it again the next night, and then asked if the entire band would be interested in four northern summer dates. Malcolm still had a set-in-stone policy that AC/DC supported no one, and he'd knocked back The Stones in 1981, but this time he relented: they were in. The money, which had to have been substantial, wouldn't hurt either.

The Enmore Theatre jams were great: the venue was small, and the mood was mellow and loose. But the northern summer dates were another thing altogether—shows rarely got any bigger. AC/DC had regularly been filling arenas in the US, but these stadiums were more like entire suburbs, an endless sea of faces. It seemed that everywhere Malcolm looked there was another Stones 'tongue and lip' logo on yet another T-shirt—one even adorned the stages on which they played. In Oberhausen they drew 70,000 fans, in Leipzig 65,000 and in Hockenheim 75,000 punters showed up.

In the hour of stage time they were allotted, AC/DC needed to work even harder than usual to win over such huge crowds—there were no cannons, Angus statues or

'All we did was go straight into the studio after doing the night's gig and knock up some new ideas.' Malcolm at work in 1976, recording *Dirty Deeds*.

AC/DC in 1978, two years before Bon Scott's death. 'You can't explain a death and how it affects you,' said Malcolm. 'Everything is numb.'

'The notorious Young brothers': Malcolm with Angus in Germany 1992.

Beachside before playing Rock in Rio, with new singer Brian Johnson (far left) and drummer Simon Wright (second from left), January 1985.

'The best right hand in the business.' Malcolm in action, Melbourne Park, 12 February 2001.

MARTIN PHILBEY

MARTIN PHILBEY

Also from the Melbourne Park show in 2001.

Malcolm's impressive family home, Onkaparinga, in the Sydney suburb of East Balmain. His neighbours would hear him playing guitar and know he was home.

Malcolm (far left) with the band, including a re-instated Phil Rudd (second from right), at London's Apollo Hammersmith, March 2003.

Malcolm signing autographs outside Berlin's Regent Hotel, June 2010, during the Black Ice world tour, his final journey with the band.

Guns N' Roses pay tribute to Malcolm Young on the day he died, 18 November 2017, during a show at Sacramento in California. '[He] will be sorely missed,' said their frontman Axl Rose, who stood in for Brian Johnson during the latter shows of the Rock or Bust tour.

Angus carries his brother's guitar, while pallbearers carry his body, on the day of Malcolm's funeral service at Sydney's St Mary's Cathedral, 28 November 2017. Malcolm's son Ross is to Angus's right.

Malcolm in Germany in 1995. He didn't have time for a lot of other rock bands. 'They don't understand the feel, the movement, you know, *the jungle of it all.*'

huge inflatable Rosie props to get people in the mood. When Justin Timberlake played on the bill in Toronto, impatient Stones fans hurled water bottles and toilet paper at the former Disney boy wonder. They were a tough crowd—and maybe Timberlake's Harley T-shirt was a touch too much for the audience. The boy was trying too hard.

That Toronto show was staged on 30 July at Downsview Park, the same site that had hosted Pope John Paul II the previous year. Now it was a shrine to pagan rock and roll. The gig was staged to help raise money for a city whose economy had been hit hard by the SARS virus—there'd been 42 deaths—and it drew a crowd of half a million. Even Mick Jagger was taken aback; he said it was possibly the biggest audience he'd ever fronted (although AC/DC had drawn a bigger crowd in Moscow in 1991, which was either close to, or well over, a million fans, depending on the source). As for Keith Richards, he had memories of Toronto that he'd rather forget: he'd been busted for heroin possession there in 1977 and had barely escaped doing hard time.

In a nod to the locals, Angus dropped his pants late in their set during 'The Jack' and revealed a snazzy pair of boxers adorned with a maple leaf. Even the strictly businesslike Malcolm, decked out in the same singlet-and-jeans combo he'd been favouring since about 1975, allowed himself a smirk. In honour of Bon Scott, the band dusted off 'If You Want Blood (You've Got It)', which they hadn't played since Scott's death. And it seemed as though every single person in the sprawling crowd joined in during the chant that opened 'Thunderstruck', Angus sweating up a storm while he worked hard on the song's 'deadly' opening. Plenty of bare boobs and exposed six-packs could be seen in the audience; it was a blazing hot summer's day in Toronto.

Just before The Stones took the stage, the MC made an announcement: 'You have been part of the greatest event in concert and music history worldwide.' Okay, maybe it was a bit of a stretch, but looking out over the huge gathering, at that moment it was hard to argue with the man.

AC/DC continued to jam 'Rock Me Baby' with The Stones during subsequent gigs. By the time the roadshow reached Leipzig in Germany on 20 June, the four flying guitarists had locked into something that vaguely resembled choreography: Malcolm would pair up with Richards, Angus with Wood, and they'd unleash riff after riff, lick upon lick, while Jagger flailed and gyrated nearby like a demented flamenco dancer. (In Toronto, Malcolm also squared up with The Stones' burly bassist, Darryl Jones; they were a study in contrasts.) What had started out as a bit of a laugh had fast become a highlight of the night. The mile-wide grins on the faces of The Stones, let alone the Youngs, said loads: 'Rock Me Baby' was a blast. The huge crowds loved it, too; a fan at their 22 June show in Hockenheim was moved to write: 'Thank you Mick and Angus and Malcolm for giving us "Rock Me Baby" yesterday, another highlight in my personal 25-years collection of Rolling Stones. What an absolute outstanding performance.'

On stage, Malcolm still looked good, if a little shaggy. His face may have been lined and his eyes seemed to come with their own baggage, but next to Keith Richards, whose facial wrinkles resembled crevices, he almost looked sprightly.

It may have only been four shows, but those gigs were a career high for Malcolm. It wasn't about simply playing with The Stones; now his heroes rated AC/DC, *his* band, as equals. Only the best were invited on stage by The Stones.

'Their tightness always impressed me,' Keith Richards said afterwards. 'Bless their hearts, what a great little bundle of energy they are.'

Maybe Malcolm had been right all those years before; perhaps there really were only two true rock-and-roll bands: 'The Stones and us'.

24

'I won't be able to do it anymore.'

It was Angus who first noticed the changes in his brother. It was early 2008, and he and Malcolm were working on new songs in advance of the band convening at the Warehouse Studio in Vancouver, Canada (owned by rock singer Bryan Adams), to start work on their fifteenth studio album. They hadn't made a record since 2000's *Stiff Upper Lip*, also recorded at the Warehouse, which had been co-produced by brother George. (They'd hoped to work again with 'gentleman' Bruce Fairbairn on that album, but the producer had died suddenly in 1999, aged just 49.)

In 2003, in the wake of *Stiff Upper Lip*, the band signed a new record deal that saw them switch from Atlantic Records to Columbia Records. Columbia was a giant of a label, but also provided AC/DC with some unlikely new peers: Bob Dylan, Billy Joel, Barbra Streisand, Bruce Springsteen and Destiny's Child among them. The label was projecting that revenue from the band would be somewhere around $50 million over the subsequent five years.

Black Ice, as the new album would be named, wasn't an

easy record to make. Bassist Cliff Williams injured his hand in 2005 and was unable to play for eighteen months. Angus and Malcolm, meanwhile, had begun throwing around song ideas when Angus sensed that something was up with Malcolm—'strange things . . . memory things', as he would later describe them.

Angus once told a reporter that he and Malcolm shared what he described as 'a psychic thing', an intricate understanding of each other's nature, especially when they played together, so it was natural that he would be the first to notice any changes in his brother. And the change that Angus noticed was huge. Malcolm knew how to play guitar better than just about anybody in rock, but he was having trouble in the studio. Simple performance issues, guitar basics, were eluding him. He was also forgetful and confused at times, something that Angus had never seen before. Malcolm had always been the organised one in the band.

'It was strange,' Angus said when he discussed Malcolm's condition with a reporter from ABC TV's *7.30* program in 2014. 'For the first time I saw him disorganised. That's when it hit me that something was not right with him.'

Malcolm consulted a specialist in the US, whose diagnosis was cerebral atrophy—'shrinkage of the brain', typically a condition of the elderly, rather than of a 55-year-old. He prescribed medication and provided Malcolm with what Angus described as 'good care, the best treatment'.

There may well have been signs that Malcolm's health was failing even earlier than 2008. As their tours grew in size and scope, the band were using big (and even bigger) video monitors, but Malcolm was rarely seen on screen; typically it was all about the Angus and Brian show. And on the rare occasions Malcolm did appear, he tended to look slightly disorientated, even a bit bewildered.

When the *Black Ice* record was finished, another mammoth world tour was set in place: 168 shows comprising eleven legs, starting in Pennsylvania in late October 2008 and slowly winding its way to Bilbao, Spain, for the final show in late June 2010. It was more like a military campaign than a rock-and-roll tour: band and crew would cover 29 countries, play to some five million fans and rake in mind-boggling amounts of money.

But even before the tour began, Angus knew he had to talk with Malcolm, to check that he was physically and mentally ready for such a grind. This was a long and demanding tour, and they hadn't been on the road since 2001, outside of those few dates with The Rolling Stones in 2003. Was he up for it?

Malcolm's response was emphatic. 'Shit yeah. I'll keep going until I can't.'

Angus knew his brother well enough not to question his commitment. But he also knew what Malcolm was committing to: this wasn't some quick lap of honour or a hit-and-run promo tour for the new record. Malcolm's decision to continue was every bit as crucial as the choice they had to make when Bon Scott died.

'Malcolm always wanted to finish what he started,' said Angus. 'He always had that drive.'

For Malcolm's part, he understood that a lot of people depended on the band, not only fans, but crew and many others. To drop out of a tour, perhaps even cancel the entire shebang, would have dire financial consequences. (Malcolm may have been rich, but he still watched every dollar.) And also, because they hadn't toured for so long, Malcolm probably felt it important that AC/DC remind the world that they could still bring the noise—and he wanted to be part of that.

Mind you, AC/DC supporters had been doing their own cheerleading during the band's absence. In 2006, Australian punk rockers Frenzal Rhomb released a song and an album called *Forever Malcolm Young* (key lyric: 'Always Malcolm, never Angus'), while AC/DC had ranked fourth on VH1's '100 Greatest Artists of Hard Rock' poll. AC/DC came in at number 72 on a US *Rolling Stone* poll of 'The 100 Greatest Artists of All Time' and *Back in Black* continued to sell and sell, inching its way towards becoming the highest-selling album ever by a hard rock band.

AC/DC's new label, meanwhile, had been rolling out remastered and revamped issues of the band's now substantial back catalogue, all essential purchases for serious AC/DC fans. It also didn't hurt the group's legacy that seemingly every new rock band to emerge—from The Hives to The Strokes and The Vines and Jet—name-checked AC/DC as a major influence. They were hardly silent during their break from the stage, even if they didn't play a note.

★

Yet as the *Black Ice* tour progressed, those close to Malcolm could clearly see that he was fading. In the past, he'd never felt the need to rehearse before playing, but on every night of the tour he'd sit backstage and work through songs that he knew inside out, songs he'd played hundreds of times— thousands of times, in some instances. 'Whole Lotta Rosie', 'The Jack' and 'Highway to Hell' were permanent fixtures in AC/DC sets, as were 'Dirty Deeds' and 'Let There Be Rock', songs Malcolm had been playing for too many years to remember. The set list rarely changed, which eased the pressure on Malcolm just a touch, but it was still tough going.

Occasionally singer Brian Johnson would shoot a look in Malcolm's direction to ensure he was doing okay. But Johnson knew Malcolm very well and realised that his condition was not a subject open for discussion. 'You couldn't say anything or do anything,' Johnson explained, 'because it would have been like giving pity.' And pity was the last thing that the strong-willed, madly determined Malcolm needed.

'You had to treat it like a normal day,' Johnson explained. 'So we did.'

As Angus told *Rolling Stone,* Malcolm 'was still capable of knowing what he wanted to do'. When Angus asked if he wanted to continue, his reply was classic Malcolm: 'Shit, yeah!'

There were bad nights on tour, times when Angus felt as though 'it was not Malcolm with me'. He was starting to look lost on stage, out of step with the others. 'He'd have a really great day,' said Angus, 'and he'd be Malcolm again. And other times, his mind was going. But he still held it together.'

Angus was the only one who could broach the subject with his brother. All Malcolm offered him in reply was a simple, 'I have good days and bad days.'

The final show of the tour was at San Mamés Stadium in Bilbao, Spain, on 28 June 2010. In front of 37,000 screaming fans—tickets had sold out in a remarkable four hours—Malcolm was his old defiant self, decked out in his singlet and jeans, hitting the strings hard (he'd work his way through as many as 50 guitar picks a night). The camera caught him briefly during 'For Those About to Rock', and while Malcolm still cradled his Gretsch guitar as though it had been born in his arms, there was an undeniably hollow look in his eyes. He was doing the job, but he seemed to be working harder, pushing himself even more than usual, just to get through the gig. He looked much older than his 55 years.

Not that the crowd noticed, or minded: all Malcolm would have been able to see from the stage was row upon row of bobbing heads, most of them sporting glowing red devil horns, Angus's latest trademark. Thousands of fists were raised in the air. It was a rock-and-roll love-in.

On stage in Bilbao, 'For Those About to Rock' thundered to a close, the cannons exploded one final time and the crowd began chanting for more, but by then Malcolm and the band had left the building. Fittingly, the gig was held at a football stadium, the home ground of Athletic Bilbao. Malcolm may have never played that Cup Final he'd dreamed about as a kid, but he'd filled his share of football stadiums with AC/DC.

Despite the difficulties behind the scenes, the Black Ice tour was big business: the band reaped an amazing $441.6 million at the box office, making it the fourth-highest grossing concert tour of all time. At the time of writing it's been pipped only by Roger Waters' The Wall Live ($459 million), The Stones' A Bigger Bang ($558 million), and U2's 360 Tour, which cashed in at $736 million. Malcolm had come a hell of a long way from the days of shared houses and a weekly wage of $60. But Bilbao was the last show he'd ever play.

★

Malcolm may have survived the tour, but bad news wasn't far away. Not long after the tour wound down he was diagnosed with a serious lung problem—'like a cancer', according to Angus—and underwent an operation, which Angus described to *GMI Rock* as 'critical'. Fortunately, the problem was detected early, but as he slowly recovered from that operation he was then diagnosed with a heart condition, which required the installation of a pacemaker.

'It was like everything hit him at once,' said Angus.

Brian Johnson visited Malcolm in hospital, and it was an experience he'd never forget. When Johnson came into the room, he was taken aback when Malcolm took his hand and thumped it repeatedly against his chest at the spot where he'd had a pacemaker installed. Malcolm reassured him the operation had been a success; the pacemaker was 'fucking good!' Johnson was a bit stunned, but as he admitted, it was 'typical Malcolm'. 'There was a twinkle in his eye. He was tickled pink. It was like he was showing us a new fuzzbox or something.'

Malcolm's doctors may have been able to address two life-threatening conditions in rapid succession, but they couldn't halt his mental deterioration. It was around this time, in early 2014, just as the band started talking about making another record, that Malcolm spoke with Angus. 'I won't be able to do it anymore,' he admitted.

It was a huge admission, especially for someone as doggedly determined as Malcolm.

It said a lot about the Youngs' protection of their privacy that nothing emerged about Malcolm's worsening condition until the band returned to the spotlight, in late 2014, to commence work on a new studio album, *Rock or Bust*.

By this time, Malcolm and his family were permanent residents, finally, of their Balmain mansion, where Malcolm was receiving in-home care. But he was having trouble recalling familiar faces, even communicating, and his wife began considering full-time care. His old friend from Velvet Underground days Herm Kovac caught up with Malcolm. 'He didn't look well,' Kovac recalled.

O'linda eventually settled on Lulworth House, a high-end care facility in Sydney's Eastern Suburbs, which had been the final residence of former prime minister Gough Whitlam, former New South Wales premier Neville Wran, and legendary entrepreneur Harry M. Miller. The 154-bed facility was located in a heritage-listed house, built in 1870, formerly the childhood home of Nobel Prize–winning author Patrick White. Top-end care ran to around $120,000 per year. O'linda became upset when she learned that the press had discovered where Malcolm was receiving treatment; she was very concerned about maintaining not just Malcolm's privacy but the privacy of all the Lulworth residents.

In early 2015, by which time Malcolm had moved into Lulworth House, news hit the real estate pages that the Youngs had dropped around $10 million on a waterfront Palm Beach home, which they had picked up from a retired mining executive. To protect the family's privacy, the purchase was conducted in O'linda's name. Sometimes Malcolm would leave Lulworth temporarily to spend time in Palm Beach with his family. And family became even more important to Malcolm as his health declined.

The Youngs released a short, sharp statement regarding Malcolm's condition. 'Malcolm is suffering from dementia and the family thanks you for respecting their privacy.' It was also revealed that Malcolm, as so many recent rumours had suggested, would not be returning to the band; he was now officially retired. Nephew Stevie again returned to take his place, just as he'd done back in 1988 when Malcolm was getting treatment for alcoholism. AC/DC would always be a family affair.

Alberts, the band's business and spiritual home since 1974, also released a statement that, like one of Malcolm's million-dollar riffs, got straight to the point. 'Unfortunately, due to the nature of Malcolm's illness,' it read, 'he will not be re-joining the band.'

It said a lot about Malcolm's commitment to the band, however, that he did contribute as a writer to *Rock or Bust,* which would be released in late November 2014. Malcolm and Angus co-wrote each of the album's eleven tracks, which were put together before Malcolm's condition made it impossible for him to continue playing. It seemed fitting that four of the album's tracks contained the word 'rock' in their title.

Malcolm didn't play on the record; nephew Stevie stood in for him. Brian Johnson admitted it was an odd experience: 'It was a strange feeling; my workmate of the past 35 years wasn't there anymore.' But, thankfully, as Johnson added, Stevie had the right stuff. 'They've got music running in their blood, these guys.'

*

But there were other problems within the band during the making of *Rock or Bust.* Drummer Phil Rudd, who'd rejoined the band in the mid-1990s, was in trouble. Big trouble. In May 2014, when sessions for the new record were scheduled to begin in Vancouver, Rudd was a no-show. Not much had been seen of Rudd since the end of the Black Ice tour; back in New Zealand he'd opened a restaurant in Tauranga, simply named Phil's Place.

A week passed and still no Rudd. Just as the band was preparing to send him a 'turn up or don't bother' ultimatum, he arrived. It was quite a shock.

'I've seen him in better shape,' Angus said, in an understatement. 'It was not the Phil we'd known . . . he'd let himself go.'

The man once described as 'quite the swank young jackeroo' now looked more like a homeless person. Still, he got the job done in Vancouver, but went AWOL again in October, missing a video and photo shoot.

In early November, news arrived from New Zealand: after an early-morning police raid on Rudd's waterfront home in Tauranga, he'd been arrested for 'attempting to procure the murder of two men'. He was also charged with possession of pot and methamphetamine (which may have explained his disturbing new look). The first charge was dropped, although the drug charges and a 'threatening to kill' charge remained. (Rudd was eventually given eight months home detention and ordered to pay NZ$120,000 in reparations.)

The band issued a press release: 'We've only become aware of Phil's arrest as the news was breaking . . . Phil's absence will not affect the release of our new album *Rock or Bust* and our upcoming tour next year.'

What that meant was that Rudd was fired, again, and Chris Slade was brought back into the fold, also for the second time.

It was a minor miracle that the Rock or Bust tour actually happened, or that it proved to be such a windfall for the band, because even more dramas followed the loss of Malcolm, and Rudd's exit. Singer Johnson was the next to experience misfortune. He was forced to pull out of the tour with 22 dates remaining of the planned 88 shows, after being told he risked losing his hearing if he played one more show. Guns N' Roses singer Axl Rose offered his services but broke his foot days before his debut; he was forced to play his first few shows with the band while seated on a modified rock-and-roll 'throne'. Then long-time bassist Cliff Williams, perhaps the quietest man in one of the world's loudest bands, made it known that this would be his last hurrah; he was retiring. He'd done everything he'd hoped to do with AC/DC, and considerably more. And, of course, Malcolm's absence loomed over the tour like a long, dark shadow, despite the presence of his doppelganger, nephew Stevie.

By tour's end, Angus was the only original member of AC/DC remaining.

It seemed a strange, messy way for the band to go about its business, yet AC/DC's rusted-on fans didn't appear to mind: the tour grossed some US$221 million. The album was number 1 in thirteen different countries and reached number 3 in the US and the UK. Over time, it sold close to three million copies—and this at a time when record sales had dipped dramatically. Even during its darkest hour, the band had somehow managed to stay on top.

25

'And most important of all, thanks to Mal, who made it
all possible.'

Malcolm's tragic downward spiral was briefly overshadowed
when news broke on 22 October 2017 that George Young
had died. He was 70. A frank, heartfelt statement quickly
appeared on behalf of AC/DC, making it clear that the band
wouldn't have existed if it weren't for George's 'help and
guidance'. Just as significantly, he was Malcolm and Angus's
big brother right to the end; it'd always been about family
for the Youngs.

'You could not ask for a finer brother,' read the statement.
'For all he did and gave to us throughout his life, we will
always remember him with gratitude and hold him close to
our hearts.'

The 'godfather of Australian rock and roll', Michael
Gudinski, rightfully described Vanda and Young as 'the
greatest production team in Australian music history'. Harry
Vanda, George's long-time partner in sound, kept it simple:
'Rest in peace, my dear friend.'

Alberts also released an official statement; in describing
George, they may as well have been talking about Ted

Albert, the man who, along with Vanda and Young, helped kickstart the AC/DC juggernaut back in the early 1970s. They praised George as a true gentleman 'who was unfailingly modest, charming, intelligent and loyal—a man with a wonderful sense of humour'. They also described George as a pioneer, just like his mentor Ted Albert, who helped create a 'new sound for the Australian music industry'.

Little had been heard of George since he'd worked with Malcolm and Angus on 2000's *Stiff Upper Lip*, which proved to be his final production. George spent most of his time living in semi-retired seclusion in Lisbon, Portugal, with his wife, Sandra, and daughter, Yvette. George said he liked it there because not only did people not know who he was, even if they knew, they simply didn't care. That suited him perfectly; he was as protective of his privacy as Malcolm and Angus were. The cause of George's death was not publicly reported.

★

Around the time of George's death, images had been published of Malcolm, apparently taken in May 2015, when he was spotted walking in Kings Cross not far from Lulworth (these were the images that had upset his wife O'linda). Malcolm wore a dark beanie, blue jeans and a hoodie, and was accompanied by a carer who appeared to be supporting him. In one shot it was clear the man was holding Malcolm's hand, guiding him along the street. It was almost impossible to recognise Malcolm as the same tough nut with the big guitar commanding his space on the stage with the rest of AC/DC, making the kind of noise that could raise the dead.

He looked far, far away, perhaps even already gone. It was heartbreaking.

The shock of George's death had barely sunk in when the news that everyone feared was made public: Malcolm passed away on 17 November. Dementia had taken him. He was 64.

A statement was released under the band's moniker on Facebook, which outlined how Malcolm—husband to O'linda, father to Cara and Ross, proud grandfather of three—had passed away peacefully, having suffered from dementia, with his family nearby. He'd 'inspired many', the release observed, stating how he and Angus never gave less than 'their all' every time they played. The family asked that rather than sending flowers, mourners should make a donation to the Salvation Army.

As soon as news of Malcolm's death broke, tributes poured in thick and fast. Australian *Rolling Stone* dedicated the bulk of their December issue to Malcolm (it had initially been planned as a tribute to George Young). On the front cover was a stark shot of a youthful but deadly serious Malcolm. 'Malcolm Young / 1953 2017' was the simple caption. Fittingly, a lightning bolt separated the years of his birth and death.

'Music lovers worldwide . . . are now saluting AC/DC guitarist Malcolm Young,' read the announcement in the *Sydney Morning Herald*. '[AC/DC] is arguably the nation's greatest ever musical export and is still one of the biggest acts in the world.' The *Herald* cited *The Guardian*'s Michael Hann, who explained that 'clarity' was the key to a great riff, something that Malcolm understood completely. He also mentioned that fans might be startled, given how loud the band were in concert, that Malcolm, when recording, was the opposite. 'He played with his amps turned down, but with the mics extremely close.' This was the reason, Hann explained, why on their records you didn't just hear riffs or chords, 'but their very texture, their burnished, rounded sound. It's why AC/DC are immediately recognisable, whether or not you know the song'.

In an obituary I wrote for *The Australian,* I spoke about the working-class roots that Malcolm never forgot, despite his impressive wealth (which at the time of his death sat somewhere upwards of A$100 million). I cited an interview Malcolm gave to US *Rolling Stone* in 2008, where he summed up his attitude perfectly. 'I've never felt like a pop star—this is a nine-to-five sort of gig. It comes from working in the factories, that world. You don't forget it.'

I also related a key conversation Malcolm had had with new recruit Mark Evans in 1975, which showed just how determined he was to get the band onto the world stage. 'We'll be in the UK in a year,' he had told Evans.

'I didn't think there was a snowball's chance in hell of the band being in the UK within a year,' Evans later wrote in his memoir *Dirty Deeds,* 'and I was dead right. It would take a year and 10 days.'

Jon Michaud wrote a heartfelt tribute for *The New Yorker,* in which he flashed back to 1978 and asked his readers, just for a moment, to look away from the Angus and Bon show, and observe the 'pugnacious long-haired kid (he looks like he's still in high school), wearing jeans and a white T-shirt', who was strumming his guitar and 'shaking his leg in time to the driving beat'. This was Malcolm Young, the 'mastermind of the whole operation, at once its visionary and its taskmaster. He is the soul of the band, its leader on and off the stage'.

Writing on his *Brian Johnson Racing* website, the long-time singer of AC/DC cast his mind back over the 32 years he had stood with Malcolm on stage. 'I am saddened by the passing of my friend Malcolm Young, I can't believe he's gone.' Johnson extended his heartfelt sympathies to the Young family, and also touched on Malcolm's uncomfortable relationship with fame: 'He never liked the celebrity side . . . he was too humble for that.

'I was always aware that he was a genius on guitar, his riffs have become legend, as has he. He was the man who created AC/DC because he said "there was no Rock 'n' Roll" out there. I am proud to have known him and call him a friend, and I'm going to miss him so much.'

Foo Fighter Dave Grohl, who'd loaned his 'rock-and-roll throne' to Axl Rose when he made his 2016 debut with AC/DC, was a man with a well-developed sense of music history, and perhaps one of the last musicians of the (relatively) new breed to continue to fly the flag for balls-and-all rock and roll. Upon hearing of Malcolm's death, he posted a recollection of a life-changing event on social media, how some 37 years prior he and a friend named Larry Hinkle—both 11 at the time—saw *Let There Be Rock* at a Washington DC movie house. That night, Grohl's life was turned upside down. 'That film,' he wrote, 'is everything that live [rock] and roll should be. Sweaty. Loose. Loud . . . It was the first time I lost control to music.' Grohl said that from then onwards, he no longer simply wanted to play guitar, he 'wanted to smash it'. 'Thank you, Malcolm,' he wrote in conclusion, 'for the songs, and the feel, and the cool, and the years of losing control to your rock and roll. I will do just that tonight, for you.'

True to his word, on stage that night in Mexico City, Grohl and the band were dwarfed by a huge projected portrait of Malcolm, his familiar Gretsch in hand, ready to get down to business. Grohl, as always, worked the crowd into a decent frenzy—'We're going to play some rock and roll for Malcolm tonight,' he yelled—as he and the Foo Fighters blasted into 'Let There Be Rock', a song they often performed. Grohl raced up and down the stage as though he'd channelled Angus and Malcolm and the audience went berserk.

Playing a show in Sacramento, California, Guns N' Roses' Axl Rose, who'd gotten tight with Angus during the troubled Rock or Bust tour, also gave a huge shout-out to Malcolm. 'We're gonna dedicate this to Mr Malcolm Young,' he told the crowd, 'who will be sorely missed.' And then, after a short pause: 'By none more than his brother Angus.' The band then played Bob Dylan's 'Knockin' on Heaven's Door' and 'Whole Lotta Rosie'. Guns N' Roses guitarist Slash, who'd toured with AC/DC as a solo act during the *Stiff Upper Lip* tour, provided a statement for US *Rolling Stone*. 'Malcolm Young was one of the best ever rhythm guitarists in Rock N Roll. He was a fantastic songwriter and he had a great work ethic, too . . . I found Malcolm to be a really cool, down to earth fellow. The entire rock n roll community is heart-broken by his passing.'

'It is a sad day in rock and roll,' wrote Eddie Van Halen. 'Malcolm Young was my friend and the heart and soul of AC/DC.'

Other high-profile admirers of the man lined up to give Malcolm much deserved kudos. Ozzy Osbourne, who had intervened in that German hotel bar when Geezer Butler was waving a knife at Malcolm, tweeted: 'So sad to learn of the passing of yet another friend, Malcolm Young. He will be sadly missed.'

Mötley Crüe's Nikki Sixx, whose nose Malcolm had once threatened to bite off, was equally saddened by the news. 'Heavy heart hearing of Malcolm Young's passing . . . RIP bad ass.'

Joe Walsh from the Eagles was another big fan. In his tweet, he rated Malcolm 'one of the top 10 greatest. My heart goes out to the entire AC/DC family'. Billy Idol, he of the Rebel Yell, heard the news and immediately reached for 'Thunderstruck', which he played loudly, before tweeting: 'Malcolm Young . . . rock on RIP.'

Author Stephen King, who'd worked with the band on the *Maximum Overdrive* film soundtrack, also headed to Twitter, describing Malcolm as a 'sweet, quiet man [who] made all the noise with his guitar. AC/DC night at my house, and loud'.

Other equally heartfelt messages—from Black Sabbath's Tony Iommi ('a fine player'), Megadeth's Dave Mustaine ('Malcolm, you are my hero'), KISS's Paul Stanley ('the driving engine of AC/DC . . . one of the true greats'), Def Leppard ('an incredible guitar player and the glue for that band onstage and off'), and Metallica's Lars Ulrich, among many others—fluttered around the Twitterverse. Anthrax's Scott Ian Instagrammed his Malcolm Young tattoo, stating: 'I am a rhythm guitarist because of Malcolm Young.' Of these peers, perhaps Tom Morello, who played guitar for Rage Against the Machine and Bruce Springsteen, said it best: 'Rest in rock power AC/DC's Malcolm Young. #1 greatest guitarist in the entire history of rock n roll. THANK YOU for everything.'

The messages that mattered most, of course, were from his family ('Malcolm was a songwriter, guitarist, performer, producer and visionary who inspired many') and from Angus. Malcolm would have appreciated the fact that his brother kept it short and sharp, but as last words went, it was note-perfect.

'As his brother it is hard to express in words what he has meant to me during my life, the bond we had was unique and very special. He leaves behind an enormous legacy that will live on forever. Malcolm, job well done.'

★

Friends and family said goodbye to Malcolm on a muggy Tuesday morning, 28 November 2017, at Sydney's stately St Mary's Cathedral. Among the many mourners were Harry Vanda, and Malcolm's bandmates past and present— Brian Johnson, Phil Rudd, Mark Evans, Cliff Williams, and Angus, of course, who was a pallbearer, along with Malcolm's son Ross. Also in attendance were Malcolm's peers and friends: Jimmy Barnes, Angry Anderson, the Brewster brothers from The Angels, and Malcolm's long-time buddy Herm Kovac still playing in a revitalised version of the Ted Mulry Gang. As mourners entered the cathedral, they were given a service program; inside was a plastic bag containing a plectrum, inscribed with the initials MY.

The portrait of Malcolm that stood at the altar captured him at his best, playing his beloved Gretsch in his equally beloved singlet and jeans, his long hair hanging down over his shoulders. 'In Loving Memory of Malcolm Mitchell Young,' read the caption. Malcolm's trademark Gretsch, known as The Beast, rested on his coffin.

Monsignor Tony Doherty spoke fittingly of Malcolm, describing him as 'an extraordinary Australian and an extraordinary musician'. He recalled visiting Malcolm during his sad final days in a nursing home after being diagnosed with dementia. 'This genius of music and song had been cruelly struck silent. Sitting in his room with . . . one of the best rhythm guitarists in the world, his beloved Gretsch guitar on the wall and an electric piano, it was a truly distressing moment. But somehow there was still life, vitality and great love.' (Malcolm had requested CDs of his favourite music by the 1950s rockers he'd loved so much, and he listened to them while at Lulworth. Malcolm never got to hear the finished *Rock or Bust* album, despite his input.)

Malcolm's nephew Bradley Horsburgh read a eulogy that might have surprised those who had only dealt with Malcolm via the business of AC/DC, where he could be tough, even ruthless. Horsburgh described his uncle as 'gentle and humble'—anything but the typical rock star. He was a family man. 'Above all for Malcolm came family. Even in his later years, the smile on his face at family gatherings said it all.' He recalled New Year's Eves at Onkaparinga, where Malcolm's extended family would gather to watch the Sydney Harbour fireworks. Malcolm, typically, stood to the rear, just as he did on stage. Horsburgh also spoke of Malcolm's love of bargain clothes shop Gowings, 'where Mal was very pleased to walk out with two pairs of jeans and half a dozen black T-shirts'.

David Albert, the latest scion of the Alberts music dynasty, outlined the band's massive success: more than 200 million albums sold and songs that had been streamed almost a billion times, and all from the humblest of beginnings. Yet in spite of this incredible ride, Albert reinforced the point that Malcolm the man was 'quiet, humble . . . understated'.

A boys' choir then sang 'Amazing Grace' and 'The Lord is My Shepherd'. There'd be no 'Thunderstruck' or 'Dirty Deeds' ringing out.

When the service concluded, Angus, accompanied by Ross, carried Malcolm's Gretsch to the hearse parked outside the cathedral. It had been a rough few weeks for all the Youngs; Angus was about to bury another brother. As the motorcade prepared to make Malcolm's final journey, the Scots College Pipes and Drums Band kicked into gear, blasting a few bars of 'Long Way to the Top', followed by 'Waltzing Matilda'.

As moving as this service was, perhaps the most fitting tribute of all was to be found on the artwork of the *Rock or Bust* LP. On the last page of the album booklet, a simple note stated: 'And most important of all, thanks to Mal, who made it all possible.' There was a photo of Malcolm's and Angus's guitars, side by side, propped up against a Marshall amp that had clearly done a few tours of duty. The caption, which looked as though it had been carved in stone, read: 'In Rock We Trust.' No better epitaph could be written for Malcolm Young.

Acknowledgements

The further I get into my writing career, the more I find myself thanking the same people, which is a very good sign. So, yet again, a huge thank you to Jane Palfreyman for her ongoing support, Jo Butler for her sage counsel and lively telephone manner, to Samantha Kent for a second great collaboration and to Luke Causby for his design magic— and for also knowing where to find the best seats at the SCG.

I'd also like to thank the many people who either steered me in the right direction regarding the life and times of Malcolm Young, or took the time to read the manuscript, namely: Dave Evans, Stephen Crothers, Larry Van Kriedt, Dave Meniketti, Philip Morris, Bob King, Martin Philbey, Bun E. Carlos, Mark Opitz, Jim Moginie, Lindsay McDougall and Chris Cheney. Mark Evans and Michael Browning both deserve ongoing thanks, firstly for inviting me to help document their life stories (as told in *Dirty Deeds* and *Dog Eat Dog*) but also for continuing to be there whenever I've had yet another question to ask.

And I'm especially indebted to Herm Kovac, Malcolm Young's long-time friend and former bandmate, a dead-set legend who was always willing to share his photos, his memories (including the strangest story I've ever heard involving sports socks), and to offer me expert guidance. I look forward to your book, Herm. It'll happen.

As always, there were key books I was reading that kept me inspired during the writing of *Malcolm Young*. Among them were Jeff Tweedy's terrific memoir *Let's Go (So We Can Get Back)*, Stanley Booth's *True Adventures of the Rolling Stones*, Sylvia Patterson's *I'm Not with the Band* and Roger Daltrey's *Thank You, Mr Kibblewhite*. And while there may be no obvious thematic connection, Helen Pitt's *The House* showed me how engrossing a well-written and researched work of non-fiction can be. I hope a little of that magic has rubbed off on *Malcolm Young*.

Closer to the topic at hand, Clinton Walker's *Highway to Hell*, the definitive biography of Bon Scott, and Murray Engleheart and Arnaud Durieux's *AC/DC Maximum Rock & Roll* remain the ultimate sources of all things AC/DC. Ditto AC-DC.net.

There's been an addition to my household during the writing of this book—Neela, Keiraville's bluest dog. She now sits alongside—sometimes quite literally—my wife, Diana, kids Elizabeth and Christian, Poe the wonder budgie and the cat with no name, as the most important people in my corner. Love and respect, one and all.

Selected Discography for Malcolm Young and AC/DC

TALES OF OLD GRAND-DADDY (1974)

Can't Stand the Heat/Goodbye Jane/Quick Reaction/Silver Shoes/Watch Her Do It Now/People and the Power/Red Revolution/Shot in the Head/Ape Man/Cry for Me

BONUS TRACKS (2014 RE-RELEASE)

One of These Days/Natural Man/Moonshine Blues/Louisiana Lady/Ride Baby Ride

HIGH VOLTAGE (1975)

Baby Please Don't Go/She's Got Balls/Little Lover/Stick Around/Soul Stripper/You Ain't Got a Hold on Me/Love Song/Show Business

T.N.T. (1976)

It's a Long Way to the Top (If You Wanna Rock 'n' Roll)/Rock 'n' Roll Singer/The Jack/Live Wire/T.N.T./Rocker/Can I Sit Next to You Girl/High Voltage/School Days

DIRTY DEEDS DONE DIRT CHEAP (1976)

Dirty Deeds Done Dirt Cheap/Ain't No Fun (Waiting 'Round to Be a Millionaire)/There's Gonna Be Some Rockin'/Problem Child/Squealer/Big Balls/R.I.P. (Rock in Peace)/Ride On/Jailbreak

LET THERE BE ROCK (1977)

Go Down/Dog Eat Dog/Let There Be Rock/Bad Boy Boogie/Overdose/Crabsody in Blue/Hell Ain't a Bad Place to Be/Whole Lotta Rosie

POWERAGE (1978)
Rock 'n' Roll Damnation/Down Payment Blues/Gimme a Bullet/Riff Raff/Sin City/What's Next to the Moon/Gone Shootin'/Up to My Neck in You/Kicked in the Teeth

IF YOU WANT BLOOD YOU'VE GOT IT (LIVE) (1978)
Riff Raff/Hell Ain't a Bad Place to Be/Bad Boy Boogie/ The Jack/Problem Child/Whole Lotta Rosie/Rock 'n' Roll Damnation/High Voltage/Let There Be Rock/Rocker

HIGHWAY TO HELL (1979)
Highway to Hell/Girls Got Rhythm/Walk All Over You/ Touch Too Much/Beating Around the Bush/Shot Down in Flames/Get It Hot/If You Want Blood (You've Got It)/Love Hungry Man/Night Prowler

BACK IN BLACK (1980)
Hells Bells/Shoot to Thrill/What Do You Do for Money Honey/Givin' the Dog a Bone/Let Me Put My Love Into You/ Back in Black/You Shook Me All Night Long/Have a Drink on Me/Shake a Leg/Rock and Roll Ain't Noise Pollution

FOR THOSE ABOUT TO ROCK WE SALUTE YOU (1981)
For Those About to Rock (We Salute You)/Put the Finger on You/Let's Get It Up/Inject the Venom/Snowballed/Evil Walks/C.O.D./Breaking the Rules/Night of the Long Knives/ Spellbound

FLICK OF THE SWITCH (1983)
Rising Power/This House is on Fire/Flick of the Switch/ Nervous Shakedown/Landslide/Guns for Hire/Deep in the Hole/Bedlam in Belgium/Badlands/Brain Shake

FLY ON THE WALL (1985)
Fly on the Wall/Shake Your Foundations/First Blood/Danger/ Sink the Pink/Playing With Girls/Stand Up/Hell or High Water/Back in Business/Send for the Man

WHO MADE WHO (1986)
Who Made Who/You Shook Me All Night Long/D.T./Sink the Pink/Ride On/Hells Bells/Shake Your Foundations/Chase the Ace/For Those About to Rock (We Salute You)

BLOW UP YOUR VIDEO (1988)
Heatseeker/That's the Way I Wanna Rock N Roll/Meanstreak/ Go Zone/Kissin' Dynamite/Nick of Time/Some Sin for Nuthin'/Ruff Stuff/Two's Up/This Means War

THE RAZORS EDGE (1990)
Thunderstruck/Fire Your Guns/Moneytalks/The Razors Edge/Mistress for Christmas/Rock Your Heart Out/Are You Ready/Got You by the Balls/Shot of Love/Let's Make It/ Goodbye & Good Riddance to Bad Luck/If You Dare

AC/DC LIVE (1992)
Thunderstruck/Shoot to Thrill/Back in Black/Who Made Who/Heatseeker/The Jack/Moneytalks/Hells Bells/Dirty Deeds Done Dirt Cheap/Whole Lotta Rosie/You Shook Me

All Night Long/Highway to Hell/T.N.T./For Those About to Rock (We Salute You)

BALLBREAKER (1995)
Hard as a Rock/Cover You in Oil/The Furor/ Boogie Man/ The Honey Roll/Burnin' Alive/Hail Caesar/Love Bomb/Caught With Your Pants Down/Whiskey on the Rocks/Ballbreaker

STIFF UPPER LIP (2000)
Stiff Upper Lip/Meltdown/House of Jazz/Hold Me Back/Safe in New York City/Can't Stand Still/Can't Stop Rock 'n' Roll/ Satellite Blues/Damned/Come and Get It/All Screwed Up/ Give It Up

BLACK ICE (2008)
Rock N Roll Train/Skies on Fire/Big Jack/Anything Goes/War Machine/Smash N Grab/Spoilin' for a Fight/Wheels/Decibel/ Stormy May Day/She Likes Rock N Roll/Money Made/Rock N Roll Dream/Rocking All the Way/Black Ice

BACKTRACKS (2009)
CD1—Studio Rarities: High Voltage/Stick Around/Love Song/It's a Long Way To the Top (If You Wanna Rock'n'Roll)/ Rocker/Fling Thing/Dirty Deeds Done Dirt Cheap/Ain't No Fun (Waitin' Round to be a Millionaire)/R.I.P. (Rock in Peace)/ Carry Me Home/Crabsody in Blue/Cold Hearted Man/Who Made Who (Special Collector's Mix)/Snake Eye/Borrowed Time/Down on the Borderline/Big Gun/Cyberspace

CD2 (LIVE): Dirty Deeds Done Dirt Cheap/Dog Eat Dog/ Live Wire/Shot Down in Flames/Back in Black/T.N.T./Let

There Be Rock/Guns for Hire/Sin City/Rock and Roll Ain't Noise Pollution/This House Is on Fire/You Shook Me All Night Long/Jailbreak/Shoot to Thrill/Hell Ain't a Bad Place to Be

CD3 (LIVE): High Voltage/Hells Bells/Whole Lotta Rosie/ Dirty Deeds Done Dirt Cheap/Highway to Hell/Back in Black/For Those About to Rock (We Salute You)/Ballbreaker/ Hard as a Rock/Dog Eat Dog/Hail Caesar/Whole Lotta Rosie/ You Shook Me All Night Long/Safe in New York City

DVD: Big Gun/Hard as a Rock/Hail Caesar/Cover You in Oil/Stiff Upper Lip/Satellite Blues/Safe in New York City/ Rock N Roll Train/Anything Goes

IRON MAN 2 (2010)
Shoot to Thrill/Rock 'n' Roll Damnation/Guns for Hire/Cold Hearted Man/Back in Black/Thunderstruck/If You Want Blood (You've Got It)/Evil Walks/T.N.T./Hell Ain't a Bad Place to Be/Have a Drink on Me/The Razors Edge/Let There Be Rock/War Machine/Highway to Hell

LIVE AT RIVER PLATE (2012)
CD1: Rock N Roll Train/Hell Ain't a Bad Place to Be/Back in Black/Big Jack/Dirty Deeds Done Dirt Cheap/Shot Down in Flames/Thunderstruck/Black Ice/The Jack/Hells Bells

CD2: Shoot to Thrill/War Machine/Dog Eat Dog/You Shook Me All Night Long/T.N.T./Whole Lotta Rosie/Let There Be Rock/Highway to Hell/For Those About to Rock (We Salute You)

ROCK OR BUST (2014)

Rock or Bust/Play Ball/Rock the Blues Away/Miss Adventure/ Dogs of War/Got Some Rock & Roll Thunder/Hard Times/ Baptism by Fire/Rock the House/Sweet Candy/Emission Control

Please note that track listings are for the Australian editions of each album; some international releases have different track listings. For full AC/DC discography, see www.ac-dc.net

Bibliography

Print

Cameron Adams: '10 of the most amazing AC/DC moments,' news.com.au, 15 April 2014

Ellen Aman: 'Get out the earplugs for Kiss concert', *Lexington Leader*, 16 December 1977

Anon: 'Easybeats in hysterical farewell', *The Canberra Times*, 11 July 1966

Anon: 'The Easybeats', *Good Neighbour*, 1 June 1967

Anon: 'AC/DC madness', *Juke*, 14 October 1978

Anon: 'AC/DC score heavy overseas workload', *RAM*, 9 April 1976

Anon: 'AC/DC to export an album', *TV Times*, 7 February 1976

Anon: 'Treble Exposure', *Record Mirror*, 3 June 1978

Anon: 'AC/DC Creates another rock concert riot', *TV Week*, 27 March 1976

Anon: 'AC/DC nipped', *Juke*, 25 June 1975

Anon: 'Sharpies: The Mulleted Rocker Kids of 70s Australia', www.dangerousminds.net, 24 June 2013

Anon: Phil Rudd interview: KISS were like a cartoon band, www.skiddle.com, 7 September 2017

Anon: *The Australian Women's Weekly*, 6 October 1976

Anon: George Young interview for *Let there be Light* fanzine, issues 5 and 6, February / December 1993

Anon: *Best* magazine, December 1979

Anon: *Riff* magazine, May 2003

Anon: Great Moments in Rock Criticism, *Spin*, September 1987

Anon: Interview with Bernie Bonvoisin of Trust, http://highwaytoacdc.com/index.php?zone=interviews/82bernie/index

Jeff Apter: 'High Voltage: The life of Angus Young AC/DC's Last Man Standing', *Nero* 2017

Laura Armitage: 'Forty Years Since AC/DC played Year 12 formal at Ivanhoe Grammar for $240', *Herald-Sun*, 7 May 2015

Jim Barnes & Stephen Scanes: *The Book Top 40 Research 1956–2010*, Scanes Music Research, 2011

Geoff Barton: 'AC/DC High on orange Smarties', *Sounds*, 22 May 1976

Geoff Barton: 'AC/DC: The Fastest Knees in the West', *Sounds*, 12 June 1976

Geoff Barton: 'Same Old Song and Dance (bot so what?)', *Sounds*, 20 November 1976

Geoff Barton: 'A Long way to the top: How AC/DC conquered the world from the back of a van', *Classic Rock* #68

Lachlan Bennett: 'Memories of AC/DC concerts in Queenstown', Devonport, *The Advocate*, 20 November 2017

Tom Beaujour: 'AC/DC's Angus Young discusses Bon Scott and the "Bonfire" Box Set', *Ultimate Classic Rock*, 1 December 2011

Nathan Bevan: 'Malcolm Young of AC/DC was "fearless" says the rock group's Welsh former singer', www.walesonline.co.uk, 10 October 2014

Martin Blake: 'AC/DC's Malcolm Young The Lost Interview', *Classic Rock*, 15 April 2016

Joe Bonomo: 'The night AC/DC stormed CBGBs', www.salon. com, 5 November 2017

Robert Brinton: Spanish Fly, *Disc*, 21 April 1973

David Brown: 'The dirtiest group in town', *Record Mirror*, 13 November 1976

Michael Browning: *Dog Eat Dog*, Allen & Unwin, 2014

Alesha Capone: 'High Voltage for AC/DC anniversary at St Albans Secondary College', *Herald-Sun*, 4 March 2016

Roy Carr: 'Is Britain ready for the human kangaroo?', *NME*, 16 October 1976

Paul Cashmere: 'AC/DC's first setlist from 40 years ago', www. noise11.com, 31 December 2013

Tony Catterall: 'Magnificent Assault on Eardrums', *The Canberra Times*, 13 December 1976

John Conroy: 'Vintage Voltage: When AC/DC rocked Albury', *The Border Mail*, 11 February 2010

Caroline Coons: Live review, *Melody Maker*, 8 May 1976

Creem Seventies Archive: https://superseventies.com/creem. html Toby Creswell / Craig Mathieson / John O'Donnell: *The Best 100 Australian Albums*, Hardie Grant books, 2010

Ian Cross: 'Tiny Angus is Cult Figure', *The Canberra Times*, 14 December 1978

Roger Daltrey: *Thanks a Lot Mr Kibblewhite*, Allen & Unwin 2018

Defending Axl Rose (an abnormal music blog): Classic Albums Revisited: Dirty Deeds Done Dirt Cheap, 30 July 2012

Robert Dimery (ed): *1001 Albums You Must Hear Before You Die*, Quintet Publishing 2005

Giovanni Dodomo: 'Destroy your brain with AC/DC', *Sounds*, 15 May 1976

Harry Doherty: AC/DC Marquee London live review, *Melody Maker*, 21 August 1976

Harry Doherty: Current Affairs: Harry Doherty travels to Cardiff to see how AC/DC are steadily working their way to the top, *Melody Maker*, 5 March 1977

Harry Doherty: 'The Who / The Stranglers / AC/DC / Nils Lofgren, Wembley Stadium—Close encounters of the Wembley kind', *Melody Maker*, 25 August 1979

Malcolm Dome: 'AC/DC's first British gig', *Classic Rock*, 23 April 2014

Patrick Donovan: 'For a piper, it's a long way to the top from the back of a flatbed truck', *The Age*, 13 February 2010

Bruce Elder: 'AC/DC by name and nature', *The Age*, 29 January 2010

Christie Eliezer: 'AC/DC Spray their Piece', *RAM*, 11 December 1976

Paul Elliott: 'AC/DC: Cash for Questions', *Q*, September 2003

Murray Engleheart & Arnaud Durieux: *AC/DC: Maximum Rock & Roll*, HarperCollins, 2006

Mark Evans: *Dirty Deeds: My Life Inside and Outside AC/DC*, Allen & Unwin, 2011

Luis Feliu: 'More than a Little Sunburn, *Powerage* album review', *The Canberra Times*, 1 December 1978

John Finley: 'Kiss, Kiss, bang, bang, at Fairgrounds Concert', *The Courier-Journal*, 11 December 1977

Ian Flavin: 'AC/DC hiding from a gunman', *Rock Star*, 5 March 1977

David Fricke: 'AC/DC Shrug off a Death and Rock On', *Rolling Stone*, 30 October 1980

Gary Graff: 'The Lost Malcolm Young interview: AC/DC in 2003', *Billboard*, 20 November 2017

Bob Granger: 'The Lusts of AC/DC—Band Bids for Supreme Punkdom', *RAM*, September 20 1975

Andy Greene: Readers' Poll: The 10 Best AC/DC Songs, *Rolling Stone*, 15 October 2014

Andy Greene: '10 Classic Albums Rolling Stone Originally Panned', *Rolling Stone*, 25 July 2016

Kory Grow: 'Metallica's Lars Ulrich: My 15 Favourite Metal and Hard Rock Albums', *Rolling Stone*, 22 June 2017

Kory Grow: 'Hipgnosis' Life in 15 Album Covers', *Rolling Stone*, 2 May 2017

Michael Hann: 'Implacable, immutable, irreplaceable: Why Malcolm Young was a rock and roll great'; *The Guardian*, 19 November 2017

Michelle Hoctor: 'It's a long way to the top . . . from AC/DC's early days in Corrimal', *Illawarra Mercury*, 5 February 2010

Andrew Hornery: 'Hard rocker Malcolm Young's "high voltage" life in sleepy suburbia', *Sydney Morning Herald*, 24 November 2017

Ira Kaplan: 'AC/DC's high-voltage sonic assault', *Rolling Stone*, 16 November 1978

David Kent: *Australian Chart Book 1970–1992*, Ambassador Press, 1993

Howie Klein: 'AC/DC Hit California', *New York Rocker*, November 1977

Greg Kot: 'Malcolm Young, the driving force of AC/DC, dead at 64', *Chicago Tribune*, 29 June 2018

Julie Kusko: 'A Family Reunion for the Easybeats', *The Australian Women's Weekly*, 15 October 1969

Dave Lewis: 'Sex + Drugs + Rock & Roll = AC/DC?', *Sounds*, 20 May 1978

Melissa Locker: 'Catching up with Cheap Trick's Rick Nielsen, 35 Years after Live at Budokan', *Time*, 3 May 2013

Vince Lovegrove: Australian Music to the World www.youtube.com/watch?v=g3LKdpOeXwQ

Vince Lovegrove: 'Fraternity: 5+1+1=7 More than Just a Pop Group', *Go-Set*, 18 September 1971

Lucy Macken: 'AC/DC's Malcolm Young splashes $10 million in Palm Beach', domain.com.au, 26 March 2015

Dave McAleer (ed): *The Warner Guide to US & UK Hit Singles*, Carlton/Little, Brown, 1994

Ian McFarlane: *The Encyclopedia of Australian Rock and Pop*, Allen & Unwin, 1999

Phil McNeill: 'I Wallaby Your Man', *NME*, 8 May 1976

Jon Michaud: 'Farewell to Malcolm Young, the Mastermind of AC/DC', *New Yorker*, 19 November 2017

Georgina Mitchell: 'Cheap Trick's Rick Nielsen "Would Be in the Angels or AC/DC right now" if plan to move to Australia had gone ahead', *Newcastle Herald*, 19 September 2014

Tony Moore: 'Cloudland: Inside Brisbane's dead queen of the ballrooms', *Brisbane Times*, 3 May 2017

Philip Morris: *It's a Long Way: From Acca-Dacca to Zappa 1969–1979*, Echo Publishing 2015

Dave Mustaine: 'The Record that changed my life', *Guitar World*, 15 January 2014

Ian McFarlane: *The Encyclopedia of Australian Rock and Pop*, Allen & Unwin, 1999

Ed Nimmervoll: 'AC/DC', *Juke*, 4 June 1975

Jas Obrecht: 'Angus Young Seriously', *Guitar Player*, February 1984

Anthony O'Grady, 'Australia Has Punk Rock Bands Too, You Know', *RAM*, 19 April 1975

Anthony O'Grady, 'Gonna be a rock'n'roll singer, gonna be a rock'n'roll band', *RAM*, 23 April 1976

Anthony O'Grady, 'AC/DC would really like to be as successful here as they are in England, but . . .', *RAM*, 14 July 1978

Rock Super Bowl IV http://www.rockshowvideos.com/rock-superbowl4.html

Bob Rogers (with Denis O'Brien): *Rock'n'Roll Australia*, Burbank Production Services, 2008

Irving Sealey: 'AC/DC The Lusty Boys from Down Under', *Rock Gossip*, No 1 1979

Andy Secher: 'Plug into AC/DC', *Super Rock* Vol 3 No1 1979

Sex Pistols Diary 1976 http://www.rockmine.com/Pistols/SexDates.html

Daniela Soave: 'Kerrang! Whang! Crunch! It's AC/DC!', *Sounds*, 18 August 1979

Sylvie Simmons: 'AC/DC Celebrate their Quarter Century', *MOJO*, December 2000

David Sinclair: 'AC/DC: Phew! Got Away With It, Readers!', *Q*, December 1990

Tony Stewart: Review of Hammersmith Odeon show, *NME*, 20 November 1976

Phil Sutcliffe: 'More Songs About Humping and Booze', *Sounds*, 24 July 1976

Phil Sutcliffe: 'The Dirtiest Story Ever Told', *Sounds*, 28 August 1976

Phil Sutcliffe: AC/DC: Let There Be Rock review, *Sounds*, 22 October 1977

Phil Sutcliffe: 'AC/DC: Sex, Snot, Sweat and School Kids', live review, *The Mayfair*, Newcastle, Sounds, 29 October 1977

Phil Sutcliffe: 'No Cord Wonder', *Sounds*, 12 November 1977

John Tait: *Vanda and Young Inside Australia's Hit Factory*, New South Books, 2010

Irene Thornton: *My Bon Scott*, Pan Macmillan, 2014

Clinton Walker: *Highway to Hell: The Life & Death of AC/DC Legend Bon Scott*, Pan Macmillan, 1994

Mick Wall: 'AC/DC: The making of Highway to Hell', 6 November 2013, *Classic Rock* 2013

Matt Wardlaw: 'AC/DC's Cheap Trick Connection: Malcolm Young was the "main man",' Ultimateclassicrock.com, 2016

Matthew Wilkening: How AC/DC brought their live show to the studio with Let There Be Rock, http://ultimateclassicrock.com/acdc-first-declared-let-there-be-rock-35-years-ago/

Matthew Wilkening: '10 Surprising Things we learned during AC/DC's 'Ask us anything' session', http://ultimateclassicrock.com/ac-dc-cool-facts/

Matthew Wilkening: 'Top 10 Bon Scott AC/DC songs', http://ultimateclassicrock.com/best-bon-scott-acdc-songs/

www.ac-dc.net—various

www.highwaytoacdc.com—various

www.acdccollector.com—various

Emma Young: Lost Perth's AC/DC memories: '3 hours straight and Angus was cranking', *Sydney Morning Herald*, 30 November 2015

Bernard Zuel: Albert Productions, the Label Behind AC/DC, Rocks up 50 years, *Sydney Morning Herald*, 10 August 2014

Video

Angus and Malcolm Young on How They Founded AC/DC: www.youtube.com/watch?v=Gwb-SNVb4Vo.

Angus talks about playing in AC/DC, 16 September 2016, www.acdc.com/news?n_id=356.

Angus Young on Why He Admires Chuck Berry So Much: www.youtube.com/watch?v=IMM_fGl3gpA.

Bethan Donnelly, *Villawood Migrant Hostel,* www.phansw.org.au/wp-content/uploads/2012/09/BethanDonnelly2008.pdf.

Beyond International/Bombora Film & Music Production Company, *Blood and Thunder: The Sound of Alberts,* 2015

Bon Scott The Classic 1978 interview: www.youtube.com/watch?v=-7Yuo-QoQi0

Countdown interview en route to London 1976: www.youtube.com/watch?v=YQIQJMhcAQU

Countdown interview with Bon Scott in London 1977: www.youtube.com/watch?v=-M-0S6B-3Zw

Funny Angus Young [talks] about AC/DC's First Singer: www.youtube.com/watch?v=GFSUySHjjzY.

'Show Business' video www.youtube.com/watch?v=dvFxTpnxk8s

Excerpts from the concert film *Let There Be Rock*: www.youtube.com/watch?v=cXS4fdof_-A www.youtube.com/watch?v=OhUQzFNwV7I

Spanish TV show Applauso 1980: www.rtve.es/alacarta/videos/aplauso/chicos-ac-dc-tocan-plato-aplauso-1980/317139/